Satellites Over Snow

Satellites Over Snow

Arctic Space Systems and the Next Surveillance Arms Race

By

Afnan Barakat

Vij Books

New Delhi (India)

Published by

Vij Books
(Publishers, Distributors & Importers)
4836/24, 3rd Floor, Ansari Road
Delhi – 110 002
Phone: 91-11-43596460
Mobile: 98110 94883
e-mail: contact@vijpublishing.com
www.vijbooks.in

ISBN: 978-93-7794-037-9 (PB)

This book was developed using advanced writing tools to support the drafting and ideation process. All content has been thoughtfully curated, refined, and reviewed to ensure quality and relevance.

Contents

Introduction

In March 2021, the *Ever Given* ran aground in the Suez Canal, and within hours, the world could watch the blockage from orbit: bright hull against brown water, a single vessel made planetary by congestion. The image travelled fast because the scene sat where the architecture of modern observation behaves as advertised. Move that same appetite for certainty north—to the Barents Sea in January, to a convoy off Murmansk, to a trawler edging along ice in the Fram Strait—and the picture changes. Snow absorbs sound. Metal cracks in the cold. The map looks cleaner than the world it claims to describe.

That is the Arctic paradox. The region is both newly central and stubbornly difficult to see. It is invoked in speeches as a corridor, a frontier, a flank, a warning line, a shipping future. Yet the closer one moves to the pole, the more the promises attached to "global" space systems begin to fray. Satellites pass, but not always when needed. Sensors collect, but not always in forms that can be trusted at once. Data exists, yet arrives late, routed through stations and queues and institutions whose quiet constraints seldom feature in glossy coverage maps. The Arctic is not a blank. It is a seam.

A seam matters because states do not act on imagery in the abstract. They act on what reaches a command post before weather shifts, before a vessel alters course, before a radio call hardens into accusation. In the High North, surveillance is rarely a matter of a single overhead asset gazing down with mechanical impartiality. It is a production chain. Orbit determines access. The sensor determines what can be distinguished. Communications determine whether the collection becomes the delivery. Ground stations, processors, analysts, and tasking authorities determine whether delivery becomes comprehension in time to matter. When any one of those links falters, awareness narrows. The effect is not theatrical. It is administrative, delayed, cumulative—and strategically decisive.

This is why the Arctic has become such a revealing theatre for contemporary surveillance. Not because it is the most technologically advanced region on earth, but because it exposes the hidden labour behind technological claims. A state may procure exquisite imagery and still fail to move from detection to identification before a contact disappears into weather or jurisdictional ambiguity. A commercial operator may advertise high revisit at latitude, while customers discover that revisit is not the same as persistence, and persistence is not the same as decision-ready knowledge. Precision has a clock attached. So does trust.

The issue is not merely that the Arctic is cold, dark, or remote, though all three matter. It is that physical conditions and political expectations collide there with unusual force. Geometry changes with latitude. Light changes with the season. Radio propagation is perturbed by ionospheric behaviour, which is no trivial footnote when communication and navigation depend on it. Ground infrastructure, meanwhile, sits on permafrost, diesel deliveries, fibre backhaul, maintenance flights, and permissions that cannot be improvised in a crisis. The public imagination tends to picture surveillance as a view from above; the Arctic insists that it is equally a matter of what can be sustained below.

One reason the seam has become harder to ignore is that the Arctic is no longer peripheral to strategic traffic. In June 2024, NATO's exercise *Baltic Operations*—BALTOPS 24—again drew attention to northern maritime awareness, even though the Baltic and the Arctic are not the same theatre and should not be lazily merged. Ships, aircraft, and undersea systems do not respect our analytic neatness. Information flows, and military planning increasingly span the spaces between the North Atlantic and the High North. A radar hit near the Norwegian coast, a navigation anomaly in Finnmark, a satellite pass over Svalbard, a cloud-processing delay in a distant operations centre: these can belong to one chain of meaning. The seam runs through institutions as much as through the atmosphere.

The temptation, especially in public debate, is to answer this growing demand with a vocabulary of abundance. More satellites. More commercial images. More data fusion. More sharing. There is truth in that instinct. The last decade has seen a dramatic expansion of Earth observation capacity, lower launch costs, denser constellations, and a new willingness among governments to buy intelligence-adjacent services from commercial firms. The war in Ukraine made that shift impossible to miss. When Maxar Technologies released satellite imagery of Russian military deployments near Ukraine in late 2021 and early 2022, public visibility altered the tempo of diplomatic argument. Images did not end deception, but they narrowed the room in which some forms of denial could operate. They also demonstrated something colder and more general: once private providers can supply timely, credible views of military activity, surveillance is no longer monopolised by states, even if state demand still shapes the market.

And yet the Arctic resists easy extrapolation from such examples. A visible armoured column near a populated frontier is not the same analytic object as a vessel moving through broken ice under low light, intermittent cloud, and sparse corroborating traffic. Broad-area maritime awareness over high latitudes often depends less on a single exquisite picture than on a sequence of imperfect observations stitched across time and source: synthetic aperture radar detections, optical glimpses in better weather, automatic identification signals when present, patterns of movement inferred from prior behaviour, local reports, airborne patrol inputs, perhaps undersea sensing, perhaps not. Knowledge accumulates by comparison. It is assembled, then tested. Often it remains provisional.

That distinction between image and awareness will prove decisive throughout this book because surveillance outputs are not interchangeable. Detection is not identification. Identification is not tracking. Tracking is not attribution. Each demands a different blend of resolution, revisit, context, and confidence. An architecture optimised to sweep vast areas for anomalies may be excellent at finding candidate events and poor at explaining them. A system built for high-detail imagery may produce magnificent evidence too slowly or too narrowly to support persistent search. These are not technical footnotes. They are choices about what uncertainty a state is willing to live with, and what kind it is willing to pay to reduce.

Consider a more local example. In July 2020, the diesel spill near Norilsk in Siberia drew intense attention to remote sensing over the Russian Arctic. Optical and radar imagery were both used to assess the spread and environmental effects of the spill, but the event also illustrated a harder truth. Environmental monitoring, emergency response, legal accountability, and strategic awareness may draw on overlapping sensor suites, yet they do not ask identical questions on identical clocks. A plume mapped over days may suffice for one purpose and fail another. When a region is increasingly treated as both operational space and evidentiary space, time itself becomes contested. Which image counts? Which delay is acceptable? Which gap becomes politically convenient?

Here the Arctic teaches a subtle lesson about latency. Public discussions often treat latency as a technical inconvenience, a matter for engineers and operators to smooth away. In practice, it is a governing condition. There is time-to-collect, time-to-downlink, time-to-process, time-to-fuse, time-to-brief, time-to-decide. The longest of those intervals often defines the real system. A satellite can see a target at 10:03, a ground station can receive the data at 10:11, processing can flag the contact at 10:24, dissemination can stall until 10:49 because another customer holds priority, and the resulting product can reach an analyst who needs corroboration from a maritime source that does not report until midday. To speak of "near real time" in such circumstances without specifying the chain is less description than theatre.

The Arctic also places unusual weight on communication and positioning systems that appear, from a distance, secondary to the glamour of imagery. They are not secondary. Communications links decide whether sensed data becomes useful before it grows stale. Positioning, navigation, and timing underpin not only movement but geolocation, synchronisation, network discipline, and the integrity of sensor fusion. At high latitudes, geometry alters how these services behave. Auroral and ionospheric effects complicate assumptions further. When timing degrades, downstream systems wobble. When a downlink window is missed, exquisite collection can become archival rather than operational. The seam widens.

Still, it would be wrong to romanticise Arctic difficulty into impossibility. Much is knowable there, and increasingly so. Synthetic aperture radar has transformed high-latitude observation by making darkness and cloud less absolute obstacles. Highly elliptical and polar low Earth orbits can serve northern missions in ways geostationary systems cannot. Inter-satellite links and relay architectures have shortened delivery times that once depended entirely on local ground access. Commercial marketplaces have widened access to imagery and analytics that were once scarce. To say that the Arctic is hard to surveil is not to say it is opaque. It is to say that opacity varies by task, by season, by architecture, and by the institutional discipline behind the system.

That last point matters because technology alone does not settle surveillance outcomes. The same constellation may serve one customer as a reassurance tool and another as an escalation engine, depending on who controls tasking, exclusivity, release, and interpretation. A public image can be deterred by showing that concealment is difficult; it can also harden narratives before uncertainty has been properly reduced. A dual-use network can improve efficiency in peacetime and create severe priority conflicts in crisis. Shared ground stations and hosted payloads can expand access while entangling sovereignty, dependence, and hidden vetoes. Power resides not only in collection but in queue position.

There is a tendency, especially among those who prefer elegant diagrams, to imagine resilience as a matter of simple redundancy: add satellites, add links, add stations, add backups. In polar surveillance, redundancy helps, but diversity often matters more. A constellation whose nodes all depend on one style of downlink, one processing provider, one timing assumption, or one governance arrangement may appear dense and remain brittle. The weakest link in the chain is rarely the most expensive component. Sometimes it is the remote antenna whose maintenance window was missed. Sometimes it is a software update that changes dissemination paths. Sometimes it is a legal arrangement that gives one actor priority at the worst possible moment. Systems fail socially as well as technically.

This is one reason the emerging surveillance competition in the Arctic is best understood not as a race for sheer visibility, but as a race over usable persistence. Persistence sounds straightforward. It is not. Continuous coverage, frequent revisit, event-driven monitoring, and investigatory follow-up are different conditions disguised by one convenient word. A coastguard, a naval planner, an environmental regulator, and an intelligence service may each invoke persistence while seeking quite different outputs. Confusion flourishes when one meaning is implied and another is procured. The result is disappointment at best, strategic miscalculation at worst.

The language of arms racing enters here with some care. The Arctic is not simply replaying older Cold War scripts in icy costume. Commercialisation has altered who can collect, who can buy, who can publish, and who can verify. Networking has changed what counts as coverage. Congestion in polar low Earth orbit has turned persistence into a traffic management problem as well as an observational one. Interference, jamming, spoofing, and cyber compromise need not destroy spacecraft to erode confidence across the chain. A service can appear present while its integrity decays. Outage and attack are not always cleanly separable. Attribution is often slower than suspicion.

That uncertainty feeds the politics of the region. Arctic governance has real achievements, yet many of its institutional forms were not built to absorb dense, dual-use, commercially mediated surveillance competition. Space law establishes broad responsibilities and registrations; it does not dissolve the ambiguities that arise when commercial constellations support public monitoring, military procurement, crisis signalling, and private analytics all at once. Confidence-building measures may help, but transparency itself is not neutral. To reveal can reassure. To reveal can provoke. Much depends on timing, framing, and the degree to which those watching trust the chain that produced the image before them.

The seam returns here, not as metaphor alone but as diagnosis. Where exactly does a state's sightline fray? At the angle of view over high latitude? At the sensor's struggle with darkness or glare? At the relay link? At the station in Svalbard or Alaska or northern Scandinavia? In a cloud-processing queue? In the handoff between civilian operator and security customer? In the legal caution surrounding release? Different architectures answer those questions differently, and that is why claims of Arctic awareness should be examined less like slogans than like supply chains. One asks not only what can be seen, but who can route it, sustain it, authenticate it, and act on it before it curdles into hindsight.

For readers trying to make sense of the High North's new strategic visibility, the decisive question is therefore not whether the Arctic can be watched. It plainly can. The harder question is what kind of watching survives contact with latitude, weather, remoteness, congestion, contestation, and institutional friction. A slow, high-detail system may support accountability after an incident and fail to shape the incident itself. A fast, coarse system may trigger alarm without yielding identification strong enough for public attribution. Neither is useless. Both carry risk.

That trade-off is now moving from specialist circles into the centre of statecraft. Governments and firms are making choices—about orbits, relay, ground access, commercial partnerships, tasking rights, interference resilience, and the meaning of persistence—that will determine not merely how often the Arctic is observed, but how confidently events there can be interpreted under pressure. The region's next surveillance arms race will not be won by whoever possesses the most dramatic satellite imagery. It will be shaped by whoever best understands the chain, narrows the seam, and knows which delays are tolerable and which are fatal.

Chapter 1

Arctic Surveillance as a Space-ground System

What does it mean to watch a place when the image arrives after the decision? The question sounds narrow until one looks north, where confidence often attaches itself to the wrong object. A satellite pass can look impressive on a briefing slide. A crisp frame of sea ice, a vessel wake, a strip of coast, a runway cut into white. Yet none of that guarantees timely awareness. The picture may be clear while the situation remains obscure.

That gap between seeing and knowing is easy to miss because modern surveillance is usually described from the top down. Attention settles on the platform, the payload, the orbit, and the branded image released to prove that something was indeed visible. The Arctic punishes that habit. Distance lengthens the chain between collection and use. Darkness alters what can be read. Weather does not merely interfere; it reshapes what counts as reliable evidence. A clean image can sit in a queue like an unopened envelope.

The deeper problem is conceptual. Surveillance is often imagined as a property of a machine, as though a capable sensor carries its own meaning with it. In practice, meaning is assembled. The orbit must place the sensor where it can collect something relevant. The link must carry that material onward. The ground station must be available. Processing must turn raw capture into an interpretable product. Tasking must have asked the right question in the first place, and someone must still be in a position to compare, judge, and act. When any part of that sequence slips, performance declines in ways that glossy descriptions rarely admit. Failure need not look dramatic. It can appear as hesitation, stale certainty, or misplaced confidence.

This is where the High North acquires its special force. Arctic difficulty is not reducible to cold, although cold leaves its mark on equipment, maintenance, timing, and human stamina. The region distorts assumptions that feel natural elsewhere. High latitude changes the viewing geometry.

Seasonal light alters the very terms of interpretation. Sparse infrastructure turns simple dependencies into strategic ones. A link that works comfortably farther south may become temperamental. A station map that appears complete may conceal thin redundancy. A route that seems open on paper may depend on support that arrives rarely and at high cost. Under such conditions, surveillance stops being a story about isolated excellence and becomes a story about weak joints.

The stakes follow from that shift in perspective. States do not merely want to collect information about the Arctic; they want to rely on it. They want to distinguish routine movement from anomaly, environmental change from deliberate masking, and signalling from noise. They want to do so under pressure, in places where corroboration is expensive and where delay can turn uncertainty into argument. The political and security significance of surveillance lies not in the existence of data but in the credibility of interpretation attached to it. Trust becomes visible here as behaviour: whether an aircraft is diverted, whether a patrol is launched, whether a claim is made publicly, whether a warning is issued or withheld.

Risk also changes shape when the chain is understood properly. A poor outcome may begin far from the sensor itself. It may begin with a missed downlink window, an overloaded processing queue, a tasking decision made on incomplete assumptions, or a ground node whose vulnerability was treated as an administrative detail. That is why arguments about persistence so often misfire. They speak as though endurance in orbit were enough, when actual usefulness depends on the slower, less glamorous question of whether information can move, be checked, and be trusted before the moment passes. The Arctic gives this question a sharper edge because there are fewer easy substitutes once the chain starts to fail.

A more disciplined vocabulary is needed as well. Surveillance can search broadly, discriminate finely, follow movement across time, or support judgements about responsibility, but these are not the same achievement dressed in different words. They demand different balances of coverage, fidelity, timing, and corroboration. Confusion enters when one output is promised and another is quietly delivered. The result is not just technical disappointment. Institutions plan around the wrong expectation, and operators inherit uncertainty they cannot easily reduce. In the Arctic, where space, weather, and logistics already stretch every assumption, loose language becomes its own source of error.

The path ahead begins by moving attention away from the satellite as solitary hero and towards the full production of awareness, where sensing, transmission, infrastructure, prioritisation, and analysis belong to one system rather than to adjacent specialisms. From there the argument tightens around the High North itself, not as a romantic landscape but as a set of physical and operational conditions that reward some architectures and expose others. Only then does the distinction between outputs come fully into focus, because the difference between noticing something, naming it, following it, and attributing meaning to it is the difference between a striking image and a surveillance posture that can bear weight.

The question that presses at the threshold is therefore not whether the Arctic can be watched. It can. The harder question is what kind of watching remains intact once the image leaves the sensor and enters the world of links, stations, queues, analysts, and authority. If the envelope arrives late, damaged, or in the wrong hands, what exactly has been gained by collecting it at all?

From platforms to systems

In March 2021, when the container ship *Ever Given* blocked the Suez Canal, satellite images circulated with astonishing speed. Maxar Technologies published clear overhead views from Egypt that helped turn a local obstruction into a global public event. The pictures were sharp, legible, and immediate enough to satisfy a broad hunger for proof. A stranded vessel, a narrow waterway, a world supply chain held in place by one hull: the scene seemed to demonstrate what space systems now do best. They see, they deliver, they settle the argument. At least, that is how it looked.

Move the same expectation north, and the confidence begins to thin. A synthetic aperture radar image of a vessel near sea ice may be technically excellent and still arrive too late to shape any useful response. An optical image may show a lead in the ice, a heat plume near a remote facility, a track across snow, yet the decisive question remains unanswered: who received it, when, in what form, with what context, and under whose authority? The image alone does not carry those answers. The file travels. That is the point.

The habit of speaking about surveillance as though it were embodied in a satellite is understandable. Satellites are visible symbols of technical power. They launch with ceremony, carry recognisable instruments, and lend themselves to neat claims about coverage, resolution, and revisit. Procurement cultures encourage the simplification. So do marketing brochures. A platform can be named, displayed, and counted. A chain of orbit design, tasking rules, antenna availability, processing queues, analytic standards, dissemination pathways, and institutional priorities is harder to compress into a slogan. Yet in the Arctic, that untidy chain usually determines what can be seen in any operational sense. The platform may be the most expensive part of the system; it is rarely the whole explanation.

This shift in emphasis matters because it changes the object of analysis. Instead of asking what a satellite can, in principle, detect, one asks what a surveillance system can reliably produce under pressure. That difference sounds minor until a decision depends on it. A sensor may collect imagery of a remote maritime contact in poor weather. That is a collection. It becomes surveillance only when the image is moved, processed, interpreted, compared with other information, and placed in front of someone able to decide whether the contact is routine, suspicious, misidentified, or simply unknown. Each step introduces delay, uncertainty, and the possibility of a mismatch between technical capacity and practical need. The Arctic magnifies those mismatches because distance, weather, and infrastructure make every hand-off more consequential.

A good image is not enough. That sentence deserves to be kept plain, because so much strategic misunderstanding grows from refusing its simplicity. A good image may satisfy a press office, a procurement official, or an external audience looking for reassurance that something is being watched. Actionable awareness is harsher. It requires timing that matches the decision. It requires enough contextual information to distinguish an anomaly from noise. It requires delivery into an institution that can absorb ambiguity without either freezing or overreacting. In the High North, where windows of observation are narrow and corroboration is often costly, the distance between those two outcomes can be the whole story.

Consider a familiar pattern in maritime surveillance. A satellite passes over a northern sea lane and captures a clear radar image of a vessel operating near the edge of ice. The target is visible. Its wake can be measured. Its position can be plotted. That sounds decisive until one asks harder questions. Was the vessel expected there? Was its identity already known from other sources? Did the product reach a maritime operations centre before the vessel changed course or entered a zone where follow-up became harder? Could the image be compared quickly with automatic identification transmissions, patrol aircraft data, coastguard reporting, or earlier passes? If not, the result may still be valuable, but it belongs to a different category of value. It aids reconstruction more than intervention.

It informs pattern analysis more than immediate response. The distinction is not semantic. It shapes how institutions should judge performance.

The language of systems helps because it forces surveillance to be treated as a production process. Orbits decide not only where a sensor flies but when and from what angle it looks. Ground stations determine whether collected data must wait for the next pass or can be downlinked quickly enough to retain operational meaning. Tasking determines whether the sensor was pointed at the right place with the right urgency. Processing determines whether raw data remains raw for too long. Analytics determine whether interpretation is disciplined or careless. Dissemination determines whether a finished product reaches the intended recipient rather than a general repository. Each component can be technically sound and still produce a poor result when joined badly to the others. Systems fail in the joins.

That is why Arctic constraints so often shift the bottleneck away from the sensor itself. At lower latitudes, analysts can sometimes treat communications, ground access, and processing as background functions because infrastructure is denser and alternatives more plentiful. The High North is less forgiving. Downlink opportunities can be constrained by station geography and pass timing. Ground terminals must survive wind, ice, power limits, maintenance delays, and physical remoteness. Fibre routes, backhaul capacity, and staffing arrangements matter more than they appear to matter from orbit. When these conditions tighten, the elegant discussion of sensor performance begins to lose explanatory power. One can possess exquisite sensing and poor awareness at the same time.

A concrete case helps. During the search for Malaysia Airlines Flight 370 in March 2014, satellite communications metadata from Inmarsat became central to reconstructing the aircraft's final track. The episode did not concern the Arctic, but it made visible a truth that applies with even greater force there: awareness often emerges from the interaction of systems not originally designed to produce a single coherent surveillance picture. Signals, orbital geometry, ground processing, model assumptions, and institutional interpretation had to be combined before any operationally meaningful account could be advanced. The value lay not in a single platform but in the chain that narrowed the field of action from fragments. The lesson is not that all surveillance resembles accident investigation. It is that the useful unit of analysis is larger than the spacecraft.

A second example comes from northern maritime monitoring around Svalbard, where remote sensing, vessel reporting, and state authority meet in a compressed strategic space. In such environments, a satellite image can reveal politically and operationally significant activity, but it rarely speaks for itself. A contact near fisheries grounds or sensitive infrastructure may trigger attention, yet the image has to be paired with legal jurisdiction, vessel identity, previous movement patterns, weather conditions, and the availability of assets that can respond. If the image reaches decision-makers after the vessel has moved, or if it arrives stripped of sufficient context, it becomes evidence of visibility rather than evidence of control. That difference often separates surveillance that reassures from surveillance that merely advertises effort.

The temptation at this point is to treat system thinking as an argument for endless complexity, as though the solution to every weakness were simply to add more layers. That would be a mistake. More links can reduce one vulnerability while creating another. Data relay can cut latency while deepening dependence on shared networks. Greater automation can move products faster while making interpretation harder to audit. More commercial inputs can widen access while obscuring who holds priority when demand spikes. Systems thinking should not be confused with systems worship. The purpose is not to celebrate complexity but to locate the real constraints that simple platform-centred narratives hide.

A credible limitation has to be admitted as well. Not every surveillance task requires the full chain to operate at peak speed. Some missions tolerate delay. Environmental monitoring, long-term pattern analysis, treaty verification after the fact, and retrospective investigation may all benefit from high-quality imagery that arrives hours or even days later. For such purposes, the platform can appear closer to the centre of value, because the urgency attached to delivery is lower. This is a genuine counterpoint, not an inconvenience to be brushed aside. It reminds us that actionable awareness is not one thing on one clock. What counts as timely depends on the question being asked.

And yet the concession strengthens rather than weakens the systems argument. The reason delay is acceptable in some cases is precisely that the chain still exists and still has to be judged against the decision it supports. A slow pipeline may be entirely fit for long-horizon monitoring and dangerously unfit for tactical cueing or crisis response. The problem begins when institutions slide between those uses without noticing. They praise a system for producing excellent retrospective knowledge and then quietly assume it can also sustain rapid operational judgement. In the Arctic, where conditions already erode margin, that confusion becomes expensive. Not always in money. Sometimes in credibility, sometimes in response time, sometimes in the gap between what governments say they can see and what they can actually act upon.

The file returns here as a useful motif because it is so ordinary. A satellite does not deliver awareness any more than a camera delivers understanding. It produces material. That material must move. It must be opened, sorted, compared, argued over, trusted, or distrusted. The file can be pristine and still fail at its moment. A snow-covered runway, a drifting contact, an unexpected plume, a gap in ice, a signal anomaly near a remote northern coast: each may be captured beautifully and handled badly. Surveillance begins earlier than the image and ends later than its receipt.

Once that is accepted, familiar debates look different. Questions about coverage become questions about usable coverage. Questions about persistence become questions about what can be kept current across orbit, link, ground, and analysis. Questions about sovereignty become questions about who owns stations, who controls tasking, who sets priority, and who can verify a product before it enters a political argument. Even trust takes on a clearer shape. It is no longer an airy principle. It appears in queue rules, access permissions, formatting standards, analyst confidence, and the speed with which one agency shares with another. A system can be technologically advanced and institutionally slow. It can be widely distributed and tightly bottlenecked. It can collect magnificently and decide badly.

The Arctic exposes these truths because it strips away the comforting illusion that sensing and knowing are close neighbours. Sometimes they are separated by minutes that matter. Sometimes, by organisations that do not speak smoothly to one another. Sometimes, the infrastructure is too sparse to absorb disruption gracefully. The question that follows is not whether the next image will be good. The more serious question is whether the chain behind it is disciplined enough, fast enough, and honest enough about its own limits to turn that image into something a state can bear to act upon.

What makes the High North distinct

In October 2018, during NATO's Trident Juncture exercise in northern Norway, civil aviation authorities and military officials reported disruptions to GPS signals in Finnmark. The event drew attention for obvious security reasons, yet its deeper significance lay elsewhere. It showed how quickly the Arctic strips away the fiction that surveillance and navigation are separate technical conveniences, each quietly doing its own job in the background. In the High North, a signal problem is rarely just a signal problem. It changes routes, timings, confidence, and the willingness to act.

The horizon rules everything here. That is not poetic indulgence but an operational fact. The Arctic imposes itself through angle, distance, and delay long before it does so through spectacle. Maps tempt outsiders into thinking of the region as an empty white field waiting to be overlaid with global systems that already work elsewhere. What the map hides is the stubborn materiality of high latitude: low look angles, unstable radio conditions, long winters of poor light, ice that reshapes movement, and infrastructure so sparse that a missed flight, a failed generator, or a damaged cable can change the practical meaning of coverage.

Cold matters, of course, but cold alone explains little. A surveillance architecture designed for temperate latitudes can fail in the Arctic even when its hardware performs exactly as advertised. The reason is that performance in the High North emerges from the interaction of conditions that are easy to discuss separately and dangerous to separate in practice. Geometry governs what can be seen and from where. Illumination governs what can be interpreted. Radio behaviour governs what can be linked, timed, and trusted. Logistics governs whether any of those gains can be sustained long enough to matter. The Arctic becomes distinct not because it presents one extreme variable, but because it combines several and forces them into the same decision.

Start with geometry. A satellite passes over high latitudes is not simply a more northerly version of a pass farther south. Look angles change. So do assumptions about what "overhead" means. A system may offer frequent opportunities to observe near the pole, yet still observe from awkward perspectives for particular tasks, especially when timing, swath, and incidence angle matter as much as mere presence. That distinction sounds technical until it reaches behaviour. Analysts choose whether to trust a detection. Operators decide whether to re-task. Commanders judge whether a contact is persistent enough to commit to an aircraft or vessel. Geometry enters those choices through confidence: not confidence in the abstract, but confidence visible in whether institutions spend scarce attention and fuel on a lead that may dissolve on closer inspection.

The limits of geometry become clearer when compared with systems designed for lower latitudes. Geostationary satellites transformed communications and meteorology over much of the globe because they appear fixed over one point on the equator. For the Arctic, that apparent convenience degrades sharply. From high latitudes, the satellite sits low on the horizon, and farther north it slips towards unusability. That is why so many northern services have depended instead on polar low Earth orbit systems, highly elliptical concepts, or constellations built to compensate for the thinness of equatorial architectures. The issue is not merely coverage on paper. It is whether a terminal can hold the link, whether terrain or structures block the path, whether the elevation angle leaves enough margin in bad weather, and whether the resulting service can be treated as dependable rather than occasional.

A concrete example sits in plain institutional view. Iridium's satellite network, completed as the Iridium NEXT constellation in 2019, has long been prized for polar communications precisely because its architecture does not abandon high latitudes to the geometry that constrains geostationary systems. That design choice made it unusually valuable to aircraft, ships, and remote users operating where equatorial satellites lose practical reach. The lesson reaches beyond one company. Arctic feasibility often begins with accepting that globally common solutions may be regionally weak, and that high-latitude service depends on architectures willing to invest orbital design effort in the problem rather than treating the far north as an afterthought.

Light produces a different kind of distinctness. Popular descriptions of the Arctic lean heavily on darkness, and for good reason, but the more interesting point is not that darkness exists. It is that illumination becomes unreliable as a basis for routine interpretation. Polar night removes the easy assumptions of optical surveillance. Low sun angles in shoulder seasons create long shadows and deceptive contrasts. Snow and ice reflect light in ways that make edges uncertain, surfaces ambiguous, and familiar visual cues less dependable. Summer does not simply solve the problem. Melt, glare, cloud, and changing surface conditions alter what can be distinguished from one pass to the next. In such a setting, visibility is seasonal in more than a meteorological sense. It is epistemic.

That matters because institutions do not ask only whether a sensor collected an image. They ask whether the image settles a question. A broad white surface with a dark interruption may indicate a lead in the ice, a vehicle track, a pressure ridge, open water, or a shadow effect, depending on season, angle, and sensor type. Interpretation, therefore, becomes inseparable from context. The High North rewards systems that compare modalities rather than rely on one stream alone. Optical imagery may provide intuitive legibility when conditions permit. Radar may cut through darkness and cloud, but it demands greater interpretive discipline. Thermal information may hint at activity while refusing to explain it fully. Arctic surveillance, then, begins to look less like a clean act of seeing and more like an act of measured comparison under unfriendly conditions.

The need for comparison appeared starkly in the response to the diesel spill near Norilsk in May 2020. Satellite imagery helped reveal the spread and environmental scale of the incident in the Russian Arctic, but no single image type exhausted the event's meaning. Colour, surface texture, weather, terrain, and time all shaped interpretation. What counted was not only that remote sensing could detect the spill, but that different forms of observation had to be assembled before decision-makers could distinguish extent, movement, and likely consequence with enough confidence to act publicly. The example belongs partly to environmental monitoring, yet that is precisely why it is instructive. The Arctic does not respect neat partitions between civil and security surveillance. The same physical conditions discipline both.

Radio propagation adds another layer of difficulty, subtler than darkness and less photogenic than sea ice, but often more consequential. The Arctic lies under ionospheric conditions that can complicate communications and navigation in ways that feel intermittent, localised, and therefore maddeningly hard to classify. Auroral activity is not a cinematic backdrop. It is a reminder that the medium through which signals travel can itself become unstable. In practical terms, this affects link quality, timing confidence, positioning integrity, and the interpretation of anomalies. A disruption may reflect natural conditions, congestion, poor geometry, equipment issues, or intentional interference. In the High North those possibilities can resemble one another just enough to slow judgement at the very moment speed is wanted.

This is why the region turns line-of-sight into a strategic condition rather than a background technical parameter. A link budget on a design sheet does not automatically become a usable service in the field. Mountains, masts, ship motion, ice accretion on equipment, low satellite elevation, and the scarcity of alternate paths all matter. When a terminal in a temperate port drops a connection, another option may be close at hand. When a terminal north of the Arctic Circle drops a connection, the nearest substitute may exist only in theory. Risk becomes visible here as a decision about margin. Does an operator overprovision power, shelter, antennas, and backhaul for a site that will be difficult to reach? Does a government accept dependence on shared infrastructure farther south? Does a commercial provider promise service that works most of the time, or only service that can survive the week when everything goes wrong?

Sparse infrastructure makes those questions harder rather than simpler. The High North is not empty, but it is thinly provisioned relative to the density of expectation now placed upon it. Ports are limited. Airfields are few. The windows are narrow. Fibre and backhaul routes may be indirect, fragile, or politically sensitive. Power can become its own operational story. A ground station on paper may look like a solved node; in practice, it depends on maintenance crews, spare parts, weather windows, access permissions, and a supply chain that can tolerate interruption. Persistence, then, is never just a matter of orbital recurrence. It is also a matter of whether the machinery below orbit can keep pace with the claim being made above it.

A useful counterpoint must be granted. The Arctic is not uniformly inaccessible, nor is every system there perpetually on the edge of failure. Some northern ground stations are highly capable. Some communications architectures have improved markedly. Polar orbiting meteorological systems have supported valuable forecasting and environmental monitoring for decades. To acknowledge this is important, because lazy writing about the region often swings from triumphalism to melodrama. The High North does not nullify technology. It simply discriminates more sharply between architectures built with polar realities in mind and those merely extended northwards with hope.

That concession, however, sharpens the central point. Capability in the Arctic tends to be specific rather than generic. A system may perform excellently for one mission and disappoint in another because the constraints do not weigh equally across tasks. Store-and-forward delivery may be entirely adequate for retrospective analysis and wholly inadequate for rapid operational cueing. A communications link may suffice for routine traffic and buckle under surge demand. A sensor may image beautifully in one season and force cautious interpretation in another. The regional mistake lies not in believing that Arctic surveillance is possible, but in treating one success as proof of universal fitness.

The horizon returns here because it joins these distinct factors into one practical image. Geometry lowers it. Darkness obscures it. Radio conditions blur it. Sparse logistics make it harder to bridge. The horizon is where physical limits turn into institutional choices. How much uncertainty will a state tolerate before acting? How much redundancy will it pay for in a place where maintenance itself is a strategic problem? How much dependence on commercial or allied infrastructure is acceptable before sovereignty begins to feel thin? Such questions rarely appear in glossy declarations about persistent awareness, yet they define whether persistence means durable presence or merely repeated opportunity.

The High North therefore imposes a discipline that more forgiving theatres allow people to postpone. It forces a separation between nominal coverage and usable coverage, between collection and delivery, between a reassuring map and a functioning chain. Demand for persistence keeps rising because governments, firms, and publics want the Arctic to be legible on command. The region keeps resisting because seeing there depends on architectures that can survive awkward geometry, variable illumination, uncertain signals, and the long logistical shadow cast by distance. The real test is not whether a system can look north. It is whether it can keep its promises once the horizon starts to take them apart.

Defining surveillance outputs

In March 2014, when the search for Malaysia Airlines Flight 370 shifted into the southern Indian Ocean, officials and analysts worked with fragments that did not all belong to the same category of knowledge. Inmarsat's satellite handshake data narrowed a vast uncertainty into a plausible arc. That was a real achievement, and a consequential one. But it did not identify the aircraft in any ordinary visual sense, did not track it continuously through its final hours, and did not by itself attribute cause. The distinction mattered. Search vessels were sent across an ocean because one kind of output had been mistaken, in public discussion at least, for several others at once.

Words do damage when they blur. A contact appears on a screen, a vessel shape emerges from radar backscatter, a thermal anomaly flares near a remote installation, and people say the same thing: we saw it. Yet "saw" conceals more than it reveals. To detect is one act. To identify is another. To track requires a further shift in time and method. Attribution demands something else again: a move from observing an object or event to attaching meaning, responsibility, or intent to it. Five plain words matter here.

The Arctic punishes loose vocabulary because it makes each of these outputs harder to produce, and costlier to confuse. Search areas are immense. Surface conditions distort familiar visual cues. Weather and light interrupt optical confidence. Radio and positioning uncertainties complicate correlation. Follow-up assets may be hours away or committed elsewhere. Under those conditions, a system designed to sweep broad areas for anomalies may prove excellent at detection and weak at identification. A system built for crisp forensic detail may offer persuasive identification and poor tracking because it cannot revisit often enough. A state that treats these outputs as interchangeable will misjudge both capability and risk.

Detection is the most elementary output, though not necessarily the easiest to achieve well. It answers a narrow question: is something there that merits attention? In practical terms, broad-area synthetic aperture radar over sea ice often excels at this task. It can mark objects or surface changes that differ from the surrounding pattern, even in darkness or cloud. The value lies in contrast. A radar scene may reveal a vessel-shaped return, an opening in ice, a disturbance along a route, or a heat-related anomaly when paired with other data. What detection does not guarantee is certainty about what the object is, whether it matters, or whether it will still matter by the time anyone responds. It is a flag, not a verdict.

That modesty should not obscure its importance. Detection governs where scarce attention goes. In the High North, attention is a resource like fuel or bandwidth: limited, rationed, often consumed by weather and distance before it reaches the contact in question. A good detection system therefore earns its worth by reducing the search field. It tells operators where *not* to look as much as where to look. Yet broad search comes with trade-offs. Wider swath and faster area coverage usually mean less fine detail, more false positives, or heavier dependence on later confirmation. A system that detects well may do so partly because it accepts ambiguity as the price of reach.

Identification raises the standard. Here the question becomes more exacting: what, specifically, is the object or activity that has been detected? That may mean distinguishing a fishing vessel from a naval auxiliary, a runway vehicle from a snow berm, a temporary melt feature from a deliberate track, or a transmission anomaly from ordinary environmental interference. Identification depends on resolution, angle, sensor type, timing, prior knowledge, and interpretive skill. It may require optical imagery where conditions permit, or high-quality radar products interpreted against known signatures, or the fusion of several data sources that each contribute only part of the answer. The crucial point is that identification does not merely add detail. It changes the institutional meaning of the observation. A generic contact invites caution. An identified one can trigger legal authority, diplomatic signalling, or operational response.

The gap between detection and identification is especially treacherous in maritime settings. A satellite may mark a dark vessel-like return north of Norway or near Svalbard, but the operational question is rarely whether *something* was present. It is whether the object belonged there, what it was doing, and whether the state now needs to act. Automatic Identification System transmissions may help if they are present and truthful. Optical imagery may help if cloud and light cooperate. Historical movement patterns may help if the contact behaves consistently. But if those aids fail, detection can remain stranded as suspicious visibility rather than usable certainty. This is why analysts who know the Arctic tend to distrust triumphalist claims based on single images. The image may be impressive; the output may still be preliminary.

Tracking introduces time. A detected or identified object becomes a track only when the system can follow it across successive observations with enough continuity to say something meaningful about movement. That sounds obvious, but continuity is expensive. It depends on revisit rates, orbit design, tasking discipline, communications, data handling, and the ability to correlate one observation with the next without drifting into guesswork. Tracking answers questions that single observations cannot: is a vessel loitering, transiting, turning away, operating in concert with another platform, or returning to a site repeatedly? For Arctic surveillance, these temporal behaviours often matter more than a single moment of recognition because the region rewards those who can interpret pattern rather than snapshot.

Consider the hunt for under-ice or near-ice activity, whether civil, commercial, or military. A broad-area system may detect recurring signatures along a route, but only repeated observations can tell whether the behaviour constitutes routine passage or something more deliberate. A contact seen once near a northern facility may amount to little. The same contact appearing over several passes, changing speed, altering route in relation to known patrol patterns, or switching emissions behaviour becomes a different analytic object. Tracking therefore depends not only on hardware but on persistence in the strict sense: enough timely observations, linked with enough confidence, to support an account of behaviour over time. This is where constellation design, ground access, and processing discipline begin to weigh as heavily as sensor quality.

Attribution is the most demanding output because it crosses from observation into responsibility and intent. It asks not simply what happened or where, but who did it, whether it was deliberate, and how strongly the evidence supports that judgement. Attribution may concern a vessel violating a restricted zone, a signal disruption affecting navigation, a surface feature linked to industrial activity, or a military movement presented publicly as routine and interpreted privately as coercive. In every case, the evidentiary threshold rises because the consequence of error rises with it. Detection can tolerate some uncertainty. Identification tolerates less. Attribution often requires corroboration from outside the original sensing chain altogether: intelligence from other domains, legal records, previous patterns, technical analysis of interference, or direct observation closer to the event.

The distinction became painfully clear in the months following the Nord Stream explosions in the Baltic Sea in September 2022. The incident did not occur in the Arctic, but it offers a disciplined lesson. Detection was immediate in one sense: something had happened. Identification of the damaged infrastructure followed quickly enough. Tracking of nearby vessel movements and maritime patterns became a major analytic task. Attribution, however, remained deeply contested because it required far more than awareness of the event and the surrounding traffic picture. That sequence matters because public discourse often collapses it. People speak as though observing aftermath, or even nearby movement, amounts to a settled account of cause. It does not. Arctic incidents will generate the same pressure to overclaim, perhaps more so because distance and environment make direct corroboration slower.

The need for distinct vocabulary also clarifies why optimising for one output often weakens another. A wide-area radar system built to detect anomalies across huge expanses of ocean and ice may accept lower resolution, coarser classification, and a higher burden of follow-up. That is not a flaw; it is an architectural choice. By contrast, a narrow-swath, high-detail optical system may support precise identification under good conditions and still fail as a tracking tool if its revisit cadence is poor or its dependence on light is too severe. The tension is not abstract. Procurement officials choose it. Tasking officers manage it. Analysts inherit it. When a government demands both broad persistent search and courtroom-grade detail from one architecture, disappointment is nearly guaranteed.

This is where efficiency must be translated into visible practice. A system that searches broadly but generates too many false leads consumes patrol time, analyst hours, and scarce downlink capacity. A system that waits for exquisite confirmation before flagging a contact may preserve confidence while missing the moment in which a low-confidence alert would have been operationally useful. Risk, likewise, should not remain an airy term. In Arctic surveillance, risk appears as a diverted aircraft, an uninspected vessel, a delayed warning, a diplomatic statement issued on thinner evidence than officials admit, or a costly deployment launched to inspect what later proves harmless. The outputs define the behaviour.

A useful limitation belongs here. In some settings, modern data fusion and machine-learning-assisted analysis can compress the distance between outputs. A system may detect and classify an object quickly enough that the gap between detection and provisional identification becomes operationally small. Commercial maritime analytics already do something like this in certain lower-latitude environments by combining imagery, vessel transmissions, and behavioural models. One should not deny the gain. Better software, denser constellations, and more disciplined fusion have changed what is possible. But the Arctic remains a stern test of those gains because it withholds the background conditions that make them look effortless elsewhere. Sparse corroboration, variable illumination, intermittent signals, and difficult ground truth all make confident automation harder to sustain.

The limitation therefore reinforces the main point. Even when outputs converge in practice, they should remain separate in thought. A "high-confidence contact" produced quickly by fused systems may still fall short of attribution. A classification may still require human confirmation before a patrol is launched or a public accusation made. Precision in language protects decision-making because it forces institutions to admit what kind of knowledge they actually possess. This is not pedantry. It is a guard against escalation born of verbal carelessness.

The Arctic amplifies the cost of that carelessness because corroboration is rarely cheap. To move from detection to identification may require another satellite pass, a different sensor, a patrol aircraft, a vessel report, or a legal cross-check. To sustain tracking may require that the contact remain observable through weather, darkness, and communications constraints. To attribute may require assembling evidence from domains whose clocks do not align neatly with orbital opportunity. Every step upward in certainty therefore carries not just technical demands but opportunity costs. One asset sent to verify one lead cannot verify another. One analyst queue devoted to a suspicious anomaly is unavailable for routine monitoring elsewhere. Vocabulary matters because it disciplines resource allocation before it disciplines prose.

The quiet motif running through all of this is the mark. A mark on radar. A mark on ice. A mark on a chart. At detection, the mark merely says: attend. At identification, it says: name me properly. At tracking, it says: follow me through time. At attribution, it says: explain why I am here and who bears responsibility. The mark remains the same only in appearance. Analytically, it changes with each question asked of it. Confusing those questions is one of the oldest habits in surveillance culture, and one of the most dangerous in a region where the cost of follow-up is so high.

What emerges is not a hierarchy in which each higher output simply improves the lower one. Detection, identification, tracking, and attribution are different products with different clocks, different evidentiary burdens, and different institutional uses. A coastguard may need rapid detection and workable identification. A military headquarters may prize tracking. A government considering a public accusation may need attribution and therefore patience. The same sensing architecture may serve all of them partially and none of them perfectly. Once that is understood, claims about persistence, coverage, and awareness become easier to test. What exactly is being promised? A mark found once, a contact named correctly, a behaviour followed over time, or a responsibility established strongly enough to act? The answer to that question will determine not just what kind of system the Arctic requires, but what kind of uncertainty its operators must still learn to live with.

Chapter 2

High Latitude Geography and Physics

How can a place receive more satellite passes and still remain hard to watch? That is the High North's first correction to lazy language about coverage. A map of orbital tracks can suggest abundance. The operational picture often says otherwise: near the pole, geometry stops behaving as intuition expects.

A satellite may pass frequently over Arctic latitudes and still provide only awkward views of the object that matters. "Overhead" becomes a misleading comfort word. The angle of view shifts. Shadows lengthen. Surfaces that appear simple on a map become elusive when seen through low light, glare, snow, clouds, or radio interference. A pass is not the same thing as a useful look, and a useful look is not the same thing as a dependable service.

The distinction matters because political and institutional claims often outrun physical reality. Governments, firms, and publics like the language of persistence because it sounds settled, almost administrative. Persistent awareness appears to promise continuity, confidence, and speed. Yet the Arctic keeps pressing a harder question: persistence of what, under which conditions, and sustained by which ground realities? A coverage claim that ignores viewing angle, illumination, signal behaviour, or maintenance access is less a description than an aspiration.

This is the chapter's central tension. The Arctic invites ambitious surveillance promises even as it exposes the material limits behind them. High latitude does not merely make ordinary systems work a little worse. It changes the terms under which they should be judged. Geometry alters what can be seen clearly. Seasonal light alters what can be interpreted with confidence. The auroral and ionospheric environment alters what can be linked, timed, and trusted. Remoteness alters what can be installed, repaired, powered, and kept alive through bad weather and worse luck.

Those constraints do not sit in separate boxes. They collide. A sensor may collect usable data, while the link carrying it degrades. A terminal may stand in the right place geographically and prove hard to sustain logistically. A region may appear transparent for one season and become interpretively treacherous in another. This is why the High North resists any account that treats space systems as self-contained technical marvels. Physics shows up in operations. Logistics shows up in latency. The horizon keeps the score.

The stakes are not only military, though military planning sharpens them. Civil aviation, maritime safety, fisheries enforcement, environmental monitoring, search and rescue, infrastructure protection, and diplomatic signalling all depend on surveillance outputs that must survive Arctic conditions rather than merely reach them. Trust, in this setting, becomes visible in behaviour: whether an aircraft changes route, whether a coastguard launches, whether a warning is issued, whether a report is treated as provisional or acted upon. Efficiency becomes visible too: in the choice to re-task a sensor, to accept degraded data, to wait for corroboration, or to spend scarce bandwidth on one product instead of another.

Later pressures only deepen the problem. A system built without respect for Arctic physics may still function impressively in calm conditions and fail at the exact moment demand becomes politically charged. That is when hidden dependencies stop being background details. A low elevation angle becomes a missed contact. Seasonal darkness becomes a dispute over interpretation. A disturbed signal becomes uncertainty about timing and position at once. A remote station becomes the weak hinge on which a grander claim of coverage quietly swings.

The path forward begins with the shape of the Earth itself and the uncomfortable truth that latitude changes the meaning of a pass, a look, and a revisit. From there the argument moves into the unstable bargain between light and surface, where snow, ice, shadow, and season alter what images can bear. The radio environment then intrudes, reminding us that awareness depends not only on sensing but on links and timing that remain vulnerable to the sky through which they travel. The line eventually reaches the ground, where remoteness ceases to be scenery and becomes a design variable governing which nodes can be sustained at all.

The Arctic is often described as harsh, and that is true but incomplete. Its sharper quality is selectiveness. It rewards architectures that acknowledge angle, season, signal, and distance as one intertwined problem, and it punishes those that treat them as manageable afterthoughts. The question that follows is therefore not whether a satellite can reach the High North. The harder test is whether the geometry of that reach can withstand the claims built upon it.

Polar geometry and viewing angles

On 23 July 1972, NASA launched Landsat 1 from Vandenberg Air Force Base in California, beginning a civil Earth observation record that taught generations of analysts a deceptively simple lesson: a satellite pass is not the same as an all-purpose view. The satellite came north and south, again and again, laying down a disciplined archive of the planet. Yet even with such regularity, what it could show depended on angle, timing, and the ground beneath the track. Near the pole, those conditions stop behaving like background details. They become the story.

The map lies politely. That is the quiet problem. A coverage diagram can make the Arctic look saturated with opportunity because so many orbital tracks seem to converge there. Lines crowd together as they approach the top of the globe. To an untrained eye, this suggests abundance bordering on omniscience. More passes, more access, more knowledge. But the geometry of polar surveillance is less generous than the map implies. A pass may be frequent and still badly shaped for the target in question. It may come at an awkward angle, with a swath that misses the object of interest, or with viewing conditions that complicate interpretation just when speed matters most.

Latitude changes the meaning of "overhead". At mid-latitudes, people often imagine a satellite as if it arrives from above in a clean, almost vertical relation to the surface. In the far north, that intuition needs correction. The satellite may indeed pass nearby in orbital terms, yet the useful look can still be oblique rather than comfortably direct. For some sensors and some targets, that difference is manageable. For others, it is decisive. A vessel, an airstrip, a coastal installation, a line in the ice, a communications site near broken terrain: each responds differently to angle. The same orbit that appears to promise repetition can therefore produce very uneven surveillance value.

This is the first conceptual distinction to keep firm. Frequency of access and quality of geometry are related, but they are not identical. Show the orbital ground tracks of a near-polar satellite, and the Arctic appears privileged. Name the concept properly, and the picture sharpens: track density does not automatically yield favourable observation geometry for every task. Explain why, and the reason becomes plain enough. The Earth curves away, targets present different shapes depending on aspect, and sensors have their own constraints on swath, pointing, distortion, and interpretability. The implication is strategic. Political claims about persistent Arctic coverage often borrow the visual comfort of dense orbital tracks while passing over the harder question of what kind of look those tracks actually provide.

A simple comparison between roughly 70 degrees north and 85 degrees north helps. The same satellite in the same orbit may revisit both latitudes often, but not in the same operational sense. Around 70 degrees north, a target sits within a region where geometry can still support relatively workable combinations of swath, angle, and follow-up for many missions, depending on the system. By 85 degrees north, orbital convergence may increase opportunities in one narrow sense while also complicating others. Passes bunch. Angular relationships shift. The temptation to speak of near-constant access grows stronger just as the practical meaning of each access window becomes more conditional. A system may notice more often and understand less clearly.

That tension matters because targets are not abstract points. They are objects and activities with shape, orientation, context, and motion. Consider a ship moving through high northern waters. A broad-area radar system may detect it readily because the geometry and sensor mode are good enough to separate the vessel from the sea or ice background. Detection is achieved. Yet if the aim is finer interpretation - the exact class of vessel, deck activity, ice escort behaviour, or a subtle interaction with nearby traffic - angle starts to matter differently. A look taken from one aspect may reveal a convincing signature; another may flatten, distort, or obscure the very features an analyst wants to compare. The pass still counts statistically. Operationally, it may fall short.

Optical systems expose the same truth in another register. A facility on land observed under a high, forgiving sun angle can often be read with comfortable confidence. Push northward, combine low solar elevation with snow cover, and geometry enters the image twice: once through the satellite's line of sight and again through the sunlight that shapes shadow, contrast, and surface texture. What seemed like a simple overhead image becomes an argument about what the shadows are actually saying. A mound of ploughed snow, a vehicle revetment, a berm, a ridge, a trench-like mark in ice or frozen ground - these can look more or less significant depending on the viewing relationship. The eye likes certainty. Geometry withholds it.

The 2019 failure of India's Chandrayaan-2 lander is a useful, if non-Arctic, reminder that geometry governs search even when the object is known, and the stakes are unambiguous. After the Vikram lander was lost near the lunar south pole in September 2019, imagery analysis depended not simply on the existence of orbital coverage by NASA's Lunar Reconnaissance Orbiter, but on the conditions under which the site could be seen and interpreted. Subsequent imaging and identification took time because angle, lighting, and surface context shaped what analysts could credibly claim. The moon is not the Arctic, and the analogy should not be strained. Still, the lesson travels well: repeated opportunity does not erase the discipline imposed by viewing geometry. It only gives more chances to negotiate with it.

Polar surveillance also complicates the meaning of revisit. Revisit sounds like a neutral measure, as if one could count passes and be done. But whether a revisit is worthy of the name depends on what needs revisiting. If the task is to maintain broad awareness over open water or ice margin, a wide-swath system may provide frequent, useful returns even when each individual look is coarse. If the task is to compare subtle changes at a fixed installation, assess damage, or distinguish one small object from another, the same revisit rate may be misleading. One can revisit a target many times without revisiting it under geometrically comparable conditions. The clock may repeat while the look does not.

This is where trust should be translated into behaviour rather than left as a comfortable abstraction. Analysts trust a system when they are willing to classify on the basis of its imagery, not merely admire it. Operators trust it when they decide not to launch another asset because the space-based view is good enough. Policymakers trust it when they are prepared to make a public claim, or to refrain from one, on the strength of the available surveillance record. Geometry enters each of those behaviours. A state that boasts of persistent coverage but quietly re-tasks aircraft for confirmation is revealing what it really trusts. A command centre that waits for another pass before escalating a report is making the same confession in operational form.

The political vocabulary of persistence, therefore, deserves suspicion. Persistence can mean frequent sampling, long dwell, rapid revisit, or a socially broader idea of dependable awareness. Geometry helps separate those meanings. A highly elliptical orbit may offer prolonged visibility over high latitudes and thereby support certain communications or observation missions with unusual effectiveness. A polar low Earth orbit may provide repeated passes valuable for mapping, search, and environmental monitoring. Neither architecture grants a universal licence to say "we see continuously" without qualifications. The claim may be defensible for one mission profile and misleading for another. Much depends on the target's location, the sensor's characteristics, the angle at which observation occurs, and the interval before a useful next look.

A credible limitation must be granted here. Modern systems are not helpless before bad geometry. Agile pointing, multi-satellite constellations, diverse sensor types, and increasingly sophisticated processing can mitigate many of the old weaknesses. Analysts can compare scenes from different passes, use radar where optical images disappoint, and fuse overhead data with maritime, airborne, or terrestrial information. That is real progress. It would be foolish to write as though Arctic surveillance were trapped in a permanently primitive state. The far north is watched more capably now than it was a generation ago.

Yet the limitation does not dissolve the underlying argument. Mitigation is not abolition. Pointing agility can improve a look while narrowing swath or complicating scheduling. Denser constellations can increase chances of useful access while multiplying demands on tasking, downlink, and analysis. Sensor diversity can reduce one form of ambiguity while introducing another. A radar image may cut through cloud and darkness but require careful interpretation of aspect and surface response. A multi-sensor fusion product may strengthen confidence while obscuring which input did the decisive work. The Arctic remains a place where geometry has to be managed rather than assumed away.

One reason this matters so much in the High North is that the penalty for misreading geometry is often paid later, somewhere else in the chain. A state persuaded by optimistic coverage claims may procure the wrong mix of satellites, underinvest in complementary sensing, or promise political reassurance that its architecture cannot regularly deliver. An operator may treat a near-polar pass as equivalent to a decisive look and then discover that the image supports detection but not reliable identification. An analyst may inherit products gathered under mismatched angles and spend precious time trying to compare what should not be compared too confidently. Geometry, in other words, converts easily into latency, doubt, and unnecessary follow-up.

The window is the motif worth keeping in view. Every pass is a window, but not every window opens the same way. Some are narrow and sharp. Some are broad and fogged. Some look straight enough to support firm judgement. Others glance across the surface and leave shadows arguing with shape. At 70 degrees north, the window may often be workable for a certain class of mission. At 85 degrees north, the same orbital design may still deliver repeated openings while altering what can be trusted through them. The difference is not merely cartographic. It governs what states can honestly claim to know.

That honesty matters because surveillance in the Arctic has become entangled with deterrence, reassurance, and public proof. To say that a region is persistently watched is to make a political promise about readiness, transparency, and control. But geometry is indifferent to political appetite. It does not bend because officials prefer the language of seamless awareness. It asks plainer questions. From what angle was the target seen? At what interval can it be seen again in a comparable way? What kind of judgement does that geometry support, and what kind does it merely tempt people to overstate? Those questions do not weaken Arctic surveillance. They discipline it. The harder problem is whether governments, firms, and publics are willing to speak about persistence in a language strict enough to survive the view from 85 degrees north.

Seasonal light and surface contrast

In May 2020, as fuel spread across land and water near Norilsk in the Russian Arctic, satellite imagery quickly became part of the public understanding of the disaster. The images mattered because they seemed to answer a simple question: what happened, and where had it gone? But the usefulness of those views did not rest on visibility alone. Snowmelt, exposed ground, water surfaces, cloud, and changing light all shaped what could be read confidently and what still required care. The Arctic offered an image, then immediately demanded interpretation.

Light is not neutral here. That is the first discipline the region imposes on optical surveillance. People often speak as if an optical image were a transparent slice of reality, a direct visual settlement of doubt. In the Arctic, light behaves more like an argument. For part of the year, darkness withdraws the familiar visual world almost entirely. For other periods, the sun skims the horizon, stretching shadows, flattening some surfaces while exaggerating others. Snow and ice do not simply brighten a scene. They alter contrast, wash out edges, conceal depth cues, and turn ordinary acts of seeing into comparative judgement. An image may be clear and still remain uncertain in meaning.

Polar night is the bluntest example. When the sun drops below the horizon for extended periods, conventional optical imaging loses the ordinary conditions on which its intuitive power depends. This does not mean all optical observation stops or that every scene becomes useless. Twilight conditions, moonlight, atmospheric glow, artificial illumination, and specialised low-light systems can still produce material of value. Yet the practical point is harsher than that technical caveat. A state cannot build claims of routine visual transparency around conditions that repeatedly remove the visual basis of confidence. During polar night, optical systems cease to be universal witnesses and become conditional ones. They may still contribute; they no longer dominate.

That shift matters because optical imagery has a peculiar political authority. People trust what resembles eyesight. A colour image of a ship, a runway, a camp, a scar in the snow, or machinery gathered on a frozen shore appears easier to interpret than radar backscatter or signal data. Public narratives often move on that ease. Officials release visible imagery because it persuades audiences more readily than a technical explanation of alternative sensing. Transparency, in this register, is not merely a matter of collection. It is a matter of what can be shown to others and understood without long mediation. The Arctic weakens that public style of proof for months at a time, and weakens it further by complicating interpretation even when light returns.

Low sun angles create a second and subtler difficulty. An object seen under a high sun often separates itself from the background in familiar ways. Edges look stable. Height reads more naturally. Surface features belong to the object rather than to shadow cast across it. In the High North, especially outside the brief generosity of summer, sunlight arrives shallow and slanting. The result can be visually dramatic and analytically awkward. Long shadows may reveal relief that would otherwise go unnoticed, which can help. The same shadows can also make a low berm resemble a vehicle line, make stored material appear larger than it is, or turn surface undulation into what looks like deliberate construction. A single optical frame then stops being an answer and becomes a prompt for comparison.

Snow deepens the problem because it changes the scene before the analyst even begins. Fresh snow can smooth the ground's visual complexity, hiding tracks, equipment, or disturbed surfaces beneath an apparently clean plane. Wind-packed snow can produce textures that mimic route marks or engineering works. Partial thaw can create dark interruptions and tonal variation that look meaningful because the eye is trained to treat contrast as evidence of structure. Ice adds its own vocabulary: leads, ridges, pressure features, melt ponds, and refrozen areas all alter the visual field. An analyst does not merely look at the Arctic; the Arctic rearranges what looking can safely infer.

The important claim, then, is not that optical imagery fails in the north. That would be crude and false. Optical systems remain indispensable. When conditions align, they offer legibility that other sensors often struggle to match, especially for human audiences who need to inspect a scene directly. A vessel's deck arrangement, the condition of a runway, the presence of vehicles near a facility, the geometry of a temporary camp, the spread of contamination, the boundary between shore and fast ice - these are often most intelligible in optical form. The real issue is the seasonality of interpretability. An image may be technically valid yet operationally weaker because the season has altered contrast, shadow, and surface response in ways that demand more restraint.

The Norilsk spill helps because it sits at the intersection of environmental and strategic observation. The incident drew attention not only because it was severe, but because remote sensing became part of the evidentiary struggle over extent, responsibility, and response. Optical imagery could reveal stained surfaces and visible spread under some conditions, but those readings had to be compared against changing ground and water states, cloud, and the pace of melt. What looked decisive in one frame might require revision in another. The case exposed a broader Arctic truth: public confidence in a visible image often outruns the environmental complexity that produced it.

A second example comes from sea-ice monitoring in the Northern Sea Route and adjacent Arctic waters, where operators, researchers, and governments have long relied on satellite imagery to judge navigability, hazards, and movement. Optical sensors have been central to that work for decades, especially when light and cloud conditions cooperate. Yet experienced users do not treat an optical sea-ice image as self-sufficient. Low-angle light can make the edge of ice appear firmer or more fragmented than it is. Melt ponds can darken ice and mimic open water in ways that confound inexperienced interpretation. Thin cloud can soften contrast without announcing itself dramatically. In such settings, the question is rarely whether the image exists. It is whether the season has made the visible scene more eloquent or more deceptive.

That is why surface contrast deserves to be treated as a physical condition rather than a pictorial one. Contrast sounds like a property of images. In Arctic surveillance, it is also a property of environment. Dark hull against bright ice, black water against white floes, a warm exhaust against frozen ground, tyre marks against fresh snow: these seem like simple oppositions. Yet each depends on angle, weather, time of day, surface age, and sensor settings. Contrast can assist detection magnificently while weakening identification. A dark mark may announce that something is present and still refuse to settle what that something is. Here again, the Arctic separates stages of knowledge that public conversation often collapses.

Risk becomes visible in decisions. Does an analyst treat a suspicious line in snow as evidence of recent movement, or wait for another image? Does a maritime centre divert an aircraft to inspect a possible lead in the ice, knowing the cost of a false alarm and the cost of delay? Does a government publish an image as proof of activity near a sensitive site, or hold it back because the seasonal conditions leave too much room for challenge? Trust in optical imagery does not live in abstract confidence scores alone. It appears that institutions commit assets, make claims, or refrain from both.

A credible limitation must be admitted. Summer can make optical surveillance in the Arctic look almost straightforward. Continuous daylight across parts of the region removes one major obstacle and can dramatically expand the tempo of visible collection. Snow retreat exposes darker surfaces and stronger separations between land, water, infrastructure, and activity. In some circumstances, this can make optical imagery unusually powerful, especially for change detection over time. A reader should not be left with the impression that the Arctic is permanently obscure. It is not.

But the limitation sharpens the main point rather than diluting it. Summer does not abolish interpretive fragility; it changes its form. Glare from water and wet surfaces can flatten detail. Broken cloud still interrupts collection. Melt processes generate new ambiguities, especially across sea ice and coastal margins. Continuous daylight can encourage overconfidence simply because visual access feels abundant. A season of easier looking may conceal how abruptly that ease will vanish, and how much a surveillance system depends on methods that do not disappear when the sun does.

This is where multi-sensor practice enters not as sophistication for its own sake, but as intellectual modesty made technical. Radar does not need sunlight and often handles clouds far better than optical systems, which is why it becomes so important in the High North. Thermal sensing can reveal activity or material differences that visible light fails to show cleanly. Optical imagery, when available under good conditions, can then restore the intuitive and forensic detail that other modes sometimes lack. The gain lies not in any one sensor replacing another, but in comparison. If optical imagery says one thing and radar suggests another, the discrepancy itself becomes information. It tells the analyst what sort of caution the scene deserves.

The move towards multi-sensor use is therefore less a triumphal story about technical abundance than a confession about optical limits. One does not add radar because optical imagery is worthless. One adds it because seasons govern what optical evidence can bear. One does not compare thermal and visible scenes because either is intrinsically superior. One compares them because the Arctic changes the scene faster than single-sensor confidence can safely keep up. A surveillance system that relies on one mode alone may perform brilliantly during favourable periods and then discover that its most publicly persuasive product has become its least dependable basis for timely judgement.

That has consequences for claims about verification. Verification sounds sturdy, even legalistic, as though the word itself could stabilise evidence. In practice, verification in the Arctic often depends on whether one image type can be checked against another before weather, light, or movement alters the scene. A visible image of a vessel near ice may persuade quickly, but its meaning strengthens when matched against radar detections over earlier passes and against positional or communications data where available. A suspected facility change may look dramatic in optical imagery and still require radar, thermal, or later seasonal comparison before analysts can distinguish construction, snow clearance, maintenance, or temporary storage. Verification, then, is not visual certainty. It is disciplined cross-checking under seasonal constraints.

The quiet motif here is glare. Not only the literal glare of low sun on ice or water, but the broader glare of apparent clarity. The Arctic often presents scenes that look obvious at a glance precisely because they are stark: white ground, dark marks, clean boundaries, empty space punctured by singular objects. That starkness flatters the eye. It encourages confidence before context. Yet glare can blind as easily as it illuminates. A scene that appears simple may in fact be seasonally loaded, with surface processes and shadows doing half the talking.

Optical imagery retains a singular place in Arctic surveillance because it satisfies a human desire no other sensor quite matches: the desire to look and feel that one has seen for oneself. That desire is not trivial. It shapes politics, public opinion, and institutional confidence. But the High North insists on a harder standard. Seeing must be compared, timed, and seasonally situated. A bright image in July and a dim uncertainty in January do not represent the same degree of transparency merely because both come from competent satellites. They belong to different evidentiary worlds.

What follows from that is uncomfortable but necessary. Any claim that the Arctic has become straightforwardly visible from space should be met with a seasonal question. Visible when? Visible to whom? Visible enough for detection, for public display, for operational action, or for contested attribution? The answer changes with the return of darkness, with the angle of the sun, with the age and texture of snow, with the condition of ice, and with the willingness of institutions to admit that optical clarity is sometimes an achievement and sometimes a trap. The real test is not whether the next image looks convincing. It is whether the season has made conviction more available than truth.

Auroral effects and radio environment

In October 2018, during NATO's Trident Juncture exercise in northern Norway, authorities reported disruptions to GPS reception in Finnmark. The incident was discussed mainly as a security matter, and understandably so. Yet it also illuminated something more basic and more durable about the High North. In Arctic operations, a signal problem rarely stays in its lane.

The sky interferes twice. That is the point to keep in view. The Arctic airspace and near-space environment do not merely carry communications and positioning signals; they can disturb them in ways that ripple through the entire surveillance chain. A radio link that fades or fluctuates changes more than data throughput. A positioning signal that becomes unreliable changes more than navigation. Timing, synchronisation, geolocation, confidence in sensor products, and the sequencing of decisions can all begin to wobble together. In the High North, the aurora is not only a visual phenomenon. It is also a systems problem.

This matters because radio systems are often discussed as though they were neutral plumbing: important, certainly, but secondary to the more glamorous business of imaging and analysis. The Arctic does not permit that hierarchy. Communications and positioning systems are foundational there precisely because so much else depends on them. A satellite image collected successfully still has to move across links shaped by latitude, weather, interference, antenna geometry, and available margin. A contact located on a map still depends on position and time references that must remain stable enough to support comparison with other sources. When the ionosphere becomes unsettled, the consequences spread laterally. A disturbance in one layer of the chain creates hesitation elsewhere.

The auroral zone sits at the centre of this problem. Charged particles from the Sun interact with the Earth's magnetic field and upper atmosphere, creating the auroral activity that so often appears in photographs of the far north as a curtain of green and red light. Beautiful, yes. Operationally awkward, also yes. Those same physical processes can produce ionospheric irregularities that affect how radio waves propagate. Signals may scintillate, refract unpredictably, weaken, drift, or suffer jumps in apparent range and phase. A radio engineer sees degraded margins. A navigator sees inconsistent positioning. An operations centre sees delay, intermittent confidence, and the unpleasant question of whether the anomaly is environmental, technical, or deliberate.

That distinction between natural disturbance and hostile interference is analytically crucial. Show the symptom - a dropped link, a corrupted data stream, degraded GNSS reception, a patch of failed communications - and several explanations may fit. Name the condition properly and the challenge sharpens: in the Arctic, the radio environment itself can mimic the operational effects of intentional disruption closely enough to slow attribution. Explain why this matters, and the answer becomes strategic rather than merely technical. If operators cannot rapidly tell whether an outage reflects auroral activity, equipment problems, congestion, poor geometry, or malicious action, then uncertainty itself becomes part of the threat picture. The implication is plain. Resilience must be built for ambiguity, not merely for attack.

A familiar example sits in aviation. Aircraft operating in high northern latitudes rely heavily on radio communications and satellite-based navigation, yet both can be stressed by ionospheric conditions. Under disturbed space-weather circumstances, high-frequency communications may degrade, satellite navigation performance may become less reliable, and the operational response may involve route changes, altitude adjustments, communication workarounds, or a greater dependence on procedural margins. The visible behaviour matters more than the abstraction. Crews repeat calls. Dispatchers wait longer for confirmation. Controllers lean more heavily on fallback practices. Confidence shrinks not because the system has vanished, but because it has become harder to trust minute by minute.

A second example comes from the large geomagnetic storm of October-November 2003, often called the Halloween storms. The event affected a range of technological systems, including satellite operations, radio propagation, and navigation performance across different regions. One need not overstate the comparison to learn from it. The lesson is not that every auroral disturbance in the Arctic resembles a major space-weather event. It is that radio and timing systems are exposed to physical conditions that can change faster than institutional language about "reliable connectivity" tends to admit. When that exposure matters operationally, the relevant question is not whether the signal failed completely. It is whether error rates, latency, and uncertainty rose enough to change behaviour.

That phrase - error rates - deserves to stay concrete. Error is not an abstract stain on performance. It appears as packets lost, messages delayed, positions that wander beyond the tolerance a task requires, clocks that no longer align cleanly across systems, and analysts who must decide whether small discrepancies can be ignored or demand re-checking. In a surveillance architecture, these frictions accumulate. A downlink that operates near its margin during quiet conditions may become unreliable when ionospheric variability increases. A navigation solution sufficient for routine transit may prove too unstable for precise geolocation of a sensor product that must later be fused with another source. The arithmetic of failure in the Arctic is often incremental before it is dramatic.

Timing sits at the quiet centre of this. Most readers think of positioning signals in terms of location, which is understandable. But timing is the hidden discipline beneath much of modern surveillance and communications. Networks synchronise to it. Data streams align by it. Sensor fusion depends on it. Logs, hand-offs, and sequence reconstruction all assume that the clocks distributed across a system remain close enough to support meaningful comparison. When Arctic ionospheric conditions disturb the signals that help maintain that temporal order, the damage may not appear as a single broken instrument. It appears as slippage across several instruments at once. A radar detection and a vessel transmission no longer line up cleanly. An image timestamp no longer supports rapid correlation with another feed. A command centre spends longer deciding whether a mismatch is real or administrative.

This is why timing and communications often degrade together in practical Arctic operations. A disrupted or noisy radio environment can make the transmission of data less dependable at the same moment that satellite-derived timing grows less certain. One problem then amplifies the other. A marginal link becomes harder to manage because synchronisation is less stable. A geolocation task becomes harder to validate because the communications path carrying the data is itself erratic. Resilience, in this setting, cannot mean merely keeping one service alive. It means preserving enough cross-system coherence that operators still know which information belongs with which event and can say so without bluffing.

The temptation, especially in policy language, is to treat such disturbances as unusual exceptions. That is too comforting. The High North teaches a sterner lesson. Environmental variability is part of the baseline, not a rare footnote appended to otherwise smooth service. Some days are quiet. Some are not. Systems intended for Arctic use therefore need more than nominal functionality. They need margin. Margin in link budgets, margin in antenna performance, margin in processing tolerance, margin in workflow expectations, and margin in the human habits that govern when to trust automated outputs and when to pause. A system designed to work beautifully only under clean conditions is not truly designed for the Arctic at all.

A useful counterpoint should be conceded. Modern systems are better at handling these conditions than older ones were. Multi-frequency GNSS receivers, improved signal processing, better ionospheric modelling, diverse communications paths, adaptive coding, and more disciplined operational procedures all reduce vulnerability. Some disturbances can be forecast or at least monitored well enough that operators adjust expectations and routing before the worst effects arrive. This is genuine progress. One would be careless to imply that the Arctic remains trapped in a permanent state of radio fragility.

But the concession does not rescue the simpler story that technology steadily erases geography. Mitigation helps, yet it rarely removes the need to choose between cost, complexity, and confidence. A more capable receiver may improve performance while demanding more power, more careful integration, or higher procurement cost. Additional communications paths may reduce dependence on one band or one geometry while adding management burdens of their own. Better forecasting of ionospheric conditions may help operators prepare, but preparation itself is a discipline: someone must watch, interpret, decide, and communicate what the forecast means operationally. Improvement does not abolish uncertainty. It redistributes it.

The radio environment in the Arctic also changes how one should think about trust in sensor products. A surveillance image is not simply an image. It arrives with metadata, timing, geolocation, and a chain of assumptions about signal integrity. If the environment supporting those assumptions has been disturbed, confidence in the product may need recalibration even when the picture still looks usable. That is why a system-level perspective matters so much. A satellite may collect perfectly. A ground station may receive most of the data. Processing may complete on schedule. Yet if timing uncertainty has widened or the communications path has introduced subtle integrity questions, the final product enters decision-making under a shadow that the image alone does not reveal. The aurora leaves fingerprints, even when it does not break the glass.

The practical consequence is that Arctic resilience must be judged by behaviour under degraded conditions, not by headline capability under favourable ones. Does a network fall back gracefully when signal quality drops? Do operators know when to widen tolerances and when to suspend confidence? Can a system compare multiple timing sources or multiple communications paths before ambiguity becomes paralysis? Can institutions tell the difference between a naturally disturbed radio environment and one that merely looks natural because a hostile actor has chosen to hide within the noise? These are not specialist afterthoughts. They are the real tests of whether a surveillance architecture can absorb the north rather than merely point at it.

The motif worth keeping is the flicker. A flicker in the sky, obvious to the eye in an auroral display. A flicker in a signal, visible only in a receiver's struggle. A flicker in confidence, harder to measure but more consequential still. The Arctic trains systems to live with flicker, but not all systems learn equally well. Some treat variability as a design requirement. Others treat it as an inconvenience to be smoothed over by assumptions imported from lower latitudes. The difference appears in moments of pressure: repeated transmissions, unexplained offsets, delayed products, extra verification steps, missed windows, longer silences.

That is why the radio environment belongs at the centre of any serious account of Arctic surveillance. Not because it is more dramatic than imagery or more politically legible than public satellite photographs, but because it is one of the places where the whole chain admits its dependence. A state may claim awareness, persistence, and rapid reaction. The harder question is whether those claims survive when the sky itself begins to interfere with the timing, linking, and positioning on which the rest of the system quietly relies. When the signal flickers, what holds together, and what merely appeared stable while the weather in near-space was kind?

Remoteness and logistics as constraints

In January 2024, a fibre-optic cable between mainland Norway and Svalbard was reported damaged for the second time in recent years, renewing attention to how a place often described in terms of orbital access still depends on a surprisingly narrow set of earthly connections. Svalbard is famous in strategic and scientific discussion because it sits well for contact with polar-orbiting satellites. That is true. It is also reachable only through an infrastructure story far less glamorous than orbital geometry: power systems that must keep running, spare parts that must arrive, personnel who must travel, links that must remain intact, and weather that does not care about the importance of the node it is interrupting. The signal may come from space. The vulnerability often starts on the ground.

A station needs a road. Or something like one. That is the quiet fact Arctic design keeps forcing back into view. People speak of coverage as if it were suspended above the region, a property of orbital mechanics and sensor performance. Yet usable coverage depends on fixed points that can receive, route, maintain, protect, and power the flow of information. A ground terminal that cannot be serviced in winter, an antenna field that loses stable power, a remote installation whose backhaul depends on one cable or one fragile relay path - these do not merely inconvenience a system. They define its real boundary. Arctic remoteness is therefore not scenery. It is an engineering and political condition that decides where surveillance capacity can exist in practice.

That change in emphasis matters because remoteness is often misdescribed as mere distance. In the High North it is more exacting than that. It combines distance with weather, sparse transport, limited local labour, short construction seasons, constrained power options, and long recovery times when something breaks. Show a map and a site may appear well placed: near the right latitude, close to a prospective shipping route, clear of obstructing terrain, available for direct downlink. Name the concept properly and the assessment shifts: a well-sited node is not necessarily a sustainable node. Explain why, and one arrives quickly at ordinary but decisive questions. Can heavy equipment be delivered there? Can generators or fuel be replaced on schedule? Can technicians reach the site safely in all relevant seasons? Can data leave the site through more than one path? The implication is strategic rather than administrative. The Arctic rewards not only those who can place nodes, but those who can keep them alive.

Power is the first discipline. A surveillance network can tolerate many inconveniences; it cannot tolerate prolonged loss of energy at the places where reception, processing, and transfer occur. In temperate and densely connected regions, power is often treated as a utility assumption. In the Arctic it becomes a design variable. Remote stations may depend on local generation, limited storage, long resupply chains, and equipment that must perform in extreme cold. Heating is not ancillary. Enclosures matter. Ice loading matters. Fuel delivery schedules matter. Redundancy becomes a material decision rather than a polite aspiration. An operator choosing between a more remote site with elegant geometry and a less ideal site with dependable power is not balancing technical against technical. They are choosing between nominal performance and sustained service.

The Svalbard case illustrates the point because it is often treated as a triumph of location, and so it is. Svalbard Satellite Station, developed by KSAT near Longyearbyen, became one of the world's most significant sites for communicating with polar-orbiting spacecraft precisely because its latitude gives repeated access to satellites whose paths sweep the High North. But its importance also reveals the other side of the equation. A strategically placed station attracts dependence. Dependence magnifies the consequences of interruption. When fibre backhaul is damaged, when local power or access is stressed, or when a limited set of nodes carries too much of the regional burden, the problem is not local inconvenience. It is regional brittleness. A strong node can become a single point of worry.

Maintenance is the second discipline, and in many Arctic systems it is the harsher one. A ground terminal in a brochure appears static and self-contained. A real terminal ages, drifts, corrodes, accumulates ice, demands calibration, and occasionally fails in ways that only people and parts can repair. Remoteness stretches each of those processes. A fault that would be solved within hours in a well-connected region may linger because flights are delayed, sea access is closed, roads do not exist, or the part in question must be carried in under awkward conditions. This is where time becomes a form of cost. Not merely financial cost, though that is obvious enough, but operational cost measured in deferred passes, longer latency, diminished confidence in continuity, and the temptation to overstate the health of a system because repair is inconvenient to discuss.

That is why maintenance planning in the Arctic cannot be treated as a downstream administrative function. It shapes architecture from the start. A system designer deciding between a cluster of smaller remote terminals and a smaller number of major stations is also deciding between different maintenance philosophies. More dispersed infrastructure may widen access and reduce dependence on single nodes, but it can multiply servicing demands across weather and terrain. Fewer major nodes may ease staffing and concentrate expertise, but they can create painful fragility when one fails. No formula resolves the tension. The correct answer depends on mission priority, available lift, tolerated downtime, and the political willingness to accept dependence on external hosts or partners.

Access, in this sense, is not a synonym for geography. It is a chain of permissions, transport, timing, and survivable working conditions. A site may exist inside the right jurisdiction and still be hard to reach when the season turns. A component may exist in storage and still arrive too late to preserve a downlink schedule that mattered. Personnel may possess the required skills and still be unable to travel because an airfield closes or weather blocks a vessel. The Arctic compresses these ordinary frictions into strategic constraints because the number of alternatives is often small. A missed maintenance window in a crowded southern corridor can sometimes be absorbed quietly. A missed maintenance window in the far north may alter what "persistent coverage" means for weeks.

A second concrete example comes from the radar warning and communications sites spread through northern North America and Greenland, including installations associated with the long history of the DEW Line and its successors. The technology and mission have changed over time, but the enduring lesson remains. Arctic sensing and communications infrastructures do not live by electronics alone. They live by fuel, shelter, transport, seasonal access, and the human capacity to sustain operations in places where the environment imposes its own schedule. The original Cold War radar chain was not simply a feat of detection architecture. It was a feat of logistics under severe geographic constraint. That remains true of modern systems, even when the equipment is smaller, more automated, and more digitally connected. Miniaturisation reduces some burdens. It does not abolish the fact that remote nodes must still be built, powered, visited, secured, and occasionally rescued from their own location.

Risk here becomes visible in specific choices. Does an operator stock more spares on site, accepting higher upfront expense in exchange for shorter repair cycles? Does a government harden power supply at a remote station rather than assume commercial service will suffice? Does a system rely on one premium high-latitude site, or commit to several less ideal sites with more modest throughput but better recoverability? Does an institution tolerate winter access limits because most missions can wait, or does it redesign the network around the few that cannot? These are not marginal questions. They are how sovereignty, reliability, and cost begin to intersect long before lawyers or diplomats enter the room.

The language of coverage often conceals this intersection because it borrows the visual ease of orbital maps. A satellite can pass over a region repeatedly. That much is true. But unless the ground segment can receive and move the resulting data, coverage exists only in a weak sense. The region was sensed. It was not necessarily served. Arctic remoteness therefore forces a sharper definition. Coverage includes the ability to sustain the nodes that translate orbital opportunity into delivered information. If a station cannot remain powered, repaired, staffed, or connected, then the apparent coverage it enables is partly theatrical. The map glows. The service thins.

A credible limitation deserves acknowledgement. Newer technologies can reduce some of the old burdens. Smaller terminals, better automation, improved remote monitoring, more capable satellite relay options, and modular equipment designs can all make Arctic nodes easier to operate than their predecessors. A highly connected network may also route around the temporary loss of one location more gracefully than earlier systems could. This matters, and it would be careless to write as though the region were frozen in an earlier era of heroic logistics and permanent scarcity.

Yet the concession changes the scale of the problem more than its nature. Automation still depends on power. Remote diagnostics still depend on communications. Modular replacement still requires transport. Relay options still rely on governance, prioritisation, and compatible ground support elsewhere. Smaller nodes may be easier to deploy and harder to defend or sustain through prolonged stress. A more distributed architecture can absorb one failure better while creating a larger field of maintenance obligations. The Arctic still asks the same question in a newer accent: not whether a node can be placed, but whether the chain supporting it remains believable when season, distance, and disruption begin to press.

The issue becomes sharper when sovereignty enters by implication. A state with limited domestic ground infrastructure can purchase access, host equipment with partners, or rely on commercial networks whose service may be technically excellent. For many missions that is rational. Sometimes it is the only workable path. But dependence on hosted or shared ground capacity changes the meaning of control. Priority rules matter. Visibility into outages matters. The location of data handling matters. Even the answer to a practical question such as who can enter a site and when can acquire political weight. Remoteness does not merely raise costs. It can thin autonomy.

This is one reason Arctic infrastructure debates often sound more abstract than they really are. People argue about presence, coverage, resilience, and deterrence, but the operative facts may concern fuel deliveries, backup generators, warehouse stock, runway availability, cable redundancy, and maintenance crews able to work in conditions that punish delay. The mundane is strategic here. A state that ignores the mundane may still procure impressive space assets and discover that its weakest point sits in a heated shelter beside an antenna whose spare component is two weeks away.

The quiet motif worth keeping is the hinge. Ground infrastructure in the Arctic functions like one: small relative to the door it moves, easy to overlook until it binds, then impossible to ignore. A hinge must be aligned, lubricated, protected, and able to bear repeated strain. The door may be heavy and handsome; the hinge decides whether it opens when required. In the same way, a terminal or station may account for little of a system's public prestige while deciding much of its practical worth. When the hinge freezes, the argument about coverage becomes embarrassingly concrete.

Remoteness therefore ought to be treated as a design variable from the outset, not as a penalty applied after the interesting work has been done. It shapes siting. It shapes staffing. It shapes maintenance cycles, backhaul choices, power redundancy, physical hardening, and the acceptable distance between failure and repair. Most of all, it shapes honesty. Governments and operators who speak seriously about Arctic surveillance must decide whether they are describing what can be sensed in principle or what can be sustained under pressure. Those are not the same claim.

The harder test lies ahead. A node in the right place can still belong to the wrong network. A station that functions brilliantly can still leave a state dependent on access it does not control. A terminal can survive winter and still fail the politics of priority when demand surges. The Arctic keeps reducing grand promises to grounded questions. Who owns the hinge, who maintains it, and who gets to use the door when it matters most?

Chapter 3

Orbits for Polar Coverage

How can a system pass over the Arctic again and again and still fail to watch it when needed? That is the orbital paradox at the heart of polar surveillance. A map dense with tracks invites confidence. It suggests repetition, access, and the comforting thought that the far north has become a place of routine observation. Yet repetition can conceal as much as it reveals. A satellite may return often, but not with the right angle, not at the right local time, not with the right dwell, and not with the right path for rapid delivery into the hands that matter.

Orbit is policy in slow motion. That is the harder truth. An orbit looks like a technical choice made early, quietly, perhaps even abstractly, in the design life of a system. In practice it governs what kinds of promises can later be made about visibility, persistence, warning time, and reassurance. Some orbits offer discipline: predictable lighting, repeatable geometry, a steady rhythm that suits comparison. Others offer patience: long northern dwell, lingering visibility, a different relation between time and place. Still others promise more than they can keep because the language around them borrows from track maps rather than from operational use.

The seduction of polar coverage begins with a genuine fact. The Arctic does favour certain orbital paths. Satellites in near-polar and related high-inclination regimes encounter the region repeatedly, and that repeated encounter has transformed what states, firms, and researchers can know about the north. But orbital opportunity is not the same thing as usable awareness. The closer one looks, the more each elegant path reveals a trade-off. Predictable illumination is not continuous presence. Long dwell is not universal flexibility. A broader swath may buy more frequent search at the cost of detail. A tighter look may buy forensic value and sacrifice persistence. Even before questions of weather, radio conditions, or ground infrastructure return, the orbit has already decided what sort of surveillance claim remains honest.

This is where the chapter's central tension sharpens. Arctic systems are often judged by the frequency with which they revisit the region, while their real value depends on how well orbital design matches the task being asked of them. A coastal installation, a shipping lane, a moving vessel, a patch of sea ice, a remote airfield, a navigation corridor, a communications mission over high latitudes: none of these demand exactly the same orbital virtues. One architecture may serve one beautifully and another only tolerably. Yet public and political language tends to compress these differences into a single word, persistence, as though every return were a form of durable watchfulness.

The stakes are larger than orbital literacy for its own sake. Surveillance claims shape procurement, alliance expectations, public reassurance, and crisis judgement. If an orbit is mistaken for a guarantee rather than a constraint, institutions may buy the wrong kind of coverage, accept the wrong kind of gap, or assume a continuity that exists mainly in graphic representation. Trust shows itself here in visible ways: whether planners are willing to depend on one system without cueing another, whether operators commit scarce tasking time to narrow detail or broad search, whether a government speaks publicly as though a region is under continuous scrutiny when the underlying architecture offers only disciplined sampling. Orbit choices are not neutral because the decisions built upon them are not neutral.

The burden also grows over time. A constellation is not finished when it reaches space. Polar architectures demand maintenance of geometry as well as hardware. Manoeuvres, ephemeris accuracy, collision avoidance, replacement planning, and traffic management all affect whether a claimed coverage pattern remains predictable enough to trust. A system can look complete at launch and become less reliable in practice as operational burdens accumulate. In the Arctic, where timing and recurrence often matter as much as raw access, that drift from design intent to lived service can alter the practical meaning of awareness without any dramatic public sign that capability has thinned.

The path ahead begins with the orbital form most familiar to Earth observation, where repeatability and lighting discipline offer one kind of order while leaving another kind of gap. It then turns to the very different logic of long northern dwell, where time over place can sometimes substitute for numbers of spacecraft but carries its own communications and ground implications. From there the argument tightens around inclination, coverage boundaries, revisit, and the arithmetic by which constellations trade detail for frequency before returning, necessarily, to the operational work of keeping such systems where they are supposed to be.

A quiet motif runs through all of this: the timetable. Some timetables reassure because they are regular. Others matter because they linger at the station long enough to be useful. Some look generous until one notices what hours they miss every day, or what destinations they never truly serve. Orbital design works in much the same way. The timetable may be elegant, but elegance does not answer the harder question of whether the train arrives when the decision needs it.

The Arctic has become a proving ground for orbital claims because it rewards precision and punishes slogans. To say that a satellite goes north is easy. To say what kind of northern service it can actually sustain is harder. The real test is not whether an orbit touches the polar region, or even how often it does, but what sort of watchfulness that motion can honestly deliver once angle, dwell, revisit, and operational upkeep are forced into the same sentence.

Sun-synchronous orbits and repeatability

On 23 July 1972, NASA launched Landsat 1 from Vandenberg Air Force Base in California, establishing a pattern of Earth observation that still shapes how much of the world imagines satellite surveillance. The achievement was not simply that a camera had been put into orbit. It was that the orbit itself imposed order. By returning over the Earth's surface at a consistent local solar time, the satellite made comparison possible in a disciplined way. A field, a coastline, a city edge, a river mouth, a patch of sea ice: each could be seen again under roughly similar lighting conditions. That regularity turned pictures into records.

The Arctic benefited from that logic and also exposed its limits. A pass repeated under comparable light can reveal change with unusual clarity. Snow retreat, ice fracture, melt pond development, shoreline movement, the appearance of new infrastructure, vessel presence near a fixed route - all become easier to compare when the sun stands in roughly the same relation to the surface from one image to the next. Repeatability matters. But the same feature that makes sun-synchronous orbits so useful for polar observation also encourages a misunderstanding that recurs in policy papers, marketing material, and public commentary: predictable lighting is not the same thing as persistent watching.

That distinction deserves care because sun-synchronous low Earth orbits have become the working grammar of much modern Earth observation. The appeal is plain enough. Show a satellite that crosses high latitudes repeatedly, name the concept properly, and one sees why designers favour it: a sun-synchronous orbit lets the satellite pass a given place at nearly the same local solar time on successive visits. Explain why that matters, and the answer is practical rather than ornamental. Analysts can compare scenes with less confusion from changing shadows. Long-term records acquire visual discipline. Surface changes become easier to attribute to the ground rather than to the wandering sun. The implication is powerful. In the Arctic, where snow, ice, and low sun angles already complicate interpretation, repeatability buys a kind of honesty.

A clock in the sky. That is the quiet motif worth keeping in view. Sun-synchronous systems behave like clocks, returning with a regularity that can make the far north look more orderly than it often feels from the ground. The clock helps because it reduces one variable. If a satellite images the same coastline, facility, or sea-ice margin again under similar light, then differences between the scenes are less likely to arise from purely visual distortion. This is why so many civil, commercial, and security-relevant Earth observation systems favour such orbits. Repeatability is not glamour. It is method.

For Arctic observation, that method has genuine strategic value. A government trying to monitor seasonal infrastructure activity, a shipping analyst comparing ice conditions along a northern route, a fisheries authority watching recurrent use of maritime zones, or a researcher measuring environmental change all benefit from images gathered under comparable illumination. The same is true for many forms of security analysis. A fixed site seen at a stable local time over weeks or months yields a cleaner record than one viewed under wildly shifting light. Tracks in snow, stockpiles, vehicle concentrations, construction progress, runway clearing, patterns of access: these often become legible not because one image is spectacular, but because several images can be compared without the sun constantly changing the terms of the argument.

The Copernicus Sentinel missions offer a good public example. Sentinel-2, operated within the European Union's Copernicus programme, uses a sun-synchronous orbit precisely to support repeat imaging under comparable lighting conditions for land and coastal observation. In Arctic and sub-Arctic settings, that repeatability helps analysts compare surface change with a steadiness that would be harder to achieve otherwise. The orbit does not solve cloud, darkness, or all questions of angle, but it gives users a disciplined temporal rhythm. That rhythm matters when interpretation depends on whether a visible difference reflects actual change on the ground or merely the misleading drama of altered sunlight.

A second example lies in the long Landsat archive itself, especially over northern landscapes where seasonal transitions are decisive. Landsat scenes of Alaska, northern Canada, Greenland, and Siberia have allowed decades of comparison because the system's orbital design favours consistency of observation. The record supports environmental science, certainly, but its lesson extends beyond science. When states speak of knowing the Arctic through space, much of what they mean in practice derives from repeatable comparison rather than continuous presence. The archive is persuasive not because it watches without interruption, but because it revisits with enough discipline to make change visible across time.

That is exactly where misunderstanding begins. Repeatability is often mistaken for persistence because both are forms of recurrence. Yet they serve different questions. Repeatability asks whether observations can be compared under similar conditions. Persistence asks whether the system can maintain timely awareness of events as they unfold. A sun-synchronous orbit excels at the first task. It may or may not satisfy the second. If a vessel enters a northern strait, departs before the next suitable pass, and leaves only a brief trace, then the orbit's disciplined lighting offers little comfort. If a remote installation changes subtly between repeat passes, the system may reveal that beautifully. If the question is what happened during the hours between those passes, the same system may say almost nothing.

This is why public coverage maps deserve suspicion. A map showing dense polar tracks can suggest omnipresence. The visual effect is seductive. Lines converge near the pole, and the eye reads the convergence as saturation. But orbital tracks do not equal uninterrupted surveillance. They show opportunity, not certainty. They show where a satellite may pass, not whether the pass will observe the right target, under the right conditions, at the right moment, with the right sensor settings, and with rapid enough delivery to shape a decision. The distinction is not pedantic. It governs what governments and publics should believe when they hear claims about routine Arctic watchfulness.

Repeat cycles sharpen the problem further because they create recurring absences as well as recurring access. A sun-synchronous satellite may return to a region with admirable regularity and still miss events that happen at roughly the same local times between passes. The pattern can become systematic. If the orbit favours morning observations over a given area, then changes that occur reliably outside that observational window may remain under-sampled. The system is not failing. It is keeping its timetable. The limitation lies in the timetable itself. What recurs visibly in the orbital schedule can produce invisible blind spots in operational awareness.

This matters especially in the Arctic because so much activity there is intermittent, mobile, or seasonally compressed. A fixed site may reward repeat imaging. A moving vessel, temporary camp, short-duration deployment, or transient surface anomaly may not. A system built around regular local solar time can detect patterned change well while remaining weak at capturing fleeting events. That trade-off is often acceptable. Sometimes it is ideal. But trouble begins when repeatability is marketed or politically interpreted as though it had solved the problem of temporal coverage in a stronger sense than it really has.

The relationship between light and persistence becomes even more complicated in high latitudes because local solar time remains meaningful only within the larger facts of Arctic seasonality. During polar night, the virtue of sun-synchronous optical observation is sharply constrained by the absence of usable daylight. During seasons of low sun, repeatability may stabilise illumination relative to itself while still leaving analysts with long shadows, glare, and difficult contrast. A repeatable optical view in poor Arctic light may still be much better than an irregular one. It does not become an all-weather, all-hour instrument by virtue of its consistency. The clock in the sky keeps good time; the Arctic does not always offer a readable scene.

A credible limitation must be granted here. Sun-synchronous systems are often embedded in broader constellations, and constellations can mitigate some of the weaknesses just described. Multiple satellites in coordinated orbital planes can increase revisit frequency. Cross-cueing with radar systems can reduce dependence on daylight. Tasking discipline and archive comparison can make even relatively sparse repeat visits strategically useful. It would be foolish to imply that sun-synchronous observation remains trapped in a solitary-satellite model inherited from an earlier era. Much has changed, and some modern constellations extract remarkable value from carefully designed repeat patterns.

Yet the concession strengthens the central point. Even when many satellites share related orbital logic, repeatability and persistence remain distinct achievements. A larger constellation may increase the number of repeat looks while still sampling the world rather than watching it continuously. A fused optical and radar architecture may provide far stronger awareness than optical repeatability alone, but that is precisely because it adds capabilities that sun-synchronous optical design does not itself guarantee. The more advanced the system becomes, the more important it is to separate which benefit comes from which layer of the architecture.

The trade-off also shapes trust. Trust, here, should be translated into visible decisions rather than left as a flattering abstraction. Analysts trust repeatable imagery when they use it to measure change across time instead of demanding new confirmation from different angles. Operators trust it when they choose not to re-task scarce resources because the next scheduled pass will likely offer a comparable view. Policymakers trust it when they make claims about patterns of activity grounded in repeated observation rather than one striking frame. But none of those behaviours implies that they would trust the same system to maintain near-continuous awareness of mobile events. A state may rely heavily on repeatable optical imagery for long-horizon monitoring and still turn elsewhere for timely warning.

This difference often appears in the contrast between broad public imagery and quieter operational architectures. Publicly released optical images from sun-synchronous systems are persuasive because they look legible and methodical. They help tell a story of what has changed. Operational users, however, often need something harsher and faster. They need to know what happened since the last pass and whether the next pass will come soon enough to matter. Repeatability excels at the first question. Persistence presses the second. The Arctic, with its weather, darkness, and mobility, forces that distinction into the open.

A further tension lies in the very virtue that makes sun-synchronous orbits attractive. By fixing local solar time, the orbit reduces interpretive noise from changing illumination. That is a major gain. But what it gains in comparability it may sacrifice in temporal diversity. The system sees a place again and again at roughly the same kind of hour. If behaviour varies by time of day, a repeatable orbit may repeatedly capture only part of the pattern. A facility active at one period and quiet at another may look more stable than it really is. A shipping route may seem orderly because the observations favour certain windows. The schedule can clarify change across scenes while still under-representing the full rhythm of activity.

That is why the most careful users treat sun-synchronous data not as a complete account but as a disciplined slice of one. The slice is valuable precisely because it is disciplined. It supports comparison, baseline building, and the detection of deviation against a stable visual record. It is less suited, by itself, to claims of seamless surveillance. A recurring morning look is not the same as an all-day watch. A beautifully repeatable archive is not a substitute for persistent cueing. A coverage map crowded with polar tracks does not dissolve the hours between them.

The clock returns at the end because it captures both the strength and the limit of the orbit. A good clock does not improvise. It returns, regular and exact, allowing other things to be measured against it. Sun-synchronous observation offers that kind of order to Arctic surveillance, and the order is precious. But a clock is not a guard standing at the door. It keeps time faithfully while events happen between its chimes. The harder question for anyone reading a claim about polar coverage is therefore simple enough to ask and difficult enough to answer honestly: does this system merely return predictably, or can it also remain present enough to matter when the Arctic refuses to wait for the next scheduled look?

Highly elliptical orbits and long dwell

On 23 April 1965, the Soviet Union launched Molniya-1 from Baikonur, opening a path that geostationary communications could not easily offer to the far north. The problem was plain. Satellites fixed above the equator appear low over high latitudes, and ever lower as one moves north. For users in the Soviet Arctic, that geometry was a practical handicap rather than an academic quirk. Molniya's answer was not to fight the pole with more of the same, but to change the orbit entirely: stretch it into a long ellipse, let the satellite race through its low point, and then linger high over northern latitudes where it could be seen for much longer.

That lingering matters. In a highly elliptical orbit, a satellite does not divide its attention evenly across the Earth. It spends disproportionate time near apogee, the high and slow part of the orbit, where orbital motion slackens and the spacecraft appears to hang over one broad region before sweeping away again. For Arctic users, this creates a distinctive kind of service. The satellite is not fixed in the sky, yet for a substantial period it behaves as though it has decided to stay. That is the promise of dwell: not omnipresence, not global equality, but sustained attention where ordinary equatorial logic begins to fail.

The appeal of highly elliptical orbits begins with a simple show-and-name discipline. Show a northern operator trying to maintain communications or awareness at latitudes where geostationary satellites sit uncomfortably low on the horizon, and the value of long northern dwell becomes immediately visible. Name the concept properly and one sees that highly elliptical orbits are not eccentric leftovers from a more improvisational space age. They are deliberate answers to a geographical problem. Explain how they work, and the reason for their continued relevance becomes clearer. By placing apogee over the northern hemisphere and allowing the spacecraft to loiter there, the orbit substitutes time over target for the constant equatorial vantage that the Arctic does not receive gracefully. The implication is strategic: in some missions, dwell can achieve with a smaller fleet what would otherwise demand a denser constellation of low Earth orbit satellites.

This does not mean that highly elliptical systems are simpler. It means they solve a different problem. A low Earth orbit constellation offers recurrence through numbers and motion: more spacecraft, more passes, more sampling opportunities. A highly elliptical architecture offers prolonged northern presence from fewer spacecraft by allowing each one to spend long intervals where the mission most needs it. That is an elegant bargain for certain communications and observation tasks, especially where users value continuity of link or regional awareness more than global uniformity. The elegance, however, resides in fit, not universality. A system built around dwell trades one set of burdens for another.

The classic Soviet Molniya and later Tundra concepts illustrate this well. Molniya orbits became associated with communications and broadcasting for high latitudes because they gave northern territories something geostationary satellites could not reliably provide: a higher look angle and a longer period of useful visibility. Tundra-style orbits pursued related aims with different orbital periods and service characteristics. The lesson that matters here is not the engineering taxonomy for its own sake. It is the institutional logic. States facing northern service gaps learned that orbital lingering could be more valuable than formal fixity. If the satellite could not stand still in the sky, it could at least spend long enough there to support real service.

That insight travels beyond communications. For Arctic surveillance, dwell can act as a substitute for sheer constellation size when the mission values sustained regional watch over broad northern areas rather than narrow, high-frequency snapshots of many unrelated points. A satellite near apogee in a highly elliptical orbit can maintain an extended relationship with a northern region, supporting continuity for communications relay, missile warning, weather observation, or other missions where long viewing time matters. The gain is not simply that the region is seen. It is that the region remains in view long enough for operators to build a steadier temporal picture than brief low Earth orbit passes alone might provide.

The visible behaviour of trust changes accordingly. Operators trust dwell when they choose to maintain a service or warning function through an apogee window rather than constantly hand off among many low-orbit assets. Planners trust it when they accept that a smaller number of spacecraft can sustain a northern mission if the orbit grants enough usable time over the area that matters. Governments trust it when they design Arctic architectures around continuity of regard rather than around the public seduction of large constellation counts. Dwell, then, should not be treated as a poetic property of an orbit. It is a practical way of redistributing attention across geography and time.

A good way to grasp the difference is to think in terms of tempo. Low Earth orbit systems often create a staccato rhythm: pass, collect, depart, return. Highly elliptical systems can create something closer to a held note over the Arctic, followed by a period of relative absence before another spacecraft rises into place. The held note is valuable because it allows a longer uninterrupted service interval. Yet it also reveals the trade-off. Continuity depends on choreography between spacecraft, and the transitions matter. If hand-offs are poorly managed, if the ground segment is not prepared to follow the moving geometry, or if mission needs demand more uniformity than the orbit can provide, the apparent grace of dwell becomes uneven service.

That is why communications constraints must sit close to any praise of highly elliptical orbits. A satellite lingering near apogee can offer favourable visibility to northern users, but it is not geostationary. The spacecraft moves. Ground antennas may need to track it. The geometry of the link changes over time. Handover between satellites becomes part of normal operations rather than an exceptional event. This can be entirely manageable. It can also impose burdens that planners accustomed to simpler metaphors of "coverage" underestimate. A link budget built around a steadily moving apogee track is not the same thing as a link budget built around a satellite that appears stationary. The service works, but it works through motion that the ground segment must actively accommodate.

This is where the ground segment implications become decisive. A highly elliptical orbit does not merely demand that a satellite be launched and maintained. It demands that the stations serving it know how to follow the moving apogee, manage switching, preserve timing across handovers, and sustain enough operational discipline that the service feels continuous to the user even when the spacecraft itself is visibly not. Show an operator with a fixed high-latitude terminal and a clean geostationary assumption, and one type of ground design follows. Show the same operator depending on a highly elliptical system, and the design changes. Antenna steering, tracking software, scheduling, and redundancy acquire a different importance. The implication reaches beyond engineering. Ground infrastructure choices begin to shape which states can use such orbits gracefully and which will find them administratively awkward.

A second checkable example comes from the Sirius satellite system serving high latitudes, historically associated with communications needs in the north Atlantic and around Greenland. The specifics of ownership and service evolution have changed over time, but the enduring point remains: high-latitude users repeatedly return to orbital designs that favour northern dwell because equatorial geometries are not enough. This recurrence across decades matters. It suggests that highly elliptical solutions are not merely historical curiosities preserved by institutional inertia. They answer a stubborn geographic problem that persists despite major changes in launch economics, satellite miniaturisation, and constellation design.

A credible limitation should be granted here. For many modern missions, especially those benefiting from mass-produced spacecraft and dense low Earth orbit constellations, highly elliptical orbits can appear less fashionable than proliferated LEO architectures. A large LEO network can provide frequent access, routing flexibility, and resilience through numbers. For Earth observation in particular, the rapid revisit of multiple low-orbit satellites often suits the demand for broad sampling and global reach. It would be careless to suggest that highly elliptical systems are the natural answer to every polar mission. They are not.

And yet the limitation helps define the orbit's real value. Highly elliptical designs are most persuasive where long northern dwell matters more than global symmetry, and where the mission can tolerate or exploit the moving geometry rather than resent it. Communications, early warning, and some regional awareness functions fit this logic better than others. If the requirement is to stare north for extended periods with relatively few spacecraft, dwell can be a powerful substitute for a much larger low

Earth orbit fleet. If the requirement is uniform, high-detail, frequently refreshed global coverage, the trade may look less attractive. The key is not to ask whether highly elliptical orbits beat LEO or vice versa, but which architecture matches the mission's clock.

That last phrase matters because "dwell" often gets confused with "persistence" in exactly the same way "repeatability" does. A long dwell can feel like persistence because the satellite remains available over the region for an extended period. Sometimes that feeling is justified. Sometimes it overpromises. A prolonged northern view is immensely useful, but it is still bounded by handover windows, communications design, sensor type, and the fact that the spacecraft eventually departs apogee. Political language about persistent Arctic awareness can quietly borrow the stability implied by dwell while obscuring the operational work needed to make that dwell usable and the limits of the periods between one long watch and the next.

Risk appears here in visible decisions rather than abstract system diagrams. Does a government choose a smaller number of more specialised satellites because the dwell profile matches its northern mission, accepting more complex ground tracking in exchange? Does an operator accept a moving communications geometry because the alternative would be dependence on low-horizon geostationary service of dubious quality? Does a defence planner prefer the continuity of a long apogee stare for warning purposes, knowing that the transition between satellites becomes a moment of special attention? These are not textbook questions. They are how architecture enters statecraft.

The moving apogee is the quiet motif that ties the orbit's strengths to its burdens. At apogee, the satellite appears patient, almost considerate, lingering where northern users need it. But the patience moves. The point of best service drifts through a pattern that the ground must know intimately. Antennas must follow. Schedulers must anticipate. Handover routines must work without drama. A system that looks sparse in orbit may therefore be surprisingly demanding on the ground. Fewer satellites do not necessarily mean simpler operations. Sometimes they mean the opposite: greater dependence on getting each long watch exactly right.

The broader strategic implication is easy to miss because public discussions of constellations tend to count. More satellites sound more modern, more resilient, more serious. Highly elliptical architectures remind us that not all useful coverage is produced by multiplication. Sometimes geometry and time do part of the work that numbers would otherwise be asked to do. That is a valuable lesson for the Arctic, where service quality depends so heavily on fit between orbit and mission. But it is also a warning. Any architecture that buys efficiency in orbit may charge for it elsewhere, in antenna complexity, operational discipline, scheduling sensitivity, and the politics of where the supporting ground infrastructure sits.

One final tension should remain unsettled. The more crowded and networked the space environment becomes, the easier it is to imagine Arctic service as something that can be brute-forced through proliferated constellations alone. Highly elliptical systems resist that assumption. They insist that some northern missions still reward lingering over counting, and that the right question is not how many spacecraft are visible on a slide but how long, how steadily, and at what ground cost a region can actually be served. The moving apogee offers a kind of northern patience. The harder question is whether institutions are willing to build the ground discipline and accept the operational asymmetry that such patience demands.

Inclination trade-offs and coverage limits

On 3 December 1999, NASA launched Terra from Vandenberg Air Force Base into a near-polar orbit designed for global Earth observation. The launch helped cement a public intuition that has only grown stronger since: if a satellite is described as polar, then the Arctic must lie comfortably within its grasp. That intuition is understandable. It is also incomplete. A spacecraft may be called polar, near-polar, high-inclination, or sun-synchronous and still not serve every northern latitude in the same way, or with the same geometry, or with the same operational usefulness.

The label hides the angle. That is the trouble. Inclination sounds like a minor orbital specification, the sort of figure left to engineers and brochure tables. In practice it decides where a satellite can go, how close it comes to the pole, what latitudes it revisits most naturally, and what sort of look it can offer while doing so. A small difference in inclination can alter not only whether a system reaches a given Arctic zone, but how convincingly it serves it. The change may look modest in a specification sheet and feel decisive in operations.

This matters because "polar" has become a permissive word in public discussion. It often functions as shorthand for northern competence, as though any orbit leaning enough relative to the equator steeply could be trusted to provide equivalent Arctic service. Show the familiar track map, and the misunderstanding becomes easy to see. Ground tracks crowd together at high latitudes, inviting the eye to treat the north as generally well-covered. Name the concept properly, and the picture sharpens: inclination governs the maximum latitude a satellite's ground track reaches and influences the geometry with which northern targets are seen. Explain why, and the strategic implication follows quickly. Arctic coverage claims should be read not as declarations of presence alone, but as claims about where the system truly goes and what kind of observation it can support once it gets there.

A true polar orbit, in the strict geometric sense, passes over or very near both poles. Many systems described in ordinary conversation as polar do something slightly different. They are near-polar, often because that inclination supports a useful compromise among launch efficiency, lighting conditions, repeat patterns, mission goals, and ground segment demands. Such orbits can be excellent for global observation. They can also leave distinctions that matter in the far north. A target at one Arctic latitude may receive frequent and useful access. A target farther north may sit near the edge of the system's practical reach, or within reach only under less favourable viewing conditions. The orbit remains highly capable. It simply does not mean the same thing everywhere in the Arctic.

This is easiest to grasp when comparing the broad middle of the Arctic with the region closer to the pole. A system serving northern Norway, Alaska, or the Barents Sea may perform quite differently when asked to support observation much farther north over the central Arctic Ocean or near the geographic pole itself. The reason is not mystical. Inclination draws a line, and the closer the mission requirement creeps towards that line, the more careful one must become about what is promised. A system can be excellent across large portions of the High North and still thin out where people are most tempted to imagine perfect convergence. The danger lies in mistaking steep inclination for unlimited northern entitlement.

The distinction between sun-synchronous and other high-inclination systems makes this clearer. Sun-synchronous low Earth orbits are often near-polar because that geometry helps maintain consistent local solar time over repeated passes. That design serves many Earth observation missions beautifully. Yet the sun-synchronous label can distract attention from a more basic question: how near to truly polar is the orbit, and what does that mean for the northern latitudes the mission actually cares about? A user focused on repeatable imaging of sub-Arctic coasts may find the answer entirely satisfactory. A user concerned with extreme high-latitude gaps, polar cap routes, or persistent support near the top of the globe may discover that the same orbit's virtues do not eliminate its boundaries.

Iridium offers a useful example because its communications constellation has long been central to high-latitude service. The system's design, based on truly polar orbital logic rather than merely steep inclination, helped it achieve the reputation that geostationary systems never fully earned in the far north. That matters because the service experience of users at very high latitude depends on more than the generic category of low Earth orbit. The orbit had to be committed enough to the pole to sustain the promise. One learns something important from this: systems built for real polar service tend to advertise it in ways grounded in architecture, not just in suggestive language about global reach.

A second example comes from Earth observation missions such as Sentinel-2 and Landsat. These systems are rightly valued for their high inclination, sun-synchronous behaviour, which delivers disciplined repeat imagery across northern regions. They support Arctic analysis extremely well for many purposes. Yet they also illustrate the need to ask the harder question. Are they serving every relevant latitude equally? Are they serving those latitudes with the same temporal rhythm and the same viewing geometry? The answer depends on what part of the Arctic one means and what kind of task is being asked of the imagery. A system optimised for repeat land and coastal observation may be entirely fit for one northern mission and noticeably less persuasive for another that pushes closer to the polar extreme or demands a different geometry of regard.

That is why inclination should be read as a mission sentence rather than as a number. It says, in effect, where the satellite spends its life and where it does not. It says how much of the north lies comfortably inside the design and how much sits near its edge. It also says something about geometry, which matters as much as reach. A satellite that approaches very high latitudes more directly can offer a different observational relationship from one that merely brushes them as part of a broader global pattern. That relationship affects trust in the data. Analysts compare scenes differently when the viewing geometry is stable and appropriate. Operators task differently when they know a northern target is not sitting at the edge of what the orbit serves well.

Trust, here, should again be translated into visible behaviour. A government that quietly supplements one "polar" system with another for the highest latitudes is admitting that the first system's inclination did not settle the matter. An operator who avoids promising routine service above a certain Arctic zone is being more honest than a brochure that uses the word polar without qualification. A planner who reads the specification sheet and asks not only whether the inclination is high, but what latitude range it truly supports with workable geometry, is doing the real intellectual work that orbit design demands. Inclination is not a label to admire. It is a boundary to interpret.

A credible limitation deserves recognition. Modern mission design can soften some of these trade-offs. Constellations can combine multiple orbital planes. Sensors can point off-nadir. Crosslinks and ground networks can make a system more useful operationally than its raw inclination figure might suggest. A mission with slightly less pole-centred geometry may still perform impressively in Arctic practice because other design choices compensate. This matters, and it should caution against a simplistic reading in which inclination alone determines everything that follows.

But the limitation does not rescue sloppy language. Compensation is not the same thing as equivalence. Off-nadir pointing may recover access at the cost of swath, distortion, or scheduling complexity. Multiple planes may improve northern service while raising cost and operational burden. A ground segment may turn a good orbit into a very useful system without changing what latitudes and angles the orbit itself naturally favours. The more one compensates, the more important it becomes to distinguish between native orbital strength and additional architectural effort. Otherwise the user cannot tell whether northern performance is inherent, contingent, or fragile.

The trade-off grows sharper in the Arctic because small differences in inclination can translate into large differences in confidence at the highest latitudes. A region around seventy degrees north is not the same design challenge as a region close to the pole, even if both sit comfortably inside a political shorthand called the Arctic. One orbit may support repeated and well-understood service over the former while delivering more constrained or awkward access over the latter. This is not a contradiction. It is the whole point of reading specifications critically. Latitude is not one thing merely because public discourse bundles it under one word.

Coverage limits also shape how one should interpret commercial and governmental claims about persistence. A constellation may legitimately provide strong northern service over inhabited or economically active Arctic margins while offering thinner support near the central polar basin. A vendor may advertise global reach with a map that is technically correct and still leave the reader unsure how the most demanding high-latitude missions perform. A policy document may speak of Arctic awareness when the underlying system really means sub-polar and lower-Arctic competence supported by selective higher-latitude access. None of this is dishonest by necessity. But it does require a reader willing to ask where the useful service begins to taper.

The quiet motif here is the edge. Every orbit has one. Not always a hard edge visible on a map, but an operational one beyond which confidence drops, angles worsen, revisit patterns change, or support becomes less routine. The edge may sit far enough north that ordinary users rarely notice it. For Arctic surveillance, that is often precisely why it matters. The most politically sensitive claims are made near edges: near the boundary of jurisdiction, near the limit of service, near the latitude where a specification remains formally impressive but practically thinner. Good analysis begins by locating the edge before accepting the slogan.

Inclination therefore belongs to the grammar of honesty in polar coverage. A reader does not need to become an orbital mechanic to use it well. One only needs to ask a stricter set of questions. Does the system truly reach the latitude being discussed? Does it serve that latitude directly or awkwardly? Does it do so by native orbital design or by compensations elsewhere in the architecture? When the answer relies on phrases such as near-polar, high-inclination, global reach, or Arctic-capable, what exactly has been promised, and what has quietly been left vague?

That last question should remain unsettled, because it points beyond orbit as such and into the politics of specification. A system can be marketed as polar because the word carries prestige, reassurance, and strategic weight. The harder test is whether the inclination behind the claim supports the particular Arctic that decision-makers have in mind, with geometry they can trust and limits they are willing to admit. The edge is always there. The question is whether anyone has bothered to read where it lies.

Revisit, persistence, and constellation size

In March 2021, when Maxar Technologies released satellite images of the *Ever Given* lodged in the Suez Canal, the pictures seemed to confirm a comforting belief about modern Earth observation: if something important happens, a satellite will be there. The scene was legible, dramatic, and easy to circulate. Yet the confidence those images inspired depended on a misunderstanding that becomes harder to sustain in the Arctic. One successful look does not prove continuous awareness. It proves that a look was obtained.

The difference matters because surveillance language often treats revisit and persistence as if they were near synonyms. They are not. Revisit describes how often a satellite, or a constellation of satellites, can observe a place again. Persistence implies something stronger: that the system can maintain useful awareness across time with gaps small enough, or consequences of those gaps mild enough, that operators feel they are not being surprised by the interval between observations. The Arctic tests that distinction mercilessly. Targets move. Weather intervenes. Downlink windows matter. A gap that appears tolerable on a coverage graphic may prove operationally expensive when the contact is a vessel, a temporary deployment, or an event whose significance lasts hours rather than days.

The heart of the matter is architectural. Show a single satellite in low Earth orbit sweeping past a northern sea lane, and the virtue of revisit appears immediately. The system can come back. Name the concept properly and one begins to see the limits as well: a return is not a watch. Explain why, and the answer lies in time, geometry, and statistical expectation. Between one pass and the next, the target may have moved, changed character, switched off a transmitter, entered cloud or darkness, or simply done whatever it was going to do and left little trace. The implication is strategic. Revisit rates are meaningful only when paired with a claim about what kind of behaviour the system is trying not to miss.

That is why constellation size looms so large in discussions of Arctic surveillance. More satellites generally mean more opportunities to look. They can reduce the average interval between observations and make it less likely that an event will occur entirely between passes. But size is only part of the answer. A constellation is not a bag of interchangeable points in space. It has orbital planes, sensor types, tasking rules, swath widths, downlink demands, and operational priorities. Two constellations of similar size may produce very different practical surveillance because one is designed for wide-area search and the other for high-detail imaging. Counting spacecraft without asking what they are built to do is like judging a library by the number of books while ignoring the language they are written in.

The trade-off between resolution and coverage sits at the centre of this problem. A narrow-swath, high-detail sensor can produce exquisitely informative imagery of a small area. It may support confident identification, infrastructure assessment, or forensic comparison. But a narrow swath means each pass covers less ground. If the mission is to search vast expanses of Arctic Ocean or ice for sparse, moving, or unexpected activity, such precision may come at the cost of missing the event entirely. A wide-swath system makes the opposite bargain. It accepts coarser detail in exchange for surveying more area more often, increasing the chance that something anomalous will be noticed at all. Neither bargain is intrinsically better. Each serves a different theory of not being surprised.

A watch with missing minutes. That is the quiet motif worth keeping in view. Persistence often sounds like seamless presence, but in practice, many surveillance systems offer something more modest and more interesting: structured sampling with intervals. A well-designed constellation does not eliminate missing minutes. It makes them shorter, more predictable, or less dangerous for the task at hand. That can be enough. A maritime search architecture may need only to detect a vessel's presence within a reasonable operational window before cueing another sensor or asset. A forensic monitoring mission may tolerate longer intervals because the purpose is not to respond instantly but to reconstruct activity credibly over time. The watch can work even with missing minutes, provided the mission understands what kind of time it can afford to lose.

Planet Labs offers a useful example because its Dove satellites helped popularise the idea that constellations can trade exquisite detail for frequent global imaging. The value of that model lies not in pretending to provide omniscience, but in making recurring looks cheap and regular enough that change becomes difficult to hide for long. For broad environmental and infrastructure monitoring, and for many kinds of open-source analysis, this is a powerful model. It turns persistence into a sampling strategy: not a guarantee that every moment has been seen, but a credible claim that many moments will be seen often enough to expose patterns and deviations. The Arctic benefits from such architectures, especially where the aim is to build a baseline of activity rather than capture every transient act as it occurs.

A second example comes from synthetic aperture radar systems used for maritime and ice observation in high latitudes, including the Sentinel-1 mission operated under the Copernicus programme. Radar brings its own strengths to the constellation problem. Because it does not depend on sunlight and handles cloud far better than optical systems, it can maintain surveillance value under conditions that would collapse purely optical persistence. Yet here too the trade-off remains. A radar system can be tasked for broad coverage or finer detail, and the choice affects revisit in practice. Wide-area modes help search large Arctic spaces for ships, ice edges, and anomalies. Finer modes support more discriminating analysis but over smaller footprints. The architecture is still deciding what kind of time and uncertainty it is willing to accept.

This is where probabilistic coverage deserves a plain explanation. Much of what is casually described as persistent surveillance is really a managed probability of seeing the target within a given interval and under given assumptions. That sounds bloodless, but it is how real systems behave. If a constellation's revisit pattern makes it highly likely that a northern shipping route will be observed repeatedly through the day, that may be operationally sufficient for some missions and wholly insufficient for others. The crucial point is that persistence is often not a binary condition but a judgement about acceptable risk. What is the chance that an event can occur and disappear between looks? How costly is that chance? What follow-on systems exist if a broad search sensor notices something but cannot resolve it fully? These are architectural questions disguised as words of confidence.

Risk, here, must be translated into visible decisions. A coastguard commits aircraft differently when it believes a constellation gives reliable broad awareness of traffic patterns. A naval planner assigns scarce higher-resolution imaging time differently when a wide-swath search has already narrowed the field. A government speaks more cautiously about persistent observation if it knows that its sampling strategy still leaves recurring windows of under-observation. The strategic implication is sobering. Surveillance claims often describe a philosophy of sampling more than a condition of omnipresence. States are not always saying, "We see everything." More often, if the claim is honest, they are saying, "We have reduced surprise to a level we think we can manage."

The Arctic makes that honesty harder and more necessary. Search areas are vast. Targets may be sparse and mobile. Corroboration is expensive. Weather and season erode the utility of some sensors and increase dependence on others. Under those conditions, persistence is frequently purchased by accepting coarser products that can be collected over broader areas with higher frequency. That bargain may be entirely rational. A wide-swath radar image showing a probable vessel track near sea ice can be far more valuable in the first instance than an exquisite optical scene of empty water collected elsewhere. The sequence matters: detect broadly, then refine where needed. The danger enters when institutions forget that they have made a sequence and begin speaking as though the first step were equivalent to the last.

A credible limitation should be granted. There are missions for which finer detail cannot be deferred. Treaty verification, damage assessment, infrastructure analysis, and some forms of public evidentiary release may depend on image quality that wide-area systems cannot provide. Likewise, small constellations of exquisite sensors can still be extremely valuable when paired with good cueing, historical knowledge, and disciplined tasking. It would be careless to suggest that broad coverage always beats detail, or that larger constellations automatically produce better surveillance. They do not. A bloated constellation built around the wrong sensor mix can sample the wrong thing with impressive regularity.

Yet the limitation reinforces the main argument rather than weakening it. The question is not whether detail or frequency matters more in the abstract. It is what kind of ignorance the system is designed to reduce first. Broad search reduces ignorance about where attention should go. Fine detail reduces ignorance about what, precisely, has been found. Tracking across time demands enough recurrence to say something stable about behaviour. Attribution requires another step again. Constellation design, therefore, becomes an argument about sequence. Which uncertainty is addressed early, which is deferred, and what kind of operational patience does that sequence assume? Arctic surveillance rewards systems that answer those questions explicitly.

This also clarifies why public coverage maps should be read with restraint. They often impressively show reach and recurrence while saying less about sensor mode, swath choice, tasking competition, and the intervals that remain uncovered for practical purposes. A map dense with orbital paths or nominal revisit promises can flatter the imagination. It encourages the idea that a larger constellation simply fills the sky until surprise becomes impossible. But surveillance rarely works like paint covering a wall. It works more like repeated glances through moving windows, each glance shaped by what the sensor values, what the orbit allows, and what the mission has chosen to sacrifice.

Constellation size carries operational burdens as well. More satellites may improve revisit, but they also create more tasking decisions, more data to route, more conjunction warnings to assess, and more opportunities for ground and processing bottlenecks to erode the gain promised by the orbital design. A proliferation strategy can therefore succeed in space and still stumble on Earth. The result is another reason to treat persistence as a system property rather than a count of spacecraft. If the data cannot be downlinked, prioritised, processed, and interpreted fast enough, the shorter revisit interval may matter less than the brochure suggests.

The quiet watch returns here. A watch with missing minutes can still be good enough if the mission accepts what those missing minutes mean. But if the wearer mistakes it for perfect continuity, error follows. In the Arctic, where activity can be intermittent and decisive, those missing minutes may contain the event that later matters most. The architecture cannot abolish that possibility. It can only decide whether to shrink the interval, widen the field, sharpen the detail, or hand the problem to another sensor layer. Every constellation is making that choice, even when its public language tries not to sound like a choice at all.

This is why persistence should be treated less as a boast than as a diagnostic question. Persistent for what? Persistent enough to find a ship? To monitor an installation? To follow a route? To support public attribution? To reassure an ally? The answer determines whether a wide-swath search constellation is the right instrument, whether a narrower high-detail system needs to be cued by something else, or whether a mix of both can produce a more honest form of awareness than either alone. Arctic surveillance is full of systems that see often and know selectively. The harder problem is deciding which selectivity a state can live with.

A final tension remains unresolved because it should. As launch costs fall and constellations grow, it becomes tempting to believe that enough satellites can dissolve the distinction between revisit and persistence. Sometimes they narrow it impressively. But the Arctic keeps reintroducing the old discipline. A system can sample more densely and still depend on choices about swath, detail, probability, and what kind of event it is most unwilling to miss. The real measure of a constellation is not how crowded it makes the coverage map appear. It is what kind of absence still survives between the looks, and whether the institutions depending on it are honest enough to say so.

Station-keeping, collisions, and operational burden

On 10 February 2009, an active Iridium communications satellite and the defunct Russian spacecraft Kosmos 2251 collided over Siberia. The event did not occur because space had suddenly become exotic or unknowable. It occurred because crowded orbital regimes punish routine inattention. For Arctic surveillance, that lesson lands with special force. A constellation designed to watch the north may look complete on launch day, its planes filled and its coverage diagrams persuasive, yet its real life begins only when operators must keep those satellites where they belong, know where everything else is, and preserve service while the orbital environment keeps changing around them.

Launch is an opening act. That sentence matters because public discussion of satellite systems still leans too heavily on deployment and too lightly on upkeep. A polar constellation seems, from the outside, like a solved geometry once the vehicles are in orbit. The spacecraft circle, the poles gather track density, and the marketing language of persistence begins to write itself. But constellations do not simply remain as designed. They drift, require corrections, face conjunction warnings, consume fuel, and depend on an unglamorous but relentless practice of prediction and response. The Arctic may be served from space, but that service depends on an earthly discipline of tracking, planning, and judgement that never really stops.

The key concept is station-keeping. Show a satellite whose orbit gradually shifts under the small but cumulative pressures of atmospheric drag, gravitational irregularities, solar radiation pressure, and operational manoeuvres, and one sees the problem at once. Name the task properly, and it becomes clear that station-keeping is not some optional refinement applied only to delicate missions. It is the deliberate maintenance of orbital position and spacing so that a constellation continues to behave as promised. Explain why this matters in the Arctic, and the implications follow quickly. If a polar system is valued because its passes recur in a particular rhythm, with particular geometry and handover timing, then any erosion of that order affects coverage predictability directly. A satellite slightly out of place is not merely untidy. It can change when and how the North is seen.

That predictability is more important in polar service than it sometimes appears. High-latitude operations often depend on known pass schedules, expected handovers, and carefully managed downlink windows. An observation architecture may already be juggling weather, illumination, communications constraints, and tasking competition. When constellation geometry itself becomes less reliable, those other burdens grow sharper. Operators may have to re-task around altered timing. Ground stations may face less convenient windows. Analysts may receive products later than expected, or in patterns that reduce the comparability on which confidence depends. Reliability, in this setting, is not an abstract virtue. It shows itself in whether people can plan around the system without constantly hedging against its own orbital drift.

Collision avoidance sits immediately beside this. The modern orbital environment, especially in low Earth orbit, requires operators to monitor close approaches and decide when a warning justifies action. A conjunction notice is not a collision. Most pass harmlessly. But the workload they impose is real because each one demands assessment, comparison of tracking data, communication where possible, and a judgement about whether the risk justifies a manoeuvre. For a polar constellation, the burden can be especially persistent because so many Earth observation and communications systems occupy high-inclination regimes that cross the Arctic repeatedly. The orbital elegance that makes the north accessible also creates traffic patterns that must be managed with care.

The Iridium-Kosmos collision remains the obvious anchor here because it exposed the consequences of a crowded environment in the bluntest possible way. Iridium 33 was an active operational satellite; Kosmos 2251 was not. Their collision created debris and demonstrated that even routine service constellations exist inside an environment where one bad meeting can permanently alter both capability and risk. The event was not about Arctic surveillance alone. Yet it carries a durable lesson for polar systems because many of the orbital regimes relevant to the High North live under similar pressures of crossing paths, shared altitude bands, and cumulative debris concern. A state may value a constellation for its northern service. It must also accept that the orbital routes providing that service are not private roads.

A second example comes from the 2019 conjunction involving ESA's Aeolus satellite and a SpaceX Starlink spacecraft. The encounter, resolved without accident after late coordination and manoeuvre decisions, showed a different aspect of the same problem. The issue was not dramatic failure but operational burden: warnings, uncertainty about the other party's likely action, human decision-making under time pressure, and the eventual need to manoeuvre to preserve safety. This is exactly the sort of episode that reveals why "space traffic management" should not be treated as a bureaucratic afterthought. A constellation's utility depends not only on where its satellites are supposed to be, but on the institutional competence that keeps them clear of others while preserving service.

Manoeuvres, however, are never free. That is where fuel enters the story. A satellite carrying propellant is carrying time, flexibility, and future decisions in compressed form. Every collision avoidance burn, every orbit maintenance correction, every inclination or phasing adjustment draws down a finite reserve. Show the satellite as a point on a map and the trade-off disappears. Name the relevant constraint - manoeuvre fuel - and the system looks different. Explain the consequence, and the strategic meaning becomes unavoidable. A satellite that spends fuel preserving safety may extend mission credibility in one sense while shortening mission life or reducing room for later corrections in another. The implication for Arctic users is that coverage promises are tied not merely to launch success but to the ongoing budget of movement each spacecraft can still afford.

This does not mean operators should hesitate to manoeuvre. Quite the opposite. Good operations depend on timely, disciplined decisions that place safety ahead of wishful thinking. But it does mean that every manoeuvre links immediate risk reduction to longer-term service quality. A constellation can remain collision-safe and still lose some of its design neatness as burns accumulate. Phasing may need restoration. Coverage windows may shift. Ground planning may have to adapt. If manoeuvres become frequent enough, the system's original coverage model can begin to look less like a stable architecture and more like a moving compromise. In the Arctic, where timing and recurrence often matter as much as raw access, such compromises can alter the practical meaning of persistence.

Ephemeris accuracy sits at the centre of this moving compromise. To know where a satellite will be, and where it is now, depends on the quality of the orbital data used by operators, users, and collision assessment systems. Show a conjunction warning based on uncertain or stale information, and the operational strain becomes obvious. Name the relevant discipline - ephemeris maintenance and dissemination - and one sees that safe, predictable service relies on accurate, current orbital knowledge. Explain the system effect, and the point grows larger. If ephemeris quality degrades, conjunction assessments become noisier, manoeuvre decisions become harder, and user planning becomes less reliable. The Arctic enters the picture because so many northern services depend on confidence in future pass times and access geometry. Bad orbital knowledge ripples outward into bad operational timing.

Trust, again, should be translated into behaviour. A ground station trusts a constellation when it schedules antenna time tightly against expected passes rather than padding every window for uncertainty. An intelligence or maritime user trusts it when they build monitoring routines around anticipated revisit and handover patterns. An operator trusts their own ephemeris when they can distinguish a serious conjunction from a false alarm without drifting into either complacency or panic. None of this trust is mystical. It is visible in planning margins, manoeuvre thresholds, data-sharing practices, and how often people resort to manual workarounds because they no longer believe the system's predictions are clean enough.

A credible limitation should be acknowledged. Modern operators possess better tools than their predecessors. Tracking networks are denser, conjunction assessment practices more mature, onboard propulsion more common, and autonomous or semi-automated manoeuvre capabilities increasingly discussed and in some cases deployed. Many constellations are therefore far more resilient to the routine pressures of low Earth orbit than a gloomy account might suggest. It would be careless to write as though every conjunction notice placed a system at the brink of failure or every manoeuvre meaningfully damaged service.

Yet the limitation reinforces the deeper claim. Better tools do not eliminate operational burden; they professionalise it. More capable tracking produces more decisions, not fewer, because a richer picture of the environment must still be interpreted. Better propulsion expands room for manoeuvre, but also creates expectations that the constellation will remain neatly maintained for longer. Automation may shorten response times while raising new questions about validation, coordination, and the consequences of simultaneous algorithmic conservatism across many operators. Progress therefore changes the texture of the burden more than its existence. Launching satellites remains only the beginning because the system's life after launch is not passive occupancy. It is managed exposure.

The Arctic sharpens that exposure because polar constellations often support missions whose value lies in timing as much as presence. If a collision avoidance manoeuvre alters the timing of a planned downlink window for imagery over northern waters, the result may be more than a slight inconvenience. It may delay a product enough to reduce its operational value. If station-keeping drifts far enough to change geometry for a high-latitude observation sequence, comparability may weaken. If ephemeris uncertainty forces larger planning margins, ground assets may be used less efficiently. The problem is rarely a single dramatic loss. More often it is a gradual thickening of friction in a surveillance chain that was already operating under Arctic constraint.

The quiet motif worth carrying through this discussion is the timetable. A constellation advertises itself through timetables: regular passes, expected handovers, recurring access, planned windows of contact. Space traffic management exists to preserve those timetables against a domain that refuses to stay still. When a satellite must dodge debris, spend fuel, or accept slightly altered phasing, the timetable absorbs the shock. Sometimes it bends invisibly. Sometimes it slips enough for users to notice. A system praised for persistence may therefore be living on a schedule whose reliability depends on hundreds of small acts of orbital housekeeping never mentioned in public claims about coverage.

This has a strategic consequence that is easy to overlook. States and firms competing over Arctic surveillance capacity are not merely competing over sensors and orbital design. They are competing over the quality of their operational discipline: how well they monitor conjunctions, preserve ephemeris accuracy, budget manoeuvre fuel, coordinate with others, and restore constellation order after inevitable perturbations. A launch campaign can produce impressive headlines. It cannot, by itself, produce enduring northern service. That requires a continuing traffic-management culture equal to the geometry it has placed in space.

The same point also unsettles the language of resilience. People often imagine resilience as redundancy: more satellites, more launch capacity, more backups. Those matter. But a badly managed large constellation can be less reliable than a smaller one with sharper operational discipline. Resilience appears in the mundane competence to predict, decide, manoeuvre, and recover without losing the timing structure on which users depend. For Arctic surveillance, where windows are precious and conditions already strain the chain, that competence becomes part of the sensing architecture itself rather than a background maintenance function.

A final tension should remain open. As constellations proliferate and polar orbits grow busier, operators face a difficult bargain. They can preserve safety through conservative manoeuvring and attentive management, but at the cost of fuel, workload, and occasional disruption to service patterns. Or they can economise on those burdens and quietly accept a thinner margin of safety and predictability. The north will not care which choice they prefer. It will simply expose the consequences. The harder question is whether the systems promising persistent Arctic awareness are being judged by how brightly they launched, or by how patiently and accurately they continue to keep their place once the traffic thickens around them.

Chapter 4

Imaging Sensors Over Ice and Sea

What counts as seeing in the Arctic when the most convincing image may be the least dependable one? The question presses because satellite pictures carry a peculiar authority. A bright optical frame of a vessel against dark water, a long scar through sea ice, a coastal facility sitting hard against snow, a plume or wake or cleared strip of ground: such images look like proof. They satisfy the eye quickly. They seem to settle argument. And yet the High North keeps prising open that certainty, because what can be pictured clearly is not always what can be interpreted safely, nor what can be monitored with the persistence that strategy demands.

A sensor never arrives alone. That should be clear by now, but it matters differently here. Over ice and sea, every imaging mode inherits the region's severe habits. Light withdraws for long periods. Cloud intrudes. Glare flattens. Snow and broken ice create backgrounds that can either expose or conceal. Surface roughness becomes meaningful, but only to those equipped to read it. Heat leaks, fades, and reappears in patterns that can point towards activity without naming it. The result is not a simple ranking of better and worse instruments. It is a harder truth: each sensor sees a different Arctic, and none sees the whole of it on its own terms.

The photograph and the X-ray. That is one useful way to think about the tension. Optical imagery often behaves like a photograph: intuitive, publicly persuasive, rich in visible detail when conditions cooperate. Radar behaves more like an X-ray: less immediately legible to the untrained eye, but often far more reliable when darkness and cloud make ordinary sight fragile. Other sensing modes complicate the picture further, adding traces of heat, material difference, and spectral signature that can settle a dispute or inflame one, depending on how firmly they are interpreted. The Arctic forces these instruments into conversation because it rarely allows any one of them to speak alone with full authority.

That matters for more than technical reasons. Imaging over ice and sea sits close to the politics of reassurance, warning, and accusation. States do not merely want data from the north; they want evidence they can trust and, at times, evidence they can show. A visible image can shape public understanding in ways a radar product seldom does, even when radar provides the more dependable record. A thermal or spectral clue may become decisive in a crisis precisely because it appears to reveal intention rather than mere presence. The stakes are therefore bound up with interpretation. Confidence does not live inside the sensor. It appears in behaviour: whether an analyst asks for corroboration, whether a patrol is launched, whether a government publishes imagery, whether an anomaly is treated as a pattern or a provocation.

The same point cuts in a second direction. The more capable a sensor appears, the easier it becomes to overstate what it has actually delivered. Radar's all-weather, day-night appeal can encourage institutions to treat it as a stand-in for persistence itself, even when resolution, latency, downlink constraints, or interpretive difficulty still impose severe limits. Optical imagery can seem transparent just when seasonal conditions make it most deceptive. Niche sensing modes can look marginal until a specific incident gives them sudden, disproportionate weight. The Arctic is full of these reversals. Instruments that appear secondary become decisive. Instruments that dominate public imagination become operationally partial. Seeing, here, is always conditional.

The stakes therefore lie not in choosing the single best imaging modality, but in learning what each one makes possible and what each one quietly distorts. Maritime awareness over open water is not the same problem as reading leads in winter ice. Monitoring a remote facility is not the same problem as following traffic across a changing ice edge. Detecting an anomaly is not the same as explaining it. A system that excels at broad search may falter when asked for forensic clarity. A system that produces exquisite detail may arrive too rarely, or too late, to support anything resembling continuous awareness. The High North sharpens these mismatches because the environment strips away the comforts that allow weaker assumptions to survive farther south.

The path ahead begins where human intuition usually starts, with visible imagery and the unstable bargain it strikes with darkness, cloud, glare, and season. From there the argument moves into radar, where apparent technical superiority over polar conditions must be tested against interpretive burden and system timing rather than admired in isolation.

It then widens to the quieter but sometimes decisive roles of thermal and spectral sensing, where the most specialised instruments can suddenly matter most when an event turns from observation to dispute.

A quiet motif runs through all of this: the window. Some sensors open a wide and familiar window, easy to look through and easy to trust too quickly. Others open a narrower, stranger one that reveals more than it first seems to. Still others offer only a brief, oblique glimpse, but one that changes the meaning of everything seen before. Arctic imaging is less a matter of finding the perfect window than of knowing which one is open, what it can honestly show, and what remains hidden just beyond its frame.

The hardest question is not which sensor performs best in a sales sheet or a demonstration scene. It is which sensor, or which combination, can carry enough confidence across ice, sea, weather, darkness, latency, and institutional caution to support a claim stronger than "we obtained an image". When a vessel enters winter darkness, when a lead opens and closes, when activity leaves a thermal trace but no obvious visual one, when a radar return looks suspiciously clear, what exactly has been seen - and what part of that confidence belongs to the sensor, rather than to the system and the season surrounding it?

Optical imaging under polar conditions

In March 1989, the *Exxon Valdez* ran aground in Prince William Sound, Alaska, and the aftermath quickly became a problem not only of law, environment, and politics, but of visibility. Aircraft photography and satellite imagery alike were called upon to show where oil had spread and how the scene was changing. The impulse was understandable: a visible image seems to settle argument faster than any other kind of evidence. Yet the north has always complicated that confidence. Light shifts abruptly, cloud intrudes, water and ice reflect unpredictably, and what looks plain from a distance can turn treacherous under closer interpretation.

That remains true across the Arctic. Optical imagery retains a special authority because it resembles ordinary sight. A ship seen in clear summer water, a camp near a shore, a line of vehicles, a scar of disturbed snow, a plume, a wake, a cleared runway: all can appear immediately legible in ways radar products and signal data rarely do for general audiences. The image seems to say, *look for yourself*. But in the High North, seeing for oneself is never quite so simple. The camera may be honest and the scene still ambiguous. The eye may be quick and the season still misleading.

The attraction of optical sensing begins with what it does genuinely well. Show an analyst a high-quality visible image of a vessel moving through open water in Arctic summer, and one sees the appeal at once. The human eye handles shape, colour, shadow, proportion, and context with remarkable speed. Name the relevant strength and the term is intuitive legibility. Explain why it matters, and the answer is not only technical. Optical images allow faster human judgement about what something appears to be, how it relates to its surroundings, and whether it is unusual enough to justify attention. The implication follows immediately: optical imagery remains the most persuasive form of overhead evidence when the task depends on public proof, rapid recognition, or close visual comparison with familiar objects.

This is why optical systems continue to matter even in a region that so often frustrates them. They are excellent at revealing spatial relationships that other sensors may mark more abstractly. A ship's deck arrangement, the visible state of sea ice around it, the presence of cranes or vehicles at a site, the way a temporary structure sits on the terrain, the difference between a wake and a crack, the broad condition of a runway or coastal facility - these are all often easier to grasp in optical form than in any other. Analysts trust optical scenes when they can compare them to lived visual expectations. Policymakers trust them when they are willing to circulate images publicly. Journalists trust them when they can print them without pages of technical explanation. That trust is not naive. It is rooted in the human preference for visible evidence that appears self-interpreting.

But the Arctic narrows that comfort quickly. Cloud is the bluntest limit. A scene hidden by cloud is simply unavailable to ordinary optical imaging, and high latitudes offer plenty of such interruptions. Yet darkness is the more strategic obstacle because it is not episodic weather; it is a seasonal fact. During polar night, the visible-light basis of ordinary optical interpretation recedes dramatically. Specialised low-light systems can sometimes recover useful material, and twilight conditions can help at the margins, but the broad point remains hard and practical. A region cannot be persistently watched by optical means alone when ordinary light disappears for long stretches of the year. Any architecture that speaks as though it can be quietly borrowing confidence from another sensor or another season.

The limit is not merely absence of light. It is the changing quality of light when it returns. Low sun angles in the Arctic create long shadows that may either expose or distort. They can reveal height, texture, and surface form with unusual clarity. They can also turn berms into apparent structures, make shallow surface undulations look like deliberate works, and conceal the true outline of objects tucked against shadowed ground. The same physical feature can look settled in one image and ambiguous in the next, not because it has changed, but because the light has. Optical interpretation in the High North therefore depends on season and geometry together. A good image in the wrong light can produce worse judgement than a less dramatic image gathered under more stable conditions.

Glare deepens the problem. Snow, sea ice, wet surfaces, and open water can all reflect light in ways that flatten detail or exaggerate contrast. The visible scene may become stark precisely when it becomes less trustworthy. A dark mark on white ice looks important because the eye is trained to treat contrast as evidence. Sometimes that instinct is right. Sometimes the mark is a shadow effect, a melt feature, a surface irregularity, or a visual artefact of the moment. This is why experienced Arctic analysts often sound more cautious than the images they study. The image can look decisive and still require discipline. The surface does not announce which contrasts matter most.

The difference between summer shipping lanes and winter leads offers a clear demonstration. In summer, optical imagery of shipping routes through open or partially open northern waters can be extraordinarily informative. Ships stand out. Wakes trace motion. Coastlines, ice margins, and vessel interactions can often be read with relative confidence when cloud allows. The visible image may support detection, identification, and broader pattern recognition all at once. Shift to winter, and the field changes. Narrow leads in the ice, partially frozen channels, pressure ridges, drifting floes, and dark interruptions in a white surface can all appear visually significant, but they do not carry the same intuitive stability. A dark line in open water is not the same interpretive object as a dark line in broken winter ice. Optical imagery still contributes, but the analyst's confidence becomes more seasonal, more conditional, and more dependent on comparison with other sources.

A second example comes from the diesel spill near Norilsk in May 2020. Visible imagery helped establish public awareness of the event and its extent. It showed stained water and damaged landscape in ways that were emotionally and politically legible. But even in such a case - one where the demand for optical evidence was obvious - interpretation depended on context. Surface condition, melt state, weather, cloud, and time separated persuasive imagery from complete understanding. The images were invaluable. They were not sufficient on their own. That distinction matters because it reveals optical sensing at its best and still shows why the Arctic resists reliance on it alone.

The real issue, then, is not whether optical imagery works. It often works beautifully. The issue is how analyst confidence changes with season, surface, and mission. Confidence is visible in behaviour. A maritime centre may act quickly on a summer optical image showing a ship where none should be. The same centre may treat a winter optical anomaly with far greater caution, waiting for radar confirmation or another pass before committing an aircraft or issuing a warning. An intelligence analyst may accept repeated summer imagery as strong evidence of a pattern of activity at a coastal site, while treating winter scenes from the same site as suggestive rather than dispositive. Confidence does not sit in the pixels alone. It appears in the willingness to act, publish, or defer judgement.

This is where optical imaging's greatest strength becomes a subtle danger. Because optical scenes are publicly persuasive, they can encourage overstatement. A visible image can travel through media and policy circles faster than a more qualified technical assessment, and the Arctic's stark visual contrasts often heighten that effect. A ship in open water, a scar in snow, a dark plume against white ground, a line through the ice - these look like plain facts. But plainness in appearance is not the same as certainty in interpretation. A system that relies heavily on optical imagery may therefore be most vulnerable not when the images fail to arrive, but when they arrive looking more definitive than they truly are.

A credible limitation must be admitted here. Arctic summer can make optical sensing look astonishingly capable. Continuous or near-continuous daylight across parts of the region removes one of the most obvious barriers, and open-water seasons can make vessel activity and coastal change strikingly visible. During such periods, optical archives and near-real-time imagery can support comparison, route monitoring, environmental analysis, and public verification with impressive authority. It would be foolish to write as though the north were permanently opaque to visible sensing. It is not.

Yet that concession only sharpens the central argument. Summer abundance can hide winter insufficiency. An architecture that performs brilliantly in bright months may still fail the test of persistence because persistence is judged across the full operational calendar, not the most photogenic slice of it. A surveillance system does not become seasonally persistent merely because one season flatters its strengths. If the same system grows intermittent, ambiguous, or dependent on luck once darkness, cloud, and glare reassert themselves, then optical success has to be named for what it is: a valuable but bounded contribution.

This is why optical imaging alone rarely supports Arctic persistence. Persistence requires more than occasional excellence. It requires continuity of usable awareness across changing conditions. Optical systems can provide high-confidence moments and strong comparative records. They can anchor public narratives, reveal visible relationships, and offer forensic detail no other sensor matches so intuitively. What they cannot do, by themselves, is sustain dependable watchfulness through the full cycle of Arctic light, weather, and surface complexity. The gap is not a defect of the camera. It is a property of the environment.

That gap explains why optical imagery in the High North so often works best as part of a sequence rather than as a sovereign answer. A broad-area radar system may first detect the anomaly. An optical system may then provide the humanly legible confirmation when conditions permit. Thermal or other sensing modes may add another layer of confidence if the event concerns activity, heat, or material distinction. In that sequence, optical imaging is not demoted. It is given its proper dignity. It becomes the visible witness rather than the sole custodian of continuity.

The quiet motif worth keeping is the horizon. In optical Arctic imagery, the horizon is sometimes literal: low light, long shadows, a world tilted towards dusk even at midday. But it is also interpretive. There is always a horizon beyond which the image cannot quite carry confidence by itself. In summer, that horizon recedes. In winter, it advances. Cloud pulls it close. Glare can make it deceptive. A skilled analyst learns to notice where it lies, and a serious system learns not to pretend it has vanished.

The harder question therefore is not whether the next optical image will be sharp, beautiful, or even operationally useful. It is whether the confidence it invites belongs to the scene itself, or to a seasonal coincidence that will not last. A vessel in a summer lane may offer itself to the eye almost too easily. A winter lead may offer just enough visible structure to tempt premature certainty. Between those two images lies the real problem of Arctic persistence: not how to obtain a picture, but how to know when a picture deserves to bear the weight placed upon it.

Synthetic aperture radar for all-weather sensing

In January 2019, the European Space Agency's Sentinel-1 satellites provided radar imagery of sea ice and ship traffic in northern waters under conditions that would have reduced ordinary optical confidence to a matter of luck. The importance of the images was not merely that they existed. It was that they existed at all when darkness, cloud, and winter surface complexity would have made visible-light interpretation intermittent or impossible. In the Arctic, that difference is not technical ornament. It changes what kind of surveillance can plausibly be sustained.

Radar does not ask permission from the sun. That is why it sits so close to the centre of high-latitude monitoring. Synthetic aperture radar, or SAR, emits its own signal and measures the returned energy. It is therefore not trapped by polar night in the way optical imaging is, and it is far less constrained by cloud. Those two facts alone would make it valuable in the High North. But SAR's real significance runs deeper. It is not simply an imaging substitute for bad weather. It sees a different Arctic: one organised by surface roughness, moisture, structure, orientation, and interaction with the radar beam rather than by visible colour and ordinary shadow.

That shift matters because the Arctic is a place where visible intuition often fails precisely when persistence is most demanded. Show a winter sea-ice field to an optical sensor and the result may depend on daylight, cloud gaps, glare, and whether the eye can trust what it thinks it sees. Show the same field to SAR and the scene changes category. Name the key strength properly and it is continuity under hostile viewing conditions. Explain how it works in practice, and the answer becomes concrete. Rough water, smooth ice, ridged pressure zones, vessel wakes, sea-state changes, and man-made objects often return radar energy differently enough to support detection when visible imaging would offer little or nothing. The implication is strategic. SAR makes the Arctic less seasonally blind.

This is why SAR has become central to maritime and cryosphere surveillance in the north. Ships can stand out against sea surfaces that look visually flat or inaccessible to optical sensors. Ice edges, leads, pressure ridges, and zones of broken or compacted ice can be mapped with a consistency that visible-light systems struggle to match across winter and cloud. Coastal monitoring benefits too. A facility near shore, a track across frozen ground, a disturbed surface, a pattern of repeated movement near infrastructure - these may each present radar signatures that invite attention even when the visible scene is unavailable. Analysts trust SAR because it keeps returning usable information when the Arctic withdraws ordinary sight.

A vessel leaves a trace. That quiet motif helps because it captures SAR's practical genius. A ship in northern waters does not merely occupy a point. It alters the surface around it. Its structure reflects energy in ways the surrounding environment does not. The wake, the disturbance, the contrast with smoother or rougher water, the interaction with nearby ice - all can become visible through radar in forms that matter operationally. This is one reason coastguards, maritime services, ice analysts, and defence users value SAR so highly. The sensor often does not need the scene to be picturesque. It needs the scene to be physically different in ways the radar can register.

The Sentinel-1 mission offers a clear public example. Operated under the Copernicus programme, Sentinel-1 has become indispensable for many users working on sea ice, maritime traffic, flooding, and land deformation because its radar imaging continues through cloud and darkness in ways optical systems cannot. In Arctic contexts, that persistence of sensing has made it especially valuable for ice services and for the observation of northern routes where weather and season repeatedly erode optical certainty. The lesson is not merely that SAR is available. It is that continuity of sensing changes the rhythm of decision-making. A user can plan around a sensor that is less vulnerable to the ordinary visual failures of the north.

A second example lies in Canada's RADARSAT programme, whose northern relevance has long been obvious. RADARSAT systems earned their place in Arctic monitoring because radar's sensitivity to sea ice conditions and ship detection made them exceptionally suited to a region where day-night capability and cloud tolerance are not luxuries but operating requirements. This mattered not only for environmental and maritime management but for the broader strategic fact that the north became more legible on more days of the year. Again, the gain should be stated carefully. SAR did not make the Arctic transparent. It made it less intermittently opaque.

Yet the very strengths that make SAR so attractive also create a familiar danger: overconfidence. Radar imagery does not arrive to the human eye as naturally as optical imagery does. A visible photograph flatters intuition. A SAR scene demands interpretation. Bright returns, dark patches, textured zones, geometric highlights, speckled backgrounds, anomalous streaks - these are not self-explaining. They emerge from the interaction between radar wavelength, incidence angle, surface roughness, moisture, object geometry, and processing choices. A ship may be obvious. A false lead may also be obvious to the unwary. Ice types can separate elegantly in one context and merge confusingly in another. The image is powerful. It is not plain.

This interpretive burden changes how SAR should be understood within a surveillance system. A strong radar image can support detection very effectively. It may support identification or classification in some cases, especially when analysts can compare patterns across time or pair the image with other data. But radar's authority is rarely the same as visible imagery's public authority, and its analytic confidence varies with context. Show a maritime analyst a radar scene of vessels against open water and the task may be straightforward. Show the same analyst complex winter ice, rough seas, mixed surface states, or infrastructure partly masked by terrain and the discipline changes. Confidence must be earned, not assumed.

Resolution and coverage sharpen that discipline further. Like all imaging systems, SAR cannot escape trade-offs. A mode designed for broad-area coverage can sweep large Arctic spaces and increase the chance of finding something unusual, but it generally gives less fine detail about whatever it finds. A mode designed for higher resolution can reveal more about a vessel, a coastal site, or a narrow area of sea ice, but it covers less ground and may reduce revisit flexibility in practice. The bargain is unavoidable. One does not simply "have radar". One chooses what kind of radar look to take, over what area, with what intended consequence.

That is why SAR fits so naturally into search-and-refine architectures. A wide-area radar mode may first detect the anomaly: a ship where one was not expected, a lead where route planners did not anticipate one, a pattern of movement near an installation, a change in surface behaviour that warrants attention. A more focused mode, or another sensor entirely, may then be tasked to resolve what the anomaly means. The sequence matters. SAR is often strongest not when it claims to do everything, but when it opens the field intelligently for the next act of interpretation. In the Arctic, where search areas are vast and time under good conditions is precious, that role is invaluable.

A credible limitation must be admitted here. SAR is not universally superior merely because it defeats darkness and most cloud. Some tasks remain better served by optical or other sensing when conditions permit. Human audiences, including policymakers and publics, often understand optical images more immediately. Fine visible details relevant to identification, public attribution, or legal presentation may not emerge from radar with the same ease. A radar return may suggest a vessel, disturbance, or activity pattern without settling the kind of question a visible image can answer in a single glance. It would therefore be wrong to cast SAR as the final word in Arctic surveillance. It is often the indispensable first word, and sometimes much more than that, but not the whole sentence.

That concession, however, strengthens rather than weakens SAR's central place. The Arctic rarely offers the luxury of waiting for ideal optical conditions. Systems built around visible imagery alone inherit a calendar of weakness that radar can partially break. The point is not that radar replaces everything else. It is that it changes the baseline. It lets operators maintain a level of awareness through darkness, cloud, and poor seasonal visibility that would otherwise collapse. Once that is understood, the question becomes less "SAR or optical?" than "What does SAR make possible for the rest of the system?" The answer often includes better cueing, more credible broad-area monitoring, and stronger continuity across the periods when other sensors become episodic.

This is where latency and downlink have to be brought back into the picture, because SAR's sensory strength can easily seduce people into forgetting the rest of the chain. A radar scene collected over northern waters at the perfect moment is not operationally meaningful merely because the sensor worked. It still has to be downlinked, processed, interpreted, and delivered. SAR data products can be large. Processing can be demanding. Tasking queues can compete. Downlink opportunities can still constrain timeliness, especially in architectures that rely on store-and-forward rather than continuous relay. A system can therefore possess a superb all-weather sensor and still fail the clock that matters to the user. The trace may be captured. It may not arrive in time to shape the decision.

Risk becomes visible here in very practical ways. A maritime centre may trust SAR enough to narrow a search field and redirect scarce patrol assets. A defence analyst may compare radar scenes across passes to judge whether a northern contact is behaving unusually. A government may decide not to wait for optical confirmation because the radar evidence, paired with context, has crossed the threshold for action. But the same users can also be misled if they assume that radar continuity equals decision continuity. A delayed SAR product can turn a live anomaly into an after-action clue. A widely praised radar constellation can still leave operators waiting on ground segments, processing queues, or tasking priorities invisible in the public celebration of its all-weather capability.

The fit between SAR and system design therefore matters as much as the sensor physics itself. A constellation intended for Arctic awareness must ask what kind of radar product it wants most often, what latency it can tolerate, how much downlink capacity it can guarantee, and what other sensors or sources will help validate ambiguous scenes. It must decide whether broad search outranks fine characterisation, whether public legibility matters as much as operational continuity, and whether its users can absorb radar-derived uncertainty without either paralysis or bravado. None of these questions diminish SAR. They place it where it belongs: at the centre of an architecture, not above one.

The vessel trace returns here because it captures both SAR's triumph and its discipline. Radar can find the trace when night and cloud have hidden the scene from ordinary sight. It can keep finding traces across seasons in ways no optical archive can match. But the trace is not the whole event. It must still be named, timed, compared, and acted upon. A bright return in a radar scene may be the beginning of clarity or the beginning of a mistake, depending on what else the system can do with it.

That is the harder test for Arctic surveillance. Not whether SAR can see through darkness - it can, and that achievement is transformative - but whether the institutions using it are careful enough not to mistake sensory continuity for complete awareness. A radar constellation can make the north vastly more observable. It can also encourage the dangerous belief that what is observable has therefore been fully understood and delivered in time. The real question is whether the next radar image will enter a system disciplined enough to turn its all-weather strength into dependable judgement, rather than just another impressive trace on a screen.

Thermal, multispectral, and hyperspectral roles

In May 2020, when fuel escaped from a storage tank near Norilsk in the Russian Arctic, visible imagery did much of the early public work. It showed stained ground and darkened water in ways that travelled quickly and persuasively. But the event also exposed a quieter truth about remote sensing in the north. Some of the most important questions did not concern what the eye could see first. They concerned temperature, material difference, spread, persistence, and the distinction between a striking image and a more disciplined account of what the surface was actually doing.

Not every clue is visible. That is the point at which thermal, multispectral, and hyperspectral sensing enter the story. They rarely command the same public imagination as optical imagery, and they do not enjoy radar's reputation for all-weather toughness. Yet in Arctic surveillance they often become decisive at exactly those moments when a broad picture must be turned into a more specific judgement. A heat anomaly may suggest activity where a visible image shows only darkness or uniform snow. A spectral signature may distinguish disturbed ground, oil, algae, meltwater, or industrial residue that ordinary colour imagery renders as ambiguous stain. A thermal pattern across repeated passes may reveal not merely that something is present, but that it is active.

These sensors matter because they change the question being asked. Show an Arctic scene to an optical system and the first issue is usually form: what does it look like? Show it to SAR and the issue shifts towards structure and surface response: how does it reflect? Show it to thermal or spectral sensors and the question becomes more discriminating. What is warmer or cooler than expected? What materials absorb and reflect across wavelengths in ways that suggest composition rather than simple appearance? What activity leaves a metabolic, industrial, or mechanical trace rather than a plainly visible shape? The implication is not that one sensor supplants the others. It is that these narrower sensing modes can push an ambiguous scene across the threshold from suspicion to a more disciplined interpretation.

Thermal sensing is the most immediately graspable of the three because its logic is intuitive. A surface or object emits heat differently depending on its composition, activity, insulation, and relation to the surrounding environment. In the Arctic that can be especially revealing because cold backgrounds increase the relative significance of warm anomalies. A vessel against freezing water, an active facility on a snowbound coast, machinery recently operated on frozen ground, a power source at a remote site, even a cleared route whose surface behaves thermally unlike the terrain around it - all may become more visible through heat contrast than through ordinary visible imaging. This does not make thermal imagery magically clear. It makes it sensitive to a different kind of evidence.

That sensitivity becomes important when visible form is insufficient. A dark object on snow may be obvious in optical imagery and still leave uncertainty about whether it is active, abandoned, newly placed, or merely differently coloured. Thermal data can change that. If the same object radiates in ways that suggest recent use, power, or heat retention distinct from the background, analyst confidence shifts. Not completely, not automatically, but materially. A maritime example makes the point. A radar pass may detect a probable vessel in difficult conditions. A thermal observation close enough in time may help distinguish an operating ship from a colder, less active object or refine interpretation of behaviour near ice. The gain lies not in theatrical revelation but in a better account of activity.

A short sequence illustrates this well. A SAR scene over northern waters detects an anomalous contact near the edge of drifting ice. The return is convincing enough to support detection, perhaps even probable vessel classification, but little more. A later thermal product shows localised heat contrast consistent with propulsion or onboard operations. That does not identify the ship fully, nor does it settle intent. But it changes the pattern from passive presence to active behaviour. An operations centre may then choose to task another sensor, compare the contact with known traffic, or elevate the anomaly for closer watch. Here thermal data does not replace radar. It completes a sentence radar began.

Multispectral sensing extends the logic by offering several discrete bands beyond ordinary visible colour, allowing analysts to compare how surfaces and materials respond across different parts of the spectrum. In Arctic environments that matters because snow, ice, water, vegetation, disturbed ground, pollution, and built infrastructure do not simply differ in appearance; they differ in spectral behaviour. A melt pond may resemble open water to the casual eye and separate more clearly in multispectral analysis. Fresh snow, older snow, wet snow, bare ice, and sediment-laden water can display distinctions that visible imagery alone compresses. A coastal discharge, burn scar, or industrial residue may emerge more clearly because the sensor reads not just colour, but how the material interacts with light beyond what human vision can comfortably parse.

This makes multispectral systems especially useful for environmental surveillance and for the interpretation of mixed natural and human activity. The Arctic is full of scenes where those categories overlap: port activity near changing shoreline, infrastructure built into permafrost terrain, shipping interacting with variable ice conditions, pollution events unfolding across snow, soil, and water. In such cases, the value of multispectral sensing is not simply higher "information content". It is the ability to discriminate between surfaces that ordinary imagery leaves entangled. A scene stops being merely visible and becomes sortable.

Hyperspectral sensing presses further by sampling many more narrow spectral bands, seeking subtle material cues that can support finer discrimination. Its promise is significant, and its use more demanding. In theory and, increasingly, in practice, hyperspectral data can help distinguish material composition, stress, contamination, or surface condition with a specificity unavailable to broader-band systems. In the Arctic, this can matter acutely during incidents. A suspected spill, exhaust residue, altered soil near infrastructure, unusual snow discolouration, or a trace of industrial activity may become politically consequential if the question turns from "did something happen?" to "what exactly happened?" Hyperspectral sensing is not a routine solution to every surveillance problem. It is a tool that can become unusually valuable when attribution begins to depend on material evidence rather than mere visual presence.

The Norilsk spill again offers a useful public anchor. Visible imagery helped establish scale and urgency. But incidents of that kind also show why material discrimination matters. The public image may confirm that a region has been affected. Multispectral and other non-visible data can help sort water from contaminated water, affected surface from unaffected, fresh spread from older residue, or active remediation from mere disturbance. The incident was environmental rather than military, yet that is precisely why it teaches well. Arctic surveillance does not divide neatly into civil and security domains. The same sensing discipline that helps characterise a pollution event may later shape judgement about industrial concealment, infrastructure stress, or operational activity around a contested site.

A second example comes from thermal monitoring of wildfires and infrastructure heat anomalies in high-latitude regions, including Alaska and Siberia. Thermal sensors have long been used to identify active fire fronts and hotspots even when visible imagery struggles with smoke, darkness, or scale. The relevance here is not that Arctic surveillance should be reduced to environmental monitoring. It is that thermal data demonstrates how activity can be inferred from energy rather than form. A surface may look quiet and still emit signs of combustion, machinery use, or subsurface processes. Once one understands that principle, its wider strategic importance becomes hard to ignore. In the High North, where visible evidence is often intermittent and public proof may lag behind operational concern, the ability to infer activity from heat can alter when and how an incident is taken seriously.

That said, these sensors are rarely universal persistence tools. This limitation matters enough to state plainly. Thermal imagery can be constrained by spatial resolution, atmospheric effects, acquisition timing, and the fact that not every meaningful activity produces a strong or interpretable heat signature. Multispectral and hyperspectral sensing often depend on lighting conditions and can generate data whose value hinges on careful calibration, processing, and expert interpretation. Their outputs may be rich yet operationally cumbersome. A sensor that distinguishes material beautifully under the right conditions may still be a poor instrument for broad, routine, all-season watch across vast Arctic spaces. That is why these systems so often feel situationally decisive rather than universally central.

The limitation should not be mistaken for marginality. In surveillance architectures, niche sensors often matter most at the moment when a broad anomaly becomes a contested incident. Optical imagery may show a suspicious change. SAR may confirm structure or persistence through weather and darkness. Thermal or spectral data may then introduce the detail that reshapes the argument: evidence of active machinery, fuel combustion, warm effluent, unusual material presence, or surface alteration inconsistent with the public explanation on offer. At that point, the sensor stops being niche in any practical sense. It becomes the difference between vague concern and a sharper judgement.

This is where escalation dynamics enter. Surveillance does not only inform action; it also informs accusation, reassurance, and denial. A state may tolerate ambiguity while an event remains at the level of broad detection. It may behave differently when thermal or spectral evidence suggests active operation, contamination, or deliberate concealment. A public statement may be withheld until a visible image can be shown, even if thermal data prompted concern earlier. Conversely, a government may act internally on thermal or spectral indications while choosing not to publish them because their evidentiary style is harder for general audiences to absorb. These are not merely communication choices. They are part of how niche sensing alters political tempo.

Trust therefore appears in specific institutional behaviour. Analysts trust thermal data when they are willing to revisit an apparently quiet site because its heat pattern has changed. Maritime operators trust it when they compare repeated heat signatures to distinguish active traffic from static clutter. Policymakers trust multispectral or hyperspectral evidence when they allow it to shape briefings, interagency warnings, or requests for corroboration. Public trust is often slower because the imagery is less intuitive than ordinary photography. That lag creates its own tension. The sensor may be operationally persuasive before it becomes politically persuasive.

A credible counterpoint must be admitted. There are many Arctic situations in which these sensors add little or add it too late to matter. A fast-moving maritime contact may leave no useful thermal or spectral signature that survives the timing of orbital passes. Atmospheric conditions, surface complexity, or coarse resolution may reduce apparent gains. A hyperspectral dataset may be scientifically rich and operationally awkward. In many routine monitoring tasks, simpler combinations of optical and radar imagery will carry more of the burden more efficiently. That is real, and any serious account should resist turning specialised sensing into mystical superiority.

But the concession clarifies rather than weakens the core argument. The value of thermal, multispectral, and hyperspectral sensing lies precisely in not asking them to be what they are not. They are not generally the workhorses of continuous Arctic watch. They are instruments of discrimination. They matter most when the question sharpens from presence to activity, from anomaly to material character, from broad surveillance to the evidentiary politics of an incident. Their strength is episodic but potentially decisive. In that sense they resemble specialist witnesses called when the ordinary account of events no longer suffices.

This also explains how they fit into system-level design. A mature Arctic surveillance architecture does not pretend that every sensor should provide constant, autonomous, self-explanatory awareness. It stages them. Broad search sensors narrow the field. More intuitive sensors provide visible confirmation when conditions allow. Specialised thermal or spectral systems are then cued for moments when activity, composition, or change in state matters enough to justify the narrower and more demanding look. The system's intelligence lies in the order of these questions, not in the fantasy that a single sensor will answer them all.

The quiet motif worth keeping is the trace. Not the obvious track left by a ship or vehicle, but the thinner trace: retained warmth, altered reflectance, a material signature that lingers after visible drama has faded. Arctic incidents often turn on such traces. A place may look inert and still hold evidence of recent power use. A surface may appear merely stained and still reveal spectral cues that change the argument about cause. A radar contact may seem generic and still, when paired with thermal contrast, suggest behaviour rather than mere presence. The trace does not settle every question. It changes which questions can honestly be asked next.

The harder problem, then, is not whether these sensors can sometimes produce remarkable insight. They can. It is whether institutions know when to call upon them, how much confidence to place in them, and how to absorb the political consequences when a once obscure sensor becomes the decisive witness in a contested Arctic event. A system that ignores them may miss the moment when broad awareness needs material proof. A system that fetishises them may mistake episodic discrimination for persistence. The real test lies in the interval between those errors: when a faint thermal or spectral trace appears, what exactly is it enough to change?

Chapter 5

Communications and Downlink Bottlenecks

What does it mean to see the Arctic if the image arrives after the moment that made it matter? That is the communications paradox at the centre of northern surveillance. The sensor may perform exactly as promised. The orbit may deliver the pass. The target may be captured cleanly. Yet none of that guarantees timely awareness. A collected image still has to travel, and the High North is where travel begins to govern truth.

The mistake is familiar. People speak about surveillance as though collection were the decisive act and delivery a secondary convenience, a matter of plumbing that follows naturally once the interesting work has been done. The Arctic does not indulge that hierarchy. At high latitudes, the path between sensing and use can be narrow, weathered, contested, and politically loaded. Elevation angles change the shape of a link. Brief windows force choices. A terminal on the ground may matter more than a celebrated sensor overhead. A system that looks rich in orbital access can still behave like a poor one if the data cannot be moved where it needs to go quickly enough.

That is why communications belongs inside the definition of capability rather than beside it. A surveillance architecture is not only a way of seeing. It is a way of moving what has been seen through links, stations, networks, queues, and institutions that each impose delay or discipline. The chapter's central tension grows from that fact. Arctic systems promise persistence, but persistence depends not merely on what can be collected; it depends on what can be delivered under adverse geometry, limited ground access, interference risk, and competing demand. The bottleneck often sits below the sensor and out of public sight.

The stakes are sharper than they first appear. A delayed product may still be valuable for pattern analysis, environmental reconstruction, or evidentiary use after the fact. It may be worthless for a decision that turns on the next hour. Communications, therefore, shape not just speed, but mission type.

It decides whether a system supports watchfulness, warning, or hindsight. Trust shows itself here in operational behaviour: whether planners rely on direct delivery or hedge with alternative sources, whether analysts accept a product as current enough to act upon, whether a maritime or defence user treats a contact as live, stale, or already lost to the gap between collection and receipt.

The issue becomes still more consequential because throughput is never simply a technical number. Under Arctic conditions, availability often matters more than peak performance. A link that is theoretically fast and practically fragile may serve the brochure better than the operator. A relay that shortens one delay can insert another dependency. A crosslinked constellation can make coverage feel broader by routing data elsewhere, but it also raises questions of control, priority, and who gets served first when civil and security users share the same mesh. The moment data begins to move, governance enters the signal.

That is where latency stops looking like physics alone. Some delay arises from orbit and geometry. Some from weather and radio conditions. Some from ground hardware. Some from prioritisation, compression, and the administrative ordering of scarcity. In the Arctic, where alternative pathways are often thin, those layers accumulate rather than cancel one another. A system may downlink only a subset of what it collects. A station may favour one customer. A relay may turn one pass into near-real-time delivery for some users and not for others. The result is a surveillance hierarchy hidden inside the network.

The path ahead begins with the link itself, where polar angles, environment, and the short life of a pass decide how much can be moved before the window closes. It then shifts into the practical logic of bands, throughput, and the difference between nominal rate and usable service, before following the escape routes systems build through relay and crosslinking when local ground access is too thin or too slow. The argument then drops to the surface, where terminals, antennas, power, and siting make or break the promise of delivery, before ending where communications always end in practice: in decisions about what to send, to whom, and with what urgency.

A quiet motif runs through all of this: the queue. Some queues are obvious, a line of packets, products, or users waiting for a narrow window. Others are hidden inside routing choices, antenna schedules, cloud processing, or interagency priority rules. The Arctic is a place where queues become strategic because the window is often short and the next chance may not arrive on terms that the decision can still use.

The harder question, then, is not whether a system can communicate with the north. Many can. It is whether the chain carrying those communications remains strong enough, fair enough, and fast enough that collection survives the trip into action. When the pass is brief, the angle poor, the weather unhelpful, the terminal remote, and several claimants all want the same downlink at once, what exactly does persistence still mean?

Link budgets and polar angles

In October 2018, during NATO's Trident Juncture exercise in northern Norway, reports of GPS disruption in Finnmark drew attention to jamming and interference, as they should have done. But the episode also pointed to a broader truth about Arctic surveillance that receives far less public attention. A system can collect something important and still fail the test that matters most: getting the result where it needs to go while it is still timely. A link does not need to collapse completely to change the meaning of awareness. It only needs to thin at the wrong moment.

The image is not the product. Not yet. In the Arctic, that sentence should be treated less as a caution than as a rule of analysis. Much of the public imagination about surveillance remains fixed on the sensor - the camera, the radar payload, the spectacular pass overhead. Yet collection is only half the act, and often less than half. A satellite gathers data, but the data must cross a radio link whose quality depends on angle, atmosphere, terminal capability, interference, and time. If that crossing becomes uncertain, slow, or selective, then excellent sensing can degrade into late knowledge. The clock starts at collection. The system is judged at delivery.

This is where link budgets become more than engineering notation. A link budget sounds technical, almost clerical: a balance of transmitted power, antenna gain, path loss, receiver sensitivity, noise, and margin. Show the problem in its Arctic form, however, and the abstraction sharpens immediately. A satellite appears low relative to a ground site. The signal travels through more atmosphere, or along a more awkward path, than a flatter map might suggest. The pass is short. Weather may not stop the link, but it can strain it. A competing transmitter, natural or deliberate, may raise the noise floor. Name the issue properly and it becomes clear that the link budget is not a back-office calculation. It is the difference between data that arrives promptly and data that waits.

Polar angles matter because geometry reaches directly into performance. At high latitudes, many space systems work under look angles that are less forgiving than non-specialists assume. A link to a satellite low on the horizon is usually harder to sustain cleanly than a link to one seen high in the sky. The path can be longer. Terrain, masts, structures, or sea state may matter more. The system may spend less time in its best geometry and more time entering and leaving it. The implication is practical rather than theoretical. Operators must decide whether a pass offers enough time and enough margin to send all the data, only part of it, or merely the most urgent summary. In that decision, communications stops being support and becomes triage.

A short window changes behaviour. That is the quiet motif running through Arctic downlink. A pass may be technically successful and still leave little room for indulgence. If a satellite carrying radar or optical products over northern waters reaches a station for only a brief interval, the system may have to choose. Full-resolution imagery or lower-fidelity quicklook? One high-priority maritime contact or several broader-area products? Raw data for later analysis or a processed alert designed to save time? The choice is not simply operational housekeeping. It determines who receives what kind of knowledge, and when. In the Arctic, the short window can decide whether a product supports action or merely enriches hindsight.

The Svalbard ground segment offers a useful public example, not because it is weak, but because it demonstrates the opposite: how valuable high-latitude station access becomes when many polar-orbiting satellites need to downlink promptly. KSAT's facilities on Svalbard have become central to global Earth observation operations precisely because high-latitude passes give repeated opportunities to contact satellites in polar orbit. Yet even strong stations do not repeal geometry. They manage it. Their significance rests on the fact that Arctic and near-Arctic ground access shortens the path from collection to delivery for many missions that would otherwise wait longer. The lesson is not that one station solves the problem. It is that link opportunity is itself a strategic resource.

A second example comes from maritime surveillance workflows that depend on synthetic aperture radar. SAR is often praised, rightly, for day-night and all-weather sensing, especially over ice and sea. But SAR also generates substantial data volumes, and those volumes have to cross the same finite windows and ground constraints as anything else. A wide-area maritime scene over northern waters may be collected at exactly the right time and still face hard delivery choices if the downlink opportunity is brief or link margin thin. In practice, this can force systems to favour compressed products, selected scenes, or prioritised contacts over comprehensive delivery. The sensor has succeeded. The link has begun to govern what success means.

Weather complicates the link without needing to destroy it. Arctic weather is often discussed in relation to visibility and logistics, but it also belongs inside communications analysis. Snow, ice accretion, moisture, wind loading on antennas, and changing atmospheric conditions can all affect how comfortably a system operates. A well-designed link may survive such conditions with no dramatic failure, yet still lose margin, throughput, or stability enough to matter. This is important because systems are rarely judged by whether they function at all. They are judged by whether they function well enough, predictably enough, that users can trust the timing of what arrives. A surveillance network that limps through poor conditions may remain technically alive and operationally disappointing.

Interference sharpens the same problem from another direction. In the High North, radio environments can be stressed by geography, sparse infrastructure, auroral and ionospheric variability, and, at times, deliberate disruption. A link budget built for clean conditions can become less forgiving when the surrounding environment grows noisier or less stable. Here again, the result need not be a theatrical blackout. It may be elevated error, retransmission, slower effective throughput, or greater caution in what the system dares to send during a narrow window. That matters because degraded communications and degraded timing often reinforce one another. When the link becomes less trustworthy, the pressure to simplify or compress the product increases. The more compressed or selective the product, the more carefully its user must interpret it.

The significance of this is easy to miss because communications problems often remain invisible to outside audiences. A satellite image released hours after collection may still look impressive. A radar-derived vessel contact may still be analytically useful. But the delay changes the class of value. A product arriving after a ship has altered course, after an aircraft has left station, or after a coastal anomaly has evolved belongs to a different decision world than one delivered quickly. Collecting without delivering does not produce the same surveillance, even when the final image is identical. The lost time has changed the system's relationship to action.

A credible limitation should be acknowledged. Modern communications architectures are not passive victims of Arctic geometry. Better antennas, adaptive coding, higher-performance terminals, relay systems, and more capable high-latitude stations can all reduce the severity of these constraints. Some missions are also tolerant of delay. Environmental monitoring, change detection, retrospective analysis, and some forms of evidentiary use may remain highly valuable even when delivery is not immediate. It would be careless to suggest that every Arctic downlink challenge amounts to operational failure. Often it does not.

But the concession clarifies the real argument. The point is not that links are always weak. It is that communications should be treated as a performance limiter whose quality determines what kind of mission the system is actually supporting. A delayed product may be perfect for reconstruction and poor for warning. A lower-fidelity alert may be ideal for cueing and inadequate for attribution. A downlink architecture that works excellently from a major station may thin dramatically when the user relies on a smaller, more deployable terminal. Once these distinctions are admitted, the glamour of the sensor gives way to the harder discipline of the chain.

This is why major stations and field terminals should never be spoken of as though they belong to the same communicative world simply because both can "receive satellite data". A large fixed station may have better tracking, more power, larger antennas, stronger backhaul, and more forgiving operational margins. A deployable or austere terminal may provide priceless flexibility while accepting narrower throughput, higher susceptibility to local conditions, or stricter limits on what can be moved during a pass. Neither is inherently superior. Each belongs to a different theory of acceptable compromise. Yet a surveillance claim that ignores this difference risks promising one kind of delivery while funding another.

Trust, once more, should be translated into visible behaviour. An operator trusts a link when they schedule delivery workflows against the expected pass without padding for likely failure. A maritime centre trusts it when it acts on a contact because the product arrived within the decision window rather than after it. A defence or coastguard user distrusts it when they insist on redundant cueing, alternative communications paths, or lower-fidelity previews because the full product may come too late. Those behavioural clues often reveal more about Arctic communications reality than any technical description of peak capacity.

The short window returns here because it joins physics to governance. When a pass is brief, the system cannot send everything at once. Someone decides. Which scene moves first? Which agency receives the higher-fidelity version? Which ally gets the alert product now and the rawer material later? Compression, prioritisation, and selection enter by necessity. This is not merely a later-stage data management issue. It begins at the link. The tighter the window, the more the communications architecture forces strategic choices about scarcity, confidence, and privilege.

That is why link budgets belong at the centre of Arctic surveillance analysis rather than in an appendix of technical concerns. They reveal where performance is actually won or lost. A system with exceptional sensing and weak delivery may look formidable and behave sluggishly. A system with modest sensing and disciplined, resilient communications may outperform expectations because its products arrive on the clock that matters. The Arctic keeps making this comparison brutal. It asks not whether the satellite saw the target, but whether the link delivered the sighting before the target, the weather, or the politics moved on.

The harder question, then, is not whether a high-latitude link can be made to work. Many can, and often impressively. It is whether the margin is large enough, the window long enough, and the interference or weather burden low enough that the system can deliver what it collected without silently converting live awareness into delayed intelligence. When the pass is brief and the queue is full, what gets sent first - and what kind of Arctic knowledge disappears into the minutes that the link could not hold open?

Frequency bands, throughput, and availability

In September 2022, NASA's Artemis I mission drew attention to the Deep Space Network for an obvious reason: even the most advanced spacecraft remain dependent on the channels through which their data returns to Earth. That lesson travels well to the Arctic, though the distances are shorter and the tempo often harsher. A satellite may collect exactly what an operator needs over ice or sea. The harder question is whether the system can move that data quickly enough, reliably enough, and often enough under northern conditions that the collection remains operationally alive by the time it arrives.

A faster link is not always a better one. That is the uncomfortable truth hiding beneath communications specifications. Public descriptions of satellite systems often encourage the reader to admire headline throughput, as if sheer rate settled the matter. In Arctic use, it rarely does. Throughput matters, certainly, especially when sensors generate large volumes of imagery or when several users compete for the same downlink window. But the north punishes any architecture that confuses peak performance with dependable service. A link that performs impressively in ideal conditions and degrades sharply under poor geometry, adverse weather, or local interference may serve a brochure well and an operator badly.

Frequency bands sit at the centre of this distinction because they shape the kind of bargain a communications system makes with the environment. Show two links on paper - one designed for high data volume, another for steadier performance under marginal conditions - and the strategic question becomes plain. Name the issue properly, and one sees that frequency choice is never just an engineering preference. It determines how readily the link can carry large products, how vulnerable it may be to atmospheric effects, how demanding its antenna and pointing requirements become, and how gracefully it survives the ordinary hostility of Arctic operations. The implication is practical: persistence depends not on theoretical capacity alone, but on usable throughput when conditions cease to flatter the design.

This is why downlink bands should be understood in operational rather than merely technical terms. Lower-frequency links often offer advantages in resilience, coverage behaviour, and tolerance for some forms of degradation, though usually at the cost of more limited raw throughput. Higher-frequency links can move more data, which is deeply attractive for radar products, high-resolution optical imagery, and dense analytic workflows. Yet the same qualities that make them appealing can also make them fussier - more dependent on link quality, cleaner pointing, stronger margins, and ground infrastructure able to support the bargain. In the Arctic, where geometry, weather, and logistics already narrow the room for error, those differences quickly stop being abstract.

X-band offers a useful public example because it has long been associated with Earth observation downlink. Many imaging satellites use it precisely because it supports substantial data return without entering the most demanding end of the communications spectrum. That balance has helped make it a practical workhorse for missions whose value depends on moving large sensor products to ground stations efficiently. In Arctic operations, the attraction is obvious: a band like this can support serious imaging demand while remaining familiar to station operators and compatible with well-established ground infrastructure. The lesson is not that one band should be canonised. It is that operators often choose bands because they represent a compromise they know how to sustain.

Ka-band illustrates the other side of the bargain. Its higher throughput potential is enormously attractive, especially for modern systems that generate more data than older architectures ever contemplated. For some missions, especially those supported by strong ground infrastructure and carefully engineered margins, the advantages are undeniable. But the Arctic is where such advantages must be tested against ordinary adversity. Weather, pointing precision, terminal quality, and link availability begin to matter with greater operational consequence. A high-rate link that loses confidence too readily under bad conditions or at awkward angles may force the system into exactly the kinds of delay and selectivity it was meant to overcome. The result is not failure in the theatrical sense. It is a narrowing of practical availability.

Availability is the word that matters most here because it captures what operators actually experience. A link may be capable of extraordinary throughput under favourable circumstances and still prove disappointing if those circumstances are too fragile, too rare, or too difficult to maintain in the north. Show the difference in behaviour, and the point becomes vivid. A station relying on a more conservative architecture may deliver products consistently enough that planners build workflows around it with confidence. Another may advertise greater capacity and still force users to hedge, compress, or prioritise aggressively because the full rate is not something they feel able to count on. In Arctic surveillance, count-on-ability often beats brilliance.

The queue returns here as a useful motif. Downlink is not only a radio event. It is a moment of selection. If throughput is narrower than the sensor's appetite, someone decides what goes first. A broad radar scene may be reduced to a quick look. A full optical product may be deferred while an alert extract is sent ahead. A lower-frequency path may carry the summary while a higher-rate route waits for cleaner conditions or a larger station. Frequency choice, therefore, shapes not only what the system can transmit, but what kind of queue it imposes on knowledge. A system with excellent sensing and unreliable high-throughput delivery may still produce a queue long enough to turn operational products into archival ones.

A second example comes from polar ground services built around high-latitude stations such as those on Svalbard. Their importance is often described in geographic terms, and rightly so, but geography alone does not explain their value. What matters is the combination of station capability, antenna systems, band support, and backhaul strong enough to make repeated polar contacts useful rather than merely possible. A station that can handle the right bands, under the right conditions, with sufficient continuity, changes what "coverage" means for an orbiting sensor. It is not just where the satellite can be seen. It is where the data can be moved at a rate that preserves its meaning.

This is why robust architectures so often look less glamorous than their peak-rate rivals. They may rely on bands and equipment combinations that appear conservative, even old-fashioned, to those drawn to ever larger capacity claims. Yet in the Arctic, conservatism can be a form of intelligence. A system built around slightly lower peak throughput but stronger operational availability may serve a decision cycle better than one designed to chase exceptional rates only when all conditions behave. This is not a romance of slowness. It is an argument about mission honesty. The system should be judged by the throughput it can deliver when weather worsens, geometry degrades, interference rises, or the only available ground node is a constrained terminal rather than a premier station.

A credible limitation deserves acknowledgement. Not every mission can afford to favour robustness over data rate. Some sensors generate volumes that will choke an architecture built too cautiously. High-resolution SAR, dense optical constellations, and increasingly sophisticated onboard processing can make higher-capacity links not merely attractive but necessary. It would be careless to imply that Arctic communications can be handled indefinitely by modest throughput simply because reliability sounds virtuous. There are real tasks that demand speed and bulk together.

But the limitation clarifies the deeper point. The serious question is not whether high-throughput bands are desirable. They are. It is whether the surrounding architecture is honest about what it takes to make those bands operationally available in the north. That means better stations, stronger backhaul, tighter pointing, more disciplined margins, more careful weather tolerance, and, often, fallback paths that prevent the system from collapsing into silence when ideal conditions disappear. Peak rate without fallback is aspiration. Peak rate with resilient alternatives begins to look like a strategy.

This is where frequency choice joins governance and not merely physics. A dual-use network serving civil and security customers may have enough aggregate capacity on paper and still confront hard prioritisation decisions when Arctic conditions reduce what can actually be delivered during a given window. Who gets the higher-fidelity product? Who receives only an alert? Which customer is moved to a more reliable but slower path? Which product is compressed to preserve timeliness? Latency, in such systems, does not arise from radio conditions alone. It emerges from administrative choice shaped by the limits of throughput under real northern operations.

Trust again becomes visible in behaviour. Operators trust a band and architecture when they stop designing every workflow around contingency and use the system as a primary path rather than a hopeful one. Analysts trust it when they expect full products to arrive within the interval that their judgement still values. Governments trust it when they promise routine awareness without quietly depending on a second, more conservative route to rescue the first. These are not symbolic gestures. They reveal what kind of throughput the institution believes it can actually count on under Arctic stress.

The deeper lesson is that persistence is communicative before it is visual. A sensor may revisit regularly, collect brilliantly, and still fail the practical meaning of persistence if the throughput behind it falters too often under bad conditions. Reliable throughput is what turns recurrence into continuity. Without it, the constellation samples the north but does not steadily serve it. This is why some of the most capable Arctic architectures look less like pure races for bandwidth and more like layered bargains between capacity and survivability.

The queue grows longest when people forget that bargain. A system built for peak rate may begin shedding detail, postponing scenes, or privileging certain users the moment conditions worsen. None of that is necessarily irrational. It can be good operations. But it should make the reader more careful with claims of persistent delivery. The relevant question is not, "How much data can this link move at its best?" It is, "What still moves when the angle worsens, the air thickens, the terminal is smaller, and the pass is already half over?"

That is the test the Arctic keeps applying. Not whether a band is advanced, but whether it is available enough, often enough, under northern strain, to preserve the decision value of what has been collected. A link that survives imperfectly may still carry the alert that matters most. A higher-rate path that arrives too late may carry more truth than anyone can still use. The harder question, then, is simple to ask and difficult to design around: when the Arctic stops rewarding theoretical throughput, which architecture still delivers something a state can act on before the queue becomes the story?

Data relay and beyond-line-of-sight delivery

In January 1983, NASA launched the first Tracking and Data Relay Satellite from Cape Canaveral, changing a basic fact of space operations: a spacecraft no longer had to wait patiently for the next convenient ground station to hand over what it knew. That shift mattered first for crewed and civil missions, but its deeper logic now reaches into Arctic surveillance. A sensor above the north may collect something important at exactly the right moment. The old question was whether it had seen enough. The newer question is whether it can hand that knowledge onward before the moment closes.

A pass is not a prison. That is the promise of relay. In a simple store-and-forward architecture, a satellite gathers data and then holds it until it comes within line of sight of a suitable ground station. Over the Arctic, that can be good enough for many tasks and painfully slow for others. Relay changes the sequence. Instead of waiting for a local downlink opportunity, the observing satellite pushes its data to another spacecraft or communications layer that can forward it onwards, often to a place far from the scene itself. The result can be dramatic: what would once have sat in onboard memory until the next pass becomes available almost at once to analysts or operators elsewhere.

This changes the politics of distance. Show a remote Arctic collection event under a traditional ground-linked model and the familiar weaknesses appear immediately. The satellite sees the target, but the value of the observation is held hostage by the next station contact, the quality of the link, the station's own queue, and the constraints of geography. Name the alternative properly and one sees that data relay is not merely a faster cable in the sky. It is a rearrangement of where dependence sits. Explain why that matters, and the implication becomes plain. Relay lowers latency by loosening the bond between observation and local ground access. In doing so, it creates new dependencies on the relay network itself.

This is precisely why relay has become so attractive for northern missions. The Arctic punishes any architecture that assumes useful stations will always sit in the right place at the right moment with the right spare capacity. High latitudes offer strong opportunities for contact with polar orbiters, but those opportunities are still bounded by local infrastructure, link conditions, and queueing. A relay layer can soften those bounds. A satellite collecting radar or optical data over ice and sea may pass its product immediately to another spacecraft with a clearer onward route, turning a fleeting overhead opportunity into something closer to continuous delivery. For users watching shipping, infrastructure, or transient events, the difference between minutes and hours is not cosmetic. It changes which decisions remain alive.

The classic NASA Tracking and Data Relay Satellite System shows the principle clearly even though its historical centre of gravity lay elsewhere. Low Earth orbiting spacecraft no longer needed to rely on brief contact with scattered ground stations alone. Relay spacecraft in higher orbits could receive data and forward it rapidly to Earth, shrinking dead zones and altering the tempo of operations. The Arctic lesson is straightforward. If relay can free a mission from waiting for the next local contact, then an observing satellite over northern waters or ice is no longer quite so captive to the geography below. The scene may still be remote. The information need not remain so.

A more contemporary example lies in the growing use of commercial relay and hosted communications services to support Earth observation missions. Operators now increasingly seek architectures in which imagery or alert data can be transferred beyond line of sight soon after collection rather than stored for the next direct ground pass. In practical Arctic terms, that can mean a vessel detection, an infrastructure anomaly, or a surface change over sea ice reaching a distant operations centre while the observing satellite has scarcely left the region. The value is not speed for its own sake. It is temporal relevance. A single pass can begin to behave like a live feed, or at least enough like one to change operational choices.

Near-real time is a dangerous phrase, and relay is one reason it can sometimes be used honestly. A radar scene gathered over northern waters need not wait for the next major polar station if the platform can hand it to a relay system with continuous or at least more frequent onward visibility. An alert product can move while the satellite still flies north. An operations centre can task follow-on collection before the original platform has completed what older architectures would have treated as a self-contained pass. That is the seduction and the achievement. Relay can make one look matter more by shortening the silence that follows it.

Yet silence does not disappear. It moves. This is the central caution. A relay architecture adds complexity, and complexity redistributes failure rather than abolishing it. The direct ground station bottleneck may shrink, but a new chain now has to function: the observing satellite must acquire the relay link, the relay network must accept and route the traffic, the onward path must remain available, and the receiving ground infrastructure must still absorb, process, and prioritise the product. Each added step can be well engineered and still become its own point of weakness. The old delay was geographical. The new delay may be architectural.

This matters because relay systems can encourage overconfidence of a new kind. Once operators grow accustomed to lower latency, they may begin to treat relay as an invisible certainty rather than as another contested layer in the chain. But the network has to be trusted in practice. That trust shows itself in visible behaviour. Do planners build workflows around relay as the primary path, or do they quietly maintain direct ground alternatives in case the relay channel proves unreliable? Do analysts expect products on the fast clock, or do they hedge against sudden reversion to store-and-forward? Do governments speak publicly as though their Arctic awareness now arrives almost instantly, without acknowledging that the new speed rests on a communications mesh whose governance and resilience may be harder to read than the orbit itself?

The governance question grows sharper because relay networks can become contested infrastructure. A direct downlink to a sovereign or trusted station feels geographically legible: one can point to the antenna, the site, the cable, the controlling authority. Relay disperses control across a more abstract system. Routing decisions matter. Priority rules matter. Shared commercial or dual-use architectures matter. A spacecraft may technically possess a path to near-real-time delivery, yet the practical value of that path may depend on who else is using the network, who controls scheduling, what kind of service agreement is in place, and what happens when civil, commercial, and security users all seek urgency at once. Latency then becomes not only a property of physics but of governance.

The queue returns here in a new form. A relay network promises to shorten the wait, but it may also create hidden queues inside the network itself. Traffic may be prioritised, compressed, delayed, or re-routed according to rules the end user does not fully see. The observing satellite may no longer wait for a station over Svalbard, Alaska, or northern Canada, but the data may still wait its turn somewhere else in the chain. The location of waiting changes. Its strategic significance does not. In the Arctic, where one shortened interval can make the difference between cueing a second asset and missing the chance entirely, those hidden queues deserve the same scrutiny once reserved for direct ground passes.

A credible limitation should be admitted. Not every Arctic mission needs relay, and not every mission benefits from its added complexity. Many forms of monitoring remain well served by store-and-forward architectures, especially when the value of the data lies in retrospective analysis, environmental baselining, or routine change detection rather than rapid operational reaction. Direct downlink can also offer simplicity, visibility of control, and a certain kind of resilience if the ground network is strong enough. It would be careless to imply that relay is the inevitable answer to every northern communications problem. Sometimes the older architecture is sufficient, cheaper, clearer, or easier to trust.

But the limitation strengthens the deeper point. Relay matters most where decision timelines are short, local ground access is thin or inconvenient, and the value of a product decays quickly with delay. In such cases, a system that can hand off data beyond line of sight may do more than improve convenience. It may change the class of mission the architecture can genuinely support. A radar image that reaches analysts quickly enough to cue another collection is a different kind of product from the same image received later for archive and review. Relay does not merely accelerate delivery. It can upgrade the operational meaning of what has been collected.

This makes relay especially significant for Arctic maritime and infrastructure surveillance. A suspicious vessel near ice, a pattern of unusual movement around a coastal site, a transient opening in sea ice, or a heat-related anomaly near remote infrastructure may all demand follow-up faster than traditional downlink allows. A relay-enabled architecture can shorten the interval between first detection and second look. It can also permit decisions about tasking, dissemination, or warning to occur while the scene remains live enough to matter. The gain may be measured less in raw minutes than in preserved opportunity.

Still, every preserved opportunity comes with a question about resilience. What happens when the relay layer itself degrades, becomes congested, or is denied? What fallback exists when a system designed around rapid beyond-line-of-sight delivery is forced back into direct-downlink habits? The answer reveals whether relay has been integrated as a disciplined enhancement or embraced as a new dependency without sufficient caution. A mature Arctic architecture does not confuse the two. It treats relay as a way to bend geography, not to abolish it.

The broader strategic implication follows naturally. As relay and beyond-line-of-sight delivery become more central to surveillance, they also become more valuable targets for interference, exclusion, commercial pressure, and political negotiation. A relay constellation or service layer is not just connective tissue. It is infrastructure with leverage over timeliness, priority, and, in some cases, visibility itself. States may own the sensors and still depend on networks they do not fully command. Commercial providers may become indispensable to public missions. Alliances may discover that information-sharing begins earlier in the chain than policy language has admitted. The Arctic makes these relationships starker because it rewards the architectures that can move data fastest out of remote conditions.

The pass remains the key motif because relay changes what a pass means. Under the older model, a pass often implied not just collection but waiting. Under a relay model, the same pass may become only the first movement in a faster chain, with the product already travelling onward before the observing satellite has left the scene. That is a remarkable gain. It is also a reminder that the critical infrastructure of Arctic surveillance may now sit not only in the satellite that sees, or the station that receives, but in the invisible hand-offs between them.

The harder test, then, is not whether relay can make Arctic surveillance faster. It plainly can. The more serious question is whether the systems now leaning on relay are prepared for what that speed costs in dependency, complexity, and new surfaces of contest. When a single pass can be turned into near-real-time delivery, who controls the route, who holds priority in the queue, and what remains of northern awareness if the relay itself becomes the bottleneck no one wanted to admit was there?

Inter-satellite links and networked constellations

In May 2024, SpaceX highlighted the growing role of Starlink's laser crosslinks in carrying traffic across space before handing it down to Earth. The commercial context was broader than Arctic surveillance, but the underlying shift was directly relevant to it. A satellite no longer needed to wait for the nearest appropriate ground station in order to become useful. Data could move sideways first. In the north, where ground access can be sparse, weathered, politically complicated, or simply mistimed, that changes the meaning of coverage more than many launch announcements ever do.

A constellation that can talk to itself behaves differently from one whose satellites merely pass over and fall silent until the next downlink opportunity. That difference matters. In a simpler architecture, observation remains tied to geography below: the satellite sees, stores, and waits for the right station. In a networked architecture with inter-satellite links, the observing spacecraft can hand data to another satellite, which may hand it to another still, until the information reaches a place where downlink is possible or preferable. Coverage then stops meaning only "where the sensor can see" and begins to mean "where the network can carry what has been seen".

The shift is profound because it relocates scarcity. Show a polar-orbiting satellite collecting imagery over the Arctic under a traditional store-and-forward model, and the bottleneck appears in a familiar place: the next contact with a capable ground station. Name the new concept properly - crosslinked or networked constellations - and the bottleneck starts to migrate into routing, network management, and access control. Explain why, and the implication becomes strategic rather than merely technical. A satellite over the Arctic may no longer depend on a local station at all. It may depend instead on whether the mesh can move its data across the constellation quickly enough, with sufficient priority, to somewhere else on Earth.

That is why "space internet" features matter so much to surveillance even when they are marketed under other names. Crosslinks are often presented as tools for connectivity, resilience, or global service reach, and they are all of those things. But in surveillance terms, they do something more specific. They turn orbiting sensors into participants in a transport network rather than isolated collectors. The Arctic benefits because its great weakness has never been only seeing. It has been seeing and then waiting. A networked constellation can shorten, or even collapse, that waiting time by moving data out of the north before the local ground segment becomes the limiting factor.

A message finds a route. That quiet motif captures the change better than most grander language does. In a store-and-forward model, the message sits where it was born until an acceptable exit appears. In a crosslinked model, it begins to travel immediately, not necessarily towards the nearest destination, but towards the best path. For Arctic users, that can be transformative. A radar scene collected over the Barents Sea or the central Arctic Ocean may no longer need to remain captive to high-latitude station schedules. It can move through the network to a downlink point with better geometry, stronger infrastructure, or lower queue pressure. The observation becomes mobile in a new way.

Iridium offers an early and important public example because its architecture long demonstrated the value of inter-satellite links for global communications, especially at high latitudes. The constellation's crosslinks helped it provide service where systems dependent on equatorial geometries and local ground access struggled. The lesson carries beyond voice and data communications, narrowly understood. When satellites can move information amongst themselves, the polar penalty associated with sparse or awkward ground access diminishes. Not disappears. Diminishes. That is an architectural difference worth taking seriously because it explains why some constellations feel truly global in use while others remain globally present only in a map sense.

A more recent example lies in proliferated commercial constellations whose crosslinks allow traffic to be routed around geography and downlinked where conditions are best. For Arctic surveillance, this means an observing platform or a hosted sensor network can potentially hand off data into a mesh that behaves less like a set of discrete passes and more like a dynamic transport fabric. A single contact over northern waters can be transmitted onward while the original satellite remains far from any ideal ground node. The gain is not only lower latency. It is freedom from one of the north's oldest constraints: the assumption that useful information must leave the region through the nearest practical door.

This is where networked constellations begin to change the meaning of persistence. Traditional discussions of persistence often focus on revisit, dwell, or sensor capability. Crosslinks add another dimension. A system may not revisit more often, but it may become more useful because each observation enters the decision chain faster. That can be enough to transform the operational value of a pass. A maritime anomaly, an ice change, or a suspicious activity pattern near northern infrastructure may still be observed only intermittently. Yet if each observation is delivered rapidly through the network rather than delayed by local ground constraints, the intermittent watch begins to behave more like active surveillance than retrospective collection.

The attraction is obvious. So is the danger of overstating it. Inter-satellite links reduce some bottlenecks while creating others. A mesh must be managed. Routing must be decided. Capacity must be shared. Prioritisation must be imposed when demand exceeds what the network can carry cleanly at a given moment. In a dual-use system, these questions acquire political force very quickly. A civil user, a commercial customer, and a security customer may all be moving data through the same orbital fabric. Who gets precedence? Which packets are delayed, compressed, or re-routed? Which missions are granted low-latency paths and which are told, quietly, to wait?

This is why governance belongs inside the technical discussion rather than appended after it. A crosslinked constellation is not just a physical mesh of satellites and laser links. It is also a policy system. Routing rules express priorities. Access rules define who counts as a full user and who remains a contingent one. Service agreements, classification regimes, sovereign restrictions, and contractual obligations all shape what the network does when it is stressed. For Arctic surveillance, where multiple agencies and allied states may seek timeliness from the same infrastructure, the mesh can become a site of hierarchy. Latency may then depend as much on governance as on orbital design.

Trust appears here in unmistakably operational ways. An intelligence or maritime user trusts the network when they route critical products through it as a primary path rather than keeping it as a convenience behind more traditional ground workflows. A government trusts it when it bases northern awareness claims on the expectation that crosslinked delivery will remain available under pressure. Operators distrust it when they quietly preserve local storage and later downlink as a safeguard against congestion, denial, or awkward prioritisation. These are not symbolic gestures. They reveal whether the network is treated as a dependable transport layer or as an impressive but politically contingent enhancement.

A credible limitation needs to be stated plainly. Not every mission benefits equally from inter-satellite links, and not every constellation needs them. Some surveillance tasks tolerate delay well enough that local ground downlink remains entirely sufficient. Some systems are small, specialised, or operationally narrow enough that the cost and complexity of full crosslinking may not be justified. Direct ground access can also offer a kind of institutional clarity that distributed routing does not. One knows where the data came down, under whose control, and through which facilities. That simplicity can be valuable, especially where sovereignty or evidentiary provenance matters as much as raw speed.

But the limitation strengthens the central point rather than softening it. The real value of crosslinks is not universal superiority. It is selective liberation from geography. In the Arctic, where ground stations can be sparse, weather can thin capacity, and local access can become politically or logistically constrained, that liberation is strategically significant. It allows a system to move information to where downlink is easier, where processing is available, where queues are shorter, or where a trusted user is already waiting. The north remains physically remote. The data becomes less so.

This also means that inter-satellite links turn constellations themselves into infrastructure whose contestability matters. A ground station can be mapped, visited, hardened, negotiated over, or denied. A mesh in orbit is more diffuse, but not less strategic. It can be congested, disrupted, governed asymmetrically, or made selectively opaque through service rules. A state may own the sensor and still depend on a transport network governed by a private actor or a coalition whose priorities shift under strain. That is not a distant possibility. It is an ordinary consequence of dual-use architectures where communications and surveillance now share the same orbital fabric.

The network's greatest promise, therefore, carries its own political burden. A crosslinked constellation can make the Arctic feel closer because it reduces the tyranny of local downlink. Yet it can also make surveillance more dependent on systems whose internal decisions are harder for outside users to see. A product that arrives quickly has already passed through a series of choices: which path, which node, which priority, which compression, which handoff, which destination. The speed flatters the experience. It can conceal the governance.

The message finds a route again, but the route is never innocent. It reflects the values and constraints embedded in the network. This matters enormously when surveillance outputs are shared across civil and security domains. A maritime safety product, an environmental alert, and a defence-relevant contact may all travel through the same mesh. The technical possibility of shared infrastructure is obvious. The difficulty lies in deciding whether those missions are truly equal when time becomes scarce. A network that solves Arctic delivery physically may still reproduce scarcity institutionally.

The broader implication is that coverage should no longer be read only as a matter of sensor footprints and pass schedules. In a crosslinked age, coverage also means path availability through the network. A target observed over the Arctic is not truly within a system's coverage in the operational sense unless the resulting data can move through the mesh to a user who can act on it. That user may be nowhere near the north. The downlink may happen thousands of miles away. The surveillance claim nonetheless depends on that path. Coverage has become topological as much as geographical.

This should change how readers interpret both commercial claims and state planning. When a provider promises low-latency polar service, the serious questions are no longer limited to orbit, sensor, and local ground access. They include network architecture, routing authority, service priority, and fallback behaviour when the mesh is stressed. When a government speaks of persistent Arctic awareness enabled by commercial or shared constellations, the relevant inquiry is not only whether the satellites can see the region, but whether the data has a protected, trustworthy route out of it. The answer may be impressive. It may also be conditional in ways the headline obscures.

The harder test lies ahead. As more constellations become networked and more surveillance products travel through meshes built partly for civil or commercial use, the distinction between connectivity infrastructure and intelligence infrastructure will continue to blur. That blur can be productive. It can also be dangerous. A route that serves everyone in peacetime may reveal sharp priorities in crisis. The Arctic will expose those priorities quickly because it rewards the systems that move data fastest out of distance and punishes those that mistake a visible mesh for a settled politics. The real question is no longer whether a satellite can reach the north. It is who controls the route home once the message starts to travel.

Ground terminals, antennas, and siting constraints

In January 2022, damage to a subsea cable serving Svalbard again drew attention to a fact that satellite rhetoric often prefers to hide: a place can be ideally positioned for polar orbit access and still depend on a small number of stubbornly terrestrial links. Svalbard matters to global space operations because satellites in polar and near-polar orbits pass within excellent reach of its ground stations. But orbital opportunity does not land on bare rock and become service by itself. It must be received, tracked, powered, enclosed, protected, and moved onwards. When one cable, one power problem, or one severe weather episode can thin the usefulness of a celebrated site, the lesson becomes difficult to ignore. The signal descends to hardware.

A dish is not scenery. That is the quiet correction Arctic surveillance keeps forcing on every grander account of constellations and downlink. The ground terminal, the antenna, the radome, the heater, the backup generator, the shelter, the backhaul route, the people who maintain them - these are often treated as logistical afterthoughts. In practice they decide how much of a space system's advertised capacity is actually usable under northern conditions. A satellite may pass overhead with perfect timing. If the terminal cannot hold the link, if the antenna cannot track cleanly, if the enclosure ices, if the power margins thin, or if the site itself cannot be sustained through the season, then orbital elegance ends in earthly insufficiency.

This matters because communications systems do not terminate at abstraction. Show an Arctic surveillance architecture on a slide and one sees satellites, arrows, ground nodes, perhaps a neat mesh of relay and backhaul. Name the real problem properly and the diagram becomes more physical than the slide admits. A ground terminal must be placed where it has usable sky, survivable access, and enough support infrastructure to function through the conditions that matter most. Explain why this becomes strategic, and the implication is plain. The capacity of a surveillance network often depends less on the nominal brilliance of the spacecraft than on whether the receiving hardware on the ground can exploit the fleeting opportunities the orbit presents.

Antenna tracking is the first place this becomes visible. Low Earth orbit satellites do not wait politely in one spot. They move quickly across the sky, and the higher the demand for throughput, the more the receiving system often depends on precise pointing, stable tracking, and clear geometry. In the Arctic, that requirement encounters awkward realities. Wind loading matters. Ice accretion matters. Snow accumulation matters. Mechanical wear matters more when maintenance windows are narrow. Terrain and structures can steal precious seconds from an already brief pass. A fixed solution that works comfortably at lower latitudes may prove less forgiving under northern weather and line-of-sight conditions. Tracking is not merely a technical accomplishment. It is the ability to keep the satellite inside the terminal's practical grasp long enough to turn opportunity into delivered data.

Power follows immediately behind it. A major station can mask this truth because its capabilities look smooth from the outside. Yet no antenna receives on rhetoric alone. Arctic sites often demand heating, enclosure protection, de-icing, redundant electricity, and stable environmental control for electronics that do not appreciate thermal extremes. A terminal that loses heat may not fail all at once, but it can drift into a state where performance degrades before anyone is ready to declare an outage. A surveillance architecture that assumes continuous power at remote northern sites without treating power as part of the mission is making an error of category. In the High North, energy is not support. It is throughput in another form.

The Svalbard Satellite Station offers the clearest public example because it combines almost every point at once. Operated by KSAT near Longyearbyen, it became one of the most important ground sites for polar-orbiting spacecraft precisely because it sits where orbital opportunity is abundant. But what makes it valuable is not latitude alone. It is also the concentration of antennas, tracking infrastructure, power resilience, radome protection, operational staffing, and onward communications needed to exploit that latitude. Svalbard is a lesson in how ground hardware can turn geography into usable capacity. It is also a warning that the capacity remains only as durable as the infrastructure and logistics sustaining it.

A second example sits at the other end of the scale: the deployable or expeditionary terminal used in remote operations, scientific campaigns, military exercises, or austere Arctic locations. Such systems are often essential. They allow a user to bring some degree of satellite access to places where no major fixed station exists and where waiting for distant infrastructure would make the mission pointless. Yet their limitations are equally instructive. A deployable terminal typically operates under tighter power, smaller apertures, less forgiving tracking, lighter enclosures, and narrower throughput expectations than a major station. It may provide priceless flexibility while accepting thinner margins. This contrast matters because people often speak of "ground access" as though a large fixed station and a portable terminal belonged to the same category of capability. They do not.

The difference shows up not in abstract engineering pride but in operational behaviour. A major station can often support higher-volume downlink, cleaner tracking across a pass, stronger integration with backhaul, and more confident scheduling under difficult conditions. A deployable terminal may force choices earlier: compressed products instead of full data, fewer simultaneous tasks, tighter weather tolerances, more cautious assumptions about which passes will be worth attempting. Neither station type is inherently superior in every sense. One offers concentration of capacity. The other offers presence where concentration does not exist. But the trade-off must be named honestly because it shapes what users think they can rely on.

This is where siting becomes more than a matter of map placement. A good site is not simply one with clear sky and useful latitude. It must also be buildable, maintainable, defensible, and connectable. Access by road, air, or sea matters because broken components and human technicians still have to reach the hardware. Terrain matters because it shapes both line-of-sight and survivability. Power availability matters because adding generation and storage changes the site's complexity and cost. Backhaul matters because a terminal that receives brilliantly and cannot move its data onward remains a bottleneck disguised as a node. In the Arctic, site selection is therefore a systems judgement masquerading as a local one.

The sovereignty implications flow directly from this materiality. A state that depends on another state's territory, a commercial host, or a shared network for high-value ground access is depending not only on friendly words but on physical installations whose control may become consequential in crisis. A station can be open in peacetime and politically awkward in tension. A commercial site can be technically excellent and still governed by priorities not fully visible to all users. Even the simple question of who can enter, service, inspect, or modify a terminal becomes sharper once the ground hardware in question sits on strategic territory or serves mixed civil and security functions. Sovereignty in Arctic surveillance is not only a matter of satellites overhead. It is also a matter of who owns the dish, the fence, the generator, the fibre route, and the key to the enclosure.

A credible limitation must be admitted. Ground hardware is not frozen in an older age of gigantic dishes and brittle mechanical systems. Modern terminals are improving. Electronic steering, smaller form factors, better automation, remote diagnostics, and modular designs are changing what can be done from austere sites. Some systems now track faster and with less visible mechanical drama than their predecessors. These advances are real, and they matter, especially in a region where every reduction in maintenance burden or deployment complexity can widen options. It would be careless to write as though Arctic ground systems remained trapped in an age of heroic logistics and static antenna fields.

But the concession only sharpens the underlying argument. Miniaturisation and automation alter the balance; they do not repeal it. A smaller terminal still needs power. A smarter enclosure still needs to survive snow, wind, and cold. Remote diagnostics still depend on a path back to somewhere that can interpret them. Electronically steered systems may reduce some mechanical vulnerabilities while introducing new dependencies on stable power, software maintenance, and thermal management. The north keeps turning innovation back into logistics because logistics is the form in which persistence becomes real on the ground.

This also explains why ground hardware is so often the quiet determinant of system capacity. Satellite systems attract attention because they are expensive, visible, and symbolically modern. Ground terminals and antenna farms appear mundane by comparison. Yet mundane infrastructure decides whether bandwidth is exploited or wasted, whether passes are fully used or partly squandered, whether remote users receive full products or alert extracts, whether a constellation's potential survives the season or frays at the edges of weather and maintenance. Capacity, in this context, is not just what the satellite can emit. It is what the ground can absorb.

The dish returns as a useful motif because it concentrates so much of the chapter's argument in one object. A dish must point accurately, survive weather, remain powered, stay connected, and be located where all those things can be true at once. It is humble-looking infrastructure carrying the burden of a much grander claim. When a state says it can monitor the Arctic, some part of that claim rests in the quiet competence of metal, motors, heaters, cables, software, and access routes that nobody photographs for publicity. The dish is not a peripheral object. It is where the constellation becomes tangible.

Risk therefore appears in visible choices rather than in generic language about resilience. Does an operator place a high-value terminal at a logistically difficult but geometrically excellent site, or accept a weaker view for easier sustainment? Does a government invest in a permanent station under national control, or rely on hosted access through a partner or commercial provider? Does a mission accept the bandwidth limits of deployable terminals in exchange for local autonomy, or build its workflows around a few powerful fixed sites whose outage would hurt more? These are the decisions through which Arctic surveillance turns from architecture into governance.

The deeper lesson is that communications bottlenecks are often grounded long before they are orbital. A constellation can be elegant, a relay layer sophisticated, a downlink band well chosen, and a routing scheme beautifully designed. But if the receiving hardware cannot exploit those advantages in the places and seasons that matter, the system's practical capacity shrinks to the level of its ground segment. Arctic conditions make that shrinkage easier to trigger and harder to repair. A terminal lost to power trouble or mechanical stress may not merely inconvenience one user. It may change the real meaning of coverage across a region.

That leaves a question worth carrying forward rather than tidying away. As Arctic surveillance grows more networked and more commercially entangled, major stations and deployable terminals will continue to coexist, each representing a different balance of reach, control, and vulnerability. One concentrates power and throughput. The other distributes presence while accepting stricter limits. The harder problem is not choosing one model in the abstract. It is deciding which compromises a state is willing to live with when the signal descends from orbit and the decisive issue is no longer whether the satellite passed overhead, but whose hardware on the ground was ready to catch it.

Prioritisation, compression, and tasking discipline

In March 2021, when Maxar and other commercial providers released imagery of the *Ever Given* wedged across the Suez Canal, the public saw a crisp lesson in modern satellite visibility: an event happened, satellites looked, and images appeared quickly enough to shape the story. What the public did not see was the queue behind the picture. Someone decided what to task, what to move first, what fidelity to preserve, and which products mattered enough to outrun the rest. Those decisions rarely become part of the image's public life. In the Arctic, they are often part of the event itself.

A system under strain never sends everything. That is the plain fact behind the smoother language of communications architecture. Satellites collect more than can always be transmitted at once. Ground stations have finite windows. Networks have finite throughput. Analysts and users have finite attention. Once scarcity enters the chain, choice enters with it. A product may be sent immediately in reduced form, held for fuller delivery later, or displaced entirely by something judged more urgent. The result is that latency stops being a neutral technical interval. It becomes, at least in part, a record of institutional priority.

This matters profoundly in the Arctic because scarcity is not exceptional there. It is routine. A pass may be brief. A link may be marginal. Weather may reduce available margin further. A major station may already be handling other traffic. A deployable terminal may only support a thinner stream. Under such conditions, a surveillance system cannot avoid choosing what to send, when, and at what fidelity. Show the problem honestly and one sees that the limiting factor is no longer just the sensor or the orbit. Name the governing process properly and it becomes prioritisation. Explain why it matters, and the implication is immediate: two users looking at the same constellation may inhabit very different timelines because one of them sits higher in the queue.

Compression belongs inside this same logic. It is often described as a technical convenience, a way to move more data through a narrow channel. In practice it is also a political instrument. To compress is to decide that a product may lose some detail in exchange for speed, storage relief, or greater distributability. Sometimes that bargain is entirely sensible. An alert product that arrives quickly at lower fidelity may be more useful than a pristine product that arrives after the contact has moved on. But the choice changes who gets what kind of truth. A coastguard may receive a fast, reduced image suitable for cueing. A central headquarters may wait for the richer version. An ally may receive only the summary. Compression, then, does not merely alter file size. It stratifies access to certainty.

The queue is the motif that best captures this part of Arctic surveillance because it keeps the analysis grounded in ordinary administrative fact. Every queue has rules, even when those rules are informal, inherited, or politely obscured. A tasking queue decides which targets are collected. A transmission queue decides which products leave first. A processing queue decides which datasets are turned into usable forms first. A dissemination queue decides who receives them and on what clock. The Arctic sharpens the consequence of those queues because the intervals are less forgiving. A delay that might be tolerable elsewhere may turn an actionable detection into a retrospective curiosity in the north.

A major claim follows from this. Surveillance latency is never only a matter of physics. Show a system with an excellent pass, a strong sensor, and a viable link, yet with several agencies requesting products from the same event window, and the outcome depends on governance as much as on hardware. Name the issue properly and one sees that latency is partly produced by prioritisation rules. Explain why, and the answer becomes institutional. If defence users hold highest precedence, their products may move first while civil maritime, environmental, or allied users wait. If commercial paying customers possess contractual priority, state actors may find their nominal access slowed by arrangements they do not control. The implication is strategic. Timeliness is distributed unevenly because power inside the system is distributed unevenly.

The war in Ukraine made this dynamic more visible to wider audiences, not because the Arctic was the theatre, but because commercial satellite imagery and analytics entered public and governmental workflows at unprecedented scale. Some products reached policymakers, media outlets, or open-source researchers rapidly enough to shape narratives. Others remained slower, narrower, or restricted. The general lesson is durable. Access to the same nominal collection environment does not mean equal access to time. In any shared surveillance architecture, prioritisation determines whose awareness arrives early enough to matter most. Arctic surveillance inherits this lesson with extra severity because sparse infrastructure and harsh conditions mean fewer alternative routes when the queue hardens.

A second example can be drawn from maritime monitoring around high latitudes, where authorities may need to distinguish among fisheries enforcement, search and rescue, environmental response, and defence-related watchfulness while drawing from overlapping data streams. A SAR scene showing several contacts near ice edge or sensitive waters may be rich enough to support several missions at once. Yet the system may not be able to move the full product set to every user immediately. One centre may receive a contact list or quicklook. Another may receive the fuller scene. A third may wait for later dissemination. The physics of the link remain the same. The meaning of the delay changes according to institutional order.

Tasking discipline is the often neglected partner to prioritisation because it acts earlier in the chain. If too many collections are requested without a disciplined theory of use, scarcity worsens downstream. Arctic systems cannot afford endless curiosity. They have to decide what kind of question a collection is meant to answer before the data burden compounds. A broad-area search product, a high-detail forensic image, a thermal cue, a repeat pass for pattern analysis - these are not equivalent requests. A disciplined system knows which one belongs to which decision and resists collecting merely because collection is technically possible. That restraint is not bureaucratic stinginess. It is how a system protects the timeliness of what genuinely matters.

This is why prioritisation should never be treated as an embarrassing sign of system weakness. Every serious surveillance architecture prioritises. The real question is whether it does so honestly, predictably, and in ways aligned with mission purpose. A good prioritisation regime makes visible distinctions between urgent cueing, evidentiary-quality delivery, routine monitoring, and archival completeness. A poor one allows urgency to be claimed by everyone and thus by no one, until hidden hierarchies decide the matter anyway. In the Arctic, where multiple agencies may each believe their need is exceptional, such confusion can be especially damaging. The queue lengthens; trust shortens.

A credible limitation must be admitted. Not every case of selective delivery is politically loaded. Often compression and prioritisation are simply sound operations. An ice service issuing navigational guidance may need broad-area situational products quickly and not care whether the imagery retains every possible detail. A scientific programme may accept slower, fuller delivery because the work depends on quality more than immediate tempo. A search-and-rescue situation may properly displace everything else. It would be careless to imply that every differential in latency reflects unfairness or hidden power. Sometimes it reflects mission logic and nothing more.

But the limitation reinforces the central argument. The fact that prioritisation is often sensible does not make it neutral. It means the politics lie in how sensible is defined, by whom, and under what pressure. A military user and a civilian environmental agency may both offer convincing reasons for urgency after an Arctic incident. Allied states may each assume privileged access when they have contributed different parts of the architecture. Commercial partners may argue that contract terms are not politics, while state users experience those terms precisely as politics when a product arrives late. Governance enters the queue whether or not the operators prefer to name it.

Compression deepens this because it changes not only timing but meaning. A compressed quick look can be enough to confirm that something happened. It may be insufficient to decide what, exactly, happened. A reduced radar product may support contact detection but not reliable interpretation of ice condition or vessel behaviour. A simplified optical scene may show presence while discarding context analysts later wish they had retained. This does not make compression suspect in itself. It means compressed delivery should be understood as a deliberate choice about what kind of judgement the system wants to support first. The first truth delivered is not always the fullest one.

This becomes especially consequential in dual-use systems where the same network may support civil safety, commercial operations, scientific work, law enforcement, and security monitoring. A "space internet" or relay-enabled mesh may appear to solve the downlink problem by expanding what can be moved where. In practice it often relocates the bottleneck into rules of routing and service class. Who gets low-latency routing? Who receives full fidelity? Who can request a retask that displaces somebody else's planned collection? The technical architecture widens possibility. Governance decides how much of that possibility any particular user may inhabit.

Trust shows itself here in ways that are easy to miss and hard to fake. An agency trusts the system when it stops building private workarounds for essential products. An allied partner distrusts it when it insists on sovereign collection channels or duplicate subscriptions rather than accepting shared queue rules. A commercial operator reveals its own hierarchy when premium customers quietly receive richer, faster products than nominally equal users. A state reveals its hierarchy when some departments act on near-live data while others receive end-of-day awareness briefings from the same underlying constellation. These behaviours are the social signature of prioritisation.

A useful counter-example lies in small, tightly bounded mission systems with a single dominant user and a clear operational clock. In such cases, prioritisation may become relatively simple because the hierarchy is known in advance. A dedicated environmental mission, a narrowly focused scientific campaign, or a sovereign military architecture with limited user diversity may avoid many of the frictions described here. The queue still exists, but its rules are clearer and its conflicts fewer. That matters because it reminds us that governance problems are not metaphysical. They intensify with complexity, plurality of users, and contested notions of urgency.

Yet Arctic surveillance increasingly lives precisely in those conditions. Shared constellations, hosted payloads, commercial analytics, allied access, dual-use relay systems, and mixed civil-security demand all push northern observation towards crowded governance. The old fantasy that latency is merely a by-product of orbital mechanics becomes impossible to sustain under such conditions. Delay may reflect weather, geometry, or link margin. It may also reflect whose request was accepted first, whose product was compressed, whose transmission path was privileged, and whose need counted as urgent when the queue tightened.

The queue returns once more because it is where the chapter's argument becomes hardest to evade. A queue is not just a line. It is a constitution in miniature. It reveals what the system values when not everyone can be served at once. Arctic surveillance systems, perhaps more than systems in gentler theatres, constantly confront that test. They must decide whether to send the broad search product or the fine-detail one, the civil alert or the defence update, the ally's request or the home agency's, the compressed preview or the fuller file that arrives later. Each decision produces a different map of timeliness.

That is why readers should treat latency as partly a governance outcome. The same physical architecture can deliver very different realities depending on who controls tasking, how scarcity is managed, and what kinds of fidelity are reserved for whom. A system may be technically superb and institutionally inequitable. It may also be technically constrained and institutionally disciplined enough to provide fairer or more transparent service. These distinctions matter because Arctic security, safety, and environmental response increasingly depend on infrastructures shared across missions that do not share the same politics.

The harder question, then, is not whether prioritisation exists. It always does. The harder question is whether the rules governing it are aligned with the decisions a state or alliance claims to care about, and whether those rules remain acceptable once several users need the same pass, the same downlink, and the same minute. When the queue hardens in the north, who receives the first version of reality - and who is told to wait for a better one after the moment has already passed?

Chapter 6

Positioning, Navigation, and Timing at High Latitudes

How can a system know where it is and still lose confidence exactly when the Arctic begins to matter most? That is the paradox at the heart of high-latitude positioning, navigation, and timing. Most users experience these services as quiet certainty. The coordinates appear, the clock aligns, the route holds, the network synchronises. Nothing seems dramatic because the achievement has been folded into routine. But the High North has a way of loosening that routine. Not by making everything fail at once, but by making the margins thinner, the geometry less forgiving, and the consequences of small errors more visible.

The difficulty is easy to underestimate because positioning is often discussed as though it were a simple gift from orbit. Signals arrive, receivers compute, and a location appears. The Arctic does not allow that simplification to survive for long. Satellite geometry changes with latitude. Ground support for improved accuracy becomes patchier and more conditional. Radio environments and timing dependencies press into one another. A system that looks stable in a southern operations room can feel markedly less certain when used on a northern air route, an ice edge, a remote coast, or a surveillance chain that depends on precise correlation across multiple sources. The signal says where. The system still has to decide how much to believe it.

That is the chapter's central tension. Positioning and timing in the Arctic rarely collapse into outright absence; more often they drift into ambiguity. The drift may be subtle in technical terms and still decisive in operational ones. A geolocation error small enough to sound negligible in a briefing may complicate image correlation, route confidence, or sensor fusion when the surrounding environment offers few cheap ways to cross-check. A timing disturbance may not stop communications or navigation outright and still unsettle the sequence by which data, tracks, and decisions are made to cohere. The High North turns slight degradations into larger questions because distance, weather, sparse infrastructure, and limited alternatives reduce the room for graceful recovery.

The stakes run well beyond navigation in the narrow sense. Ships, aircraft, remote infrastructure, scientific operations, emergency response, and surveillance architectures all rely on precise or at least trustworthy notions of position and time. Trust, here, takes visible form. It appears when a crew keeps to a route without seeking extra confirmation, when analysts align one sensor feed with another without pausing to question the clock behind them, when a command centre accepts that a contact plotted from one system truly corresponds to the object seen by another. Once that trust thins, behaviour changes. Routes are reconsidered. Corroboration is demanded. Timelines stretch. What looked like a minor technical degradation becomes operational caution.

The Arctic sharpens those consequences because it exposes the hidden dependencies under positioning services. Augmentation and correction improve performance, but they depend on communications, backhaul, and ground presence that can be thin or uneven in the far north. Timing feels invisible until it begins to wobble, and then several systems start to disagree at once. A receiver may still produce a position while the larger architecture around it grows less certain about synchronisation, integrity, or the confidence with which one event can be matched to another. This is why high-latitude PNT belongs inside the same system argument that has shaped the book so far. It is not merely a service from space. It is another chain.

The danger of overlooking that chain lies partly in habit. PNT is so deeply embedded in modern operations that many organisations treat it as background infrastructure rather than as a strategic condition. The Arctic resists that habit by making dependence visible. A remote site without reliable local correction, a northern route with variable signal quality, a surveillance process requiring precise timestamps to fuse data from different platforms - these are not edge cases. They are ordinary expressions of how the region turns quiet dependencies into active constraints. The question stops being whether position is available at all and becomes whether the available position, and the time beneath it, can still support the judgement being asked of it.

The path ahead begins with geometry, because geometry decides more than most users notice until the pole draws the constellation into a different relation with the receiver. It then moves through the uneven world of augmentation and local correction, where improved accuracy rests on terrestrial support that may be weaker or more exposed than the orbital story suggests. From there the argument drops into timing, the hidden substrate of communications, sensor alignment, and network order, before turning towards the broader question that follows whenever confidence erodes: what remains usable when precise PNT no longer behaves as a single dependable pillar?

A quiet motif runs through all of this: the clock. Not only the literal clock that keeps networks and systems aligned, but the wider sense of order it stands for. A route, a fix, a timestamp, a synchronised network, a fused surveillance picture - each depends on clocks that agree closely enough for the rest of the architecture to trust itself. The Arctic does not always break the clock. Often it merely makes the ticking less certain, and that is enough to change how people move, compare, and decide.

The harder question, then, is not whether satellites can provide position and time to the High North. They plainly can. It is whether the geometry, support infrastructure, and hidden timing dependencies behind that service remain reliable enough that operators can distinguish a small inconvenience from the beginning of broader uncertainty. When the fix still appears but confidence begins to thin, what exactly has been lost - and how much of the surveillance chain was depending on more than anyone had fully admitted?

GNSS geometry near the pole

In October 2018, during NATO's Trident Juncture exercise in northern Norway, reports of disrupted GPS reception in Finnmark drew obvious attention to jamming and interference. Yet the episode also illuminated a quieter and more durable Arctic problem. Even when no one is actively interfering, position and timing in the High North do not behave quite as they do farther south. The change is rarely theatrical. More often it arrives as a thinning of confidence: the fix still appears, the route still plots, the clock still ticks, and yet the geometry behind that apparent normality has become less forgiving.

This matters because global navigation satellite systems are usually encountered as finished certainty. A receiver produces a location. A track is drawn. A sensor product is stamped with coordinates and time. The user is spared the architecture underneath. In the Arctic, that hidden architecture begins to show through. Satellites are not merely present or absent; they stand in a particular spatial relationship to the receiver, and that relationship changes the quality of the solution. Geometry is the arrangement of those satellites in the sky at the moment the receiver tries to determine where it is. Near the pole, that arrangement can become subtly awkward in ways that do not always break service, but can still change how much trust a system deserves.

The simplest way to see the problem is to stop imagining positioning as a gift from a single satellite overhead and begin imagining it as an act of triangulation carried out with moving reference points. Show a receiver several satellites clustered in similar parts of the sky, and the solution becomes less stable than when those satellites are more usefully spread. Name the concept properly and one has geometry, not signal strength alone, as the relevant condition. Explain why it matters, and the reason is plain enough even without equations: a good position fix depends not merely on hearing enough satellites, but on hearing them from angles that help the receiver separate one dimension of uncertainty from another. The implication in the Arctic is not necessarily dramatic loss. It is that the same nominal service can yield subtly different practical confidence at different latitudes.

A wide sky is better. That short sentence is the non-technical intuition worth keeping. A receiver benefits when the satellites contributing to its solution are well distributed rather than bunched into a narrow part of the visible sky. At extreme high latitudes, the geometry behind that distribution can become less generous than users assume, especially for some constellations, some moments, and some operational settings. The receiver may still compute a perfectly usable position for ordinary purposes. But where operations depend on tighter confidence - aircraft navigation, ship movement near hazards, precise geolocation of sensor products, synchronisation of multiple data feeds - the small deterioration can become operationally meaningful.

This is one reason the Arctic does not need positioning failure to create positioning risk. The fix may remain available while continuity becomes less graceful and confidence intervals less comforting. A ship operating in open water with generous sea room may barely notice. The same system used near ice edge, in constrained waters, at a remote airfield, or as the geolocation basis for comparing several surveillance inputs may suddenly expose the consequences of geometry. Risk, here, should not be left abstract. It appears when a crew slows and cross-checks more often, when an operator refuses to trust a single solution near a hazard, when analysts hesitate before fusing two tracks because the positional agreement no longer feels strong enough to be automatic.

The high northward routes of civil aviation illustrate the point well. Aircraft operating through polar and near-polar airspace rely heavily on satellite navigation and timing, but they do so inside a procedural culture designed around the fact that service quality and continuity can vary. The practical consequence is not that every polar flight is imperilled by geometry. It is that geometry joins with ionospheric conditions, equipment performance, and operational margin to shape how navigation is monitored and trusted. A position that is perfectly acceptable for one phase of flight or one part of the route may invite stricter caution in another. The lesson travels beyond aviation. Arctic performance is often not bad in a dramatic sense. It is contingent in a way that professional users must continuously manage.

A second example comes from the geolocation of remote-sensing products themselves. A surveillance image, radar contact, or thermal anomaly over the Arctic is not operationally useful merely because it exists. It must be placed on the Earth accurately enough to compare with charts, infrastructure, previous passes, vessel transmissions, or other sensor feeds. Here geometry matters twice over: once for the platform or receiver establishing position and again for the user trying to fuse the resulting product with other data. A small positional uncertainty that sounds negligible in a briefing can become frustratingly real when two sources ought to line up and do not. The analyst then faces a familiar Arctic problem. Is the discrepancy meaningful, or is it the quiet tax of geometry?

This is why satellite geometry near the pole should be understood as a problem of arrangement, not simply of access. It is tempting to think that high latitudes are well served because many satellite tracks appear to crowd together there. That visual intuition is not useless, but it is incomplete. Track density does not automatically produce ideal navigation geometry at the receiver. A system can be very present in one sense and still present in a less helpful pattern at the moment a precise solution is required. The distinction resembles earlier Arctic lessons about coverage and viewing angles: frequency and usefulness are related, but not identical. Presence in the sky is not the same as a well-posed fix on the ground.

The temptation to overstate difficulty should be resisted. Modern multi-constellation receivers have changed the landscape substantially by drawing on more than one global navigation system where equipment and permissions allow. This often improves the practical geometry available to the user and makes Arctic solutions more resilient than older, single-system assumptions would suggest. That is a real gain, and any serious account should say so clearly. It would be wrong to imply that GNSS becomes broadly unusable near the pole. It does not. For many routine tasks, it remains highly effective.

And yet the improvement does not abolish the underlying logic. Better geometry from combined constellations still depends on what is actually visible, usable, and trustworthy in the environment at that moment. Antenna masking, vessel superstructures, terrain, signal quality, operational filtering, and receiver design all shape which satellites are contributing to the solution. More satellites available in principle does not mean everyone improves the outcome equally in practice. A system can therefore look stronger on paper than it feels to the operator at the edge of what the mission can tolerate. The Arctic excels at exposing precisely that gap between nominal sufficiency and lived confidence.

What matters most is not to turn geometry into mystique. The reader does not need equations to reason about it well. A useful mental model is simply to ask how many independent-looking lines of reference the receiver truly has, and from how varied a spread of sky. If the answer feels narrow, low, clustered, or unstable, confidence should become more conditional, even if the device still reports a neat fix. That mindset is particularly important in surveillance work because timing and geolocation often travel together. A contact seen by one system and timed by another is only as convincing as the geometry supporting both when the evidence is fused.

This is where safety and surveillance start to touch. In maritime or aviation navigation, geometry-driven uncertainty affects route confidence and operational margin. In surveillance, it affects whether one can say that an observed object was here rather than there, whether two tracks truly correspond, or whether a reported anomaly falls inside the boundary that makes it politically or legally significant. The signal may never visibly fail. The consequences may still ripple. A government does not need a dramatic positioning collapse to face trouble. It needs only enough uncertainty that attribution, warning, or response becomes harder to justify with the speed the moment demands.

A credible limitation belongs here as well. Geometry is not the only or even always the dominant source of Arctic positioning difficulty. Interference, ionospheric disturbance, receiver quality, augmentation coverage, and local operating environment may matter more in a specific case. Sometimes geometry is merely one strand in a larger tangle. This matters because it guards against the false confidence of monocausal explanation. Not every bad fix in the Arctic is a geometry story.

But that concession reinforces the main point rather than weakening it. Geometry matters precisely because it interacts with those other sources of strain. A receiver enjoying excellent spatial distribution of satellites may better absorb some disturbance than one already working with an awkward sky. A user trying to judge whether an anomaly reflects interference, atmospheric effects, or equipment trouble needs some baseline sense of how geometry should have been helping or failing in the first place. Geometry is rarely the whole story. It is often the quiet condition that makes the rest of the story harder or easier to live with.

The watchword here is continuity. Arctic users often need not only an accurate fix once, but a solution that remains stable enough across time to support route management, sensor correlation, and disciplined decision-making. A fix that wanders subtly or loses grace at intervals may be tolerable for broad transit and awkward for precise operations. Continuity, then, is not merely a feature of signal availability. It is the steadiness with which geometry keeps offering a usable arrangement of reference points as the platform moves and the sky shifts. Near the pole, that steadiness can become more conditional, and the condition matters most to those tasks least able to absorb doubt.

The quiet motif of the wide sky returns here because it captures the operational lesson without technical clutter. A wide sky gives the receiver options and spreads the burden of uncertainty. A narrower, more awkward sky may still yield a valid answer, but one that deserves more caution. The Arctic often gives users enough service to feel comfortable and just little enough margin to make that comfort hazardous when conditions deteriorate or demands tighten. That is why geometry-driven risk is easy to miss. It rarely announces itself as catastrophe. It reveals itself as the point at which ordinary confidence begins to need help.

This becomes especially important once the position fix feeds something else. A timing signal supports network order. A coordinate supports a radar track, an image footprint, a ship route, or a fused operational picture. When the geometry underneath the original fix is slightly less generous, the downstream products inherit that subtlety whether their users notice or not. Arctic systems therefore deserve to be judged not by whether they can obtain a position at all, but by what kind of action that position can honestly support under stress.

The harder question, then, is not whether GNSS works near the pole. It does, often impressively. The more serious question is how much uncertainty a particular Arctic mission can absorb before a merely adequate geometric solution becomes operationally unsafe or analytically weak. When a receiver still reports a position but the sky above it has narrowed into a less helpful arrangement, who notices first: the machine, the operator, or the event that reveals the margin was smaller than anyone wanted to admit?

Augmentation systems and local corrections

In August 2000, the United States declared WAAS, the Wide Area Augmentation System, fully operational after years of work to improve the reliability of satellite navigation for demanding civil use. The story is often told as one of technical refinement: better accuracy, better integrity, better confidence. That is all true. Yet the more revealing lesson lies elsewhere. Positioning was never improved by satellites alone. It was improved by an architecture in which the sky depended on the ground, and the ground depended on communications, siting, maintenance, and institutional discipline. The Arctic makes that dependency impossible to ignore.

A better fix needs a scaffold. That is the quiet truth behind augmentation. Ordinary satellite navigation gives a receiver a solution. Augmentation tries to make that solution more accurate, more reliable, and, crucially, more trustworthy about its own limits. It does so by adding information from outside the receiver's simple view of the sky: corrections derived from monitored conditions, integrity messages warning of problems, and local or regional signals that help the user separate a good fix from a merely plausible one. In the Arctic, where geometry, atmosphere, and sparse infrastructure already push against confidence, augmentation can be the difference between using satellite navigation comfortably and using it with a hand always hovering near contingency.

This matters because augmentation is often misunderstood as a polite upgrade layered atop an otherwise self-sufficient service. In reality it reveals that positioning has always been a chain. Show a vessel, aircraft, survey system, or surveillance workflow depending on higher confidence than standard GNSS alone can comfortably provide, and the appeal of correction becomes obvious. Name the concept properly and one sees not just "better accuracy" but a supporting network of reference stations, data links, control systems, and distribution paths. Explain why that matters, and the implication is larger than navigation alone. Positioning, like imagery and communications, becomes usable at its highest value only when the space segment and the ground segment continue to hold together under real conditions.

This is especially important in the far north because augmentation does not spread itself evenly across the map. Regional systems depend on where monitoring stations can be placed, where backhaul exists, how correction messages are transmitted, and whether the intended users can receive them with adequate continuity. A correction service that feels seamless near dense infrastructure can thin rapidly in remote northern areas, not always because the concept fails, but because the supporting chain begins to fray. The result is often subtle. The receiver may still produce a perfectly serviceable position. What changes is the degree of confidence with which operators can assume the fix is both accurate and honest about its own uncertainty.

Integrity is the word that deserves particular care here. Accuracy tells a user how close the position may be to reality. Integrity tells the user how much faith to place in the system's own warning behaviour when something is wrong. That distinction matters enormously in the Arctic because uncertainty is expensive. A pilot, ship master, or remote operator does not merely want a position; they want to know whether the system is still fit to trust under current conditions. In surveillance, the same principle takes another form. Analysts geolocating a sensor product or correlating one data stream with another need to know not simply that coordinates are available, but that the coordinates retain enough integrity to support the judgement being asked of them.

A reference station on the ground is therefore not a minor convenience. It is one of the places where confidence is manufactured. Ground monitoring sites measure local GNSS conditions, compare observed signals with known reference positions, and contribute to the corrections or warnings delivered onward to users. This sounds narrow until one follows the chain outward. The reference station must be sited well. It must be powered reliably. Its data must move through communications links that remain stable enough to keep corrections current. The resulting messages must then reach users through another distribution path. The space-ground chain reappears in full. Augmentation improves position only by adding dependencies elsewhere.

The European Geostationary Navigation Overlay Service, EGNOS, offers a useful public example because it shows both the power and the boundary of augmentation in a way readers can readily grasp. EGNOS improves GPS-based services across much of Europe through a network of ground stations and geostationary broadcast. It has delivered real benefits where coverage and geometry support the service model. Yet its utility in the far north has never been a matter of wishful map colouring alone. High latitudes raise the familiar questions: can the broadcast be received with enough quality, do the ground components cover the region adequately, and does the infrastructure behind the service remain strong where remoteness begins to bite? The lesson is not that EGNOS is weak. It is that augmentation reveals its own geography.

A second example can be found in local differential or real-time kinematic correction services used for precise operations in northern environments, from surveying and construction to infrastructure monitoring and some scientific work. These systems can provide excellent local performance when the reference site is well placed and the communications path between correction source and user remains healthy. But that "when" is doing serious work. A correction stream may depend on backhaul over fibre, radio, or satellite. It may be limited by terrain, weather, local power, or the difficulty of maintaining the reference site itself. Here one sees the Arctic's distinctive severity. The correction may exist in theory, the receiver may be ready to use it, and yet the practical service may still degrade because the terrestrial support behind it is thinner than the user assumed.

A correction that arrives late is a different kind of correction. That sentence matters because augmentation lives on timeliness as much as on content. If the communication path carrying local corrections degrades, the user may still receive something, but not something with the same operational worth. In a dense southern environment, that delay might be a nuisance. In the Arctic it can become a shift in safety margin, in route confidence, or in the reliability of geospatial products derived from the position solution. This is why backhaul is never just a telecoms detail. It is part of positioning itself. A correction system whose reference sites are well chosen but whose onward communications are brittle is not truly a finished navigation service.

Siting sharpens the same point. A local correction system is only as good as the physical logic of where its reference infrastructure sits. In the Arctic, a site may look ideal on paper because it serves a strategic coast, an air route, a mining district, or a research hub. Yet the same site may be hard to sustain through weather, access limits, and power constraints. An augmentation architecture may therefore find itself pulled between geometry and logistics. Put the station where it best serves the user, or where it can actually be maintained? The decision is rarely clean. And because augmentation is so often discussed in terms of elegant improvement, the uglier siting trade-offs that decide whether it persists tend to disappear from the story.

This is one reason augmentation belongs inside sovereignty debates even when it sounds too technical for them. A state may depend on foreign or commercially hosted correction infrastructure for high-confidence positioning in northern territory. That dependence can be perfectly practical and entirely sensible in peacetime. It can also become politically or operationally uncomfortable when access, priority, maintenance, or data-sharing rules shift. A correction service feels invisible when it works. It becomes strategic when it does not, or when users realise that the confidence of their navigation and geolocation rests partly on infrastructure they do not fully control. The Arctic amplifies this discomfort because alternatives are often sparse and the costs of losing precision are harder to absorb.

A credible limitation should be admitted. Not every Arctic operation requires augmentation, and many routine tasks remain well served by ordinary multi-constellation GNSS without elaborate correction layers. For broad transit, general situational awareness, and some forms of monitoring, the additional complexity of high-precision or high-integrity augmentation may be unnecessary. It would be careless to imply that all northern navigation collapses without it. Much does not. The ordinary service can remain useful across large parts of the Arctic for many everyday needs.

But the concession reinforces the deeper point. Augmentation matters most precisely because the tasks that rely on it are often the ones least able to absorb uncertainty cheaply. Precision approach operations, infrastructure surveying, geolocation of sensitive data products, tightly bounded routes, and the alignment of multiple sensor streams all reveal how quickly a merely adequate position becomes inadequate once the decision depends on confidence rather than rough usefulness. The Arctic multiplies that pressure because its operating margins are often narrower and its opportunities for quick verification fewer. The user may not need augmentation all day. They may need it desperately at the moment that counts.

This is also why augmentation should not be romanticised as a universal cure. It solves one set of uncertainties by building a second system around the first. That second system can fail in ways the original satellite service alone did not. Communications drop. Reference stations go offline. Backhaul becomes intermittent. Coverage becomes patchy at the edge. Users move beyond the area where corrections remain trustworthy. A mature Arctic architecture therefore treats augmentation not as magic but as disciplined scaffolding. It knows what the service can improve, what dependencies it introduces, and what operational posture remains when the improved layer thins away.

Trust shows itself clearly here. A pilot or maritime operator trusts augmentation when they are willing to tighten procedures around the improved service rather than maintaining all margins as though nothing had changed. A surveyor trusts it when work is planned around correction availability rather than around later rework. An analyst trusts it when coordinates derived from a corrected solution are treated as firm enough to support fusion or attribution tasks. Institutions distrust it when they quietly preserve manual checks, duplicate references, or fallback workflows because the correction path is too uneven to carry the weight placed upon it. Those behaviours reveal whether augmentation has become infrastructure or remains an occasional convenience.

The scaffold returns as the guiding motif because it captures both augmentation's value and its vulnerability. A scaffold allows work at levels that would otherwise be too uncertain or too dangerous. It extends reach. It does not become the building itself. And it must stand on the ground. In the Arctic, that grounding is literal: stations, cables, radios, shelters, technicians, power, snow clearance, permissions, backhaul. The improved position that appears on a receiver or inside a data product is therefore the visible end of a much larger and more fragile construction.

The harder question, then, is not whether augmentation can improve northern positioning. It plainly can, sometimes dramatically. The more serious question is what sort of chain is carrying that improvement, and how far north that chain remains intact before geography, logistics, and governance begin to thin it. When a corrected fix is treated as stronger than the base GNSS solution, who is checking whether the corrections themselves still rest on infrastructure robust enough to deserve that extra trust?

Timing as a hidden dependency

On 25 January 2016, a software update in parts of GPS-dependent infrastructure contributed to timing anomalies that disrupted networks and systems well beyond the narrow world of navigation receivers. The episode did not unfold in the Arctic, but it exposed a truth that becomes especially sharp there: many systems depend on precise time long before anyone notices that they do. A clock slip can travel farther than a map error. It can leave no dramatic visual trace and still alter how networks, sensors, and decisions fit together.

Time is the invisible alignment. That is why it deserves harder attention than it usually gets. Positioning attracts notice because it yields something people can see on a display: a coordinate, a route, a moving icon. Timing is quieter. It sits underneath communications synchronisation, timestamping, signal processing, sensor fusion, and the ordering of events inside distributed systems. When it works, it disappears into routine. When it degrades, the failure rarely announces itself as "a timing problem". It appears instead as dropped links, inconsistent tracks, disagreeing datasets, awkward handoffs, or a dawning suspicion that the system no longer knows what happened first.

In the Arctic, this hidden dependency becomes strategically important because the region already stretches the margins of communication, navigation, and verification. Show a surveillance chain trying to combine satellite imagery, maritime tracks, radio reports, and remote sensing from other platforms, and the need for shared temporal discipline is immediate. Name the concept properly and one sees that timing is not merely a support service for clocks on walls. It is the common reference that lets one piece of information be compared meaningfully with another. Explain why that matters, and the implication grows larger than engineering. Once timing confidence thins, situational awareness begins to fray even if every sensor continues collecting something.

This is easiest to understand through communication networks. Digital links often depend on timing to align transmissions, manage handoffs, preserve order, and distinguish signal from noise. A network whose components agree closely on time behaves smoothly enough that users rarely notice the effort behind that agreement. A network whose timing begins to drift may still function, but with more retransmissions, more cautious margins, more unexplained delay, and less confidence in sequence. In Arctic environments, where links are already exposed to awkward geometry, variable propagation, and infrastructure scarcity, that extra strain matters quickly. The network may not fail outright. It may simply stop behaving like a system that can be trusted under pressure.

Sensor fusion reveals the same dependency in a more analytic form. A radar detection, an optical image, an AIS transmission, an aircraft report, and a thermal anomaly are not simply piled together to make awareness. They are aligned in time as well as space. If the timestamps underlying those inputs no longer share enough common discipline, the fused picture becomes less convincing. A contact that appears to correspond across systems may in fact be a near miss in time rather than a match. A vessel may seem to have altered behaviour when what changed was the system's ability to line up observations properly. In the Arctic, where corroboration is already expensive and sparse, such slips have outsized consequences. Analysts can lose confidence not because the data vanished, but because the chronology ceased to cohere.

A network needs a pulse. That quiet motif captures timing better than more ornate language. A pulse tells separate parts of a system when to act, when to listen, when to compare, and when to trust that another component is referring to the same moment. The Arctic does not need to stop the pulse entirely to create operational trouble. It only needs to introduce enough wobble that synchronisation, fusion, or sequencing becomes more effortful and less automatic. In high-latitude operations, where communication paths may already be thin and where decisions can hinge on whether an event happened before or after another, a wobbly pulse spreads uncertainty across the whole architecture.

The practical effects are often misread because they arrive sideways. Timing degradation can resemble communications degradation, positioning degradation, or processing failure, depending on where the system notices it first. A user may see a navigation service behaving strangely. Another may see delayed or inconsistent data products. A third may observe that two streams no longer align cleanly. The hidden dependency matters because it connects these symptoms. Timing is one of the few elements in a surveillance and communications chain that can degrade many outputs without touching the primary sensor directly. One does not need to interfere with imagery collection to undermine confidence in what the imagery means alongside everything else.

The 2018 reports of GNSS disruption in northern Norway offer a useful Arctic-facing example, even though public discussion focused mainly on navigation and interference. Timing and positioning travel together in satellite navigation systems, and the degradation of one often implies consequences for the other. When a region experiences GNSS problems, the visible concern may centre on route safety or positional integrity. The quieter concern is that timing services supporting communications, network order, and data correlation may also be under strain. This is one reason Arctic disruptions can feel larger than their headline symptom. What appears to be a navigational inconvenience may in fact be a broader systems problem beginning to show itself at one visible edge.

A second example can be drawn from financial and telecommunications outages in other parts of the world when timing references failed or drifted. These events are not Arctic by location, but they are clarifying by logic. Networks dependent on precise synchronisation do not need a spectacular physical attack to misbehave. A timing anomaly alone can generate cascades: service interruptions, failed handshakes, processing delays, inconsistent records. That lesson is directly transferable northward because Arctic surveillance and communications architectures are just as dependent on the orderly sequencing of distributed components. The difference is that the north offers fewer easy substitutes and often less forgiving timelines for sorting out what has gone wrong.

This is why timing deserves to be treated as a strategic target in thought even when no one is prescribing tactics in practice. A system that loses timing confidence can become less useful in several ways at once. Navigation becomes shakier. Communication synchronisation becomes more fragile. Sensor fusion becomes slower and more doubtful. Network operations accumulate friction. The user may still receive imagery, coordinates, or contact reports, but each arrives under a growing question mark. The strategic point is unsettling and simple: one can degrade awareness without attacking the most visible part of the architecture. The imagery can remain intact. The confidence connecting it to action can still erode.

A credible limitation should be acknowledged. Modern systems often include internal clocks, holdover capabilities, buffering, and design practices that prevent small timing disturbances from becoming immediate catastrophe. Many networks can ride through temporary loss of a precise external reference, and many fusion processes can tolerate limited timing uncertainty without collapsing. It would be careless to imply that any brief disturbance in timing produces instant systemic confusion. In many cases it does not. Engineers have long understood that clocks drift, references fail, and resilient design must absorb some of that reality.

But the concession sharpens the core argument rather than weakening it. Holdover is not independence. It is a grace period. Buffers and local oscillators buy time, not exemption from the wider problem. Once the interval of degraded reference grows longer, or once several systems drift differently, the burden returns in the form of confidence loss, expanded margins, slower decision-making, or reversion to more labour-intensive cross-checking. Arctic operations are especially exposed to that burden because remoteness, sparse infrastructure, and difficult conditions often make graceful recovery slower than planners would like. A system that can tolerate timing degradation for a while is still a system whose behaviour changes under that degradation.

This is also why timing should not be discussed as though it lived only inside navigation receivers. It is a property distributed across the chain. Ground stations need it. Communications protocols depend on it. Data centres and processing environments rely on it. Remote terminals, sensor packages, and fusion systems use it to align their outputs with those of others. The Arctic's distinctive risk lies in making all these layers lean more heavily on timing at the same moment that other forms of certainty are already under pressure. When the visual scene is poor, the weather difficult, the communications path intermittent, and corroboration scarce, time becomes even more important because it is one of the few remaining ways to preserve order among partial truths.

Trust appears here in small, revealing behaviours. Analysts trust timing when they fuse data streams without manually re-examining every offset. Operators trust it when they allow automation to hand over communications or processing tasks on the assumption that timestamps remain meaningful. Planners trust it when they rely on system logs, route histories, or event chains to reconstruct what happened without building large buffers for temporal uncertainty. The moment those behaviours begin to change - extra checks, wider tolerances, slower dissemination, more reluctance to correlate - timing has already become an operational issue even if no one has yet named it aloud.

A useful counter-example lies in simpler or more localised systems that do not depend heavily on distributed synchronisation. A single platform conducting a narrow task, or a workflow with limited need to combine multiple streams, may absorb timing degradation more comfortably than a large, networked, multi-sensor architecture. That matters because it reminds us not to turn timing into a universal explanation for every weakness. Some systems can remain useful under relatively degraded temporal conditions. Others cannot. Complexity amplifies dependence.

Arctic surveillance, unfortunately or necessarily, tends towards the more dependent end of that spectrum. It asks separate systems to work together across distance, weather, sparse infrastructure, and competing institutional demands. It relies on communications networks that must coordinate across fragile paths. It increasingly fuses civil and security data sources whose timelines were not all designed with one another in mind. Under such conditions, timing becomes the hidden common language. When that language degrades, translation grows harder everywhere at once.

This is one reason resilience should be judged not only by whether a system can still collect data, but by whether it can still preserve temporal order under strain. A sensor may keep operating beautifully while the architecture around it becomes slower, noisier, and less sure of sequence. That is not resilience in the fuller sense required by the Arctic. It is sensory persistence without temporal confidence. The region punishes that distinction because decision cycles are often unforgiving, alternatives few, and misunderstandings costly.

The pulse returns at the end because it is both ordinary and indispensable. Systems do not need to be visibly attacked to lose the rhythm that keeps them trustworthy. A pulse can slow, slip, or desynchronise across components that continue to appear healthy in isolation. In the Arctic, that is often enough. The harder question is therefore not whether imagery, navigation, or communications still function after timing begins to degrade. The more serious question is whether they still function together well enough that a state can believe the order of events it thinks it sees.

Resilient PNT concepts and alternatives

In October 2018, during NATO's Trident Juncture exercise in northern Norway, reports of GPS disruption in Finnmark sharpened a lesson that Arctic operators had long understood in quieter ways: a navigation service can remain visible on a screen and still cease to deserve unqualified trust. Routes did not vanish from the world. Coordinates did not become impossible in some theatrical sense. What changed was confidence. A signal that usually sits in the background moved abruptly to the centre of operational attention, and with it came a harder question than most systems are built to ask of themselves: what still works when precise positioning, navigation, and timing become doubtful?

That question is more serious in the Arctic because the region punishes brittle dependence. A vessel can have more water around it and less room for mistake. An aircraft can have long stretches of route and fewer cheap ways to verify a fix. A remote station can continue collecting data while the timing and position references holding its products together become less certain. In such conditions, resilience does not mean pretending that GNSS can always be made perfect. It means building systems, procedures, and habits that remain useful when perfection thins.

The first step in thinking clearly about resilient PNT is to abandon the fantasy of a single sovereign source of truth. Show a modern Arctic operation - navigation, remote sensing, communications synchronisation, maritime monitoring, even routine logistics - and one sees how thoroughly it leans on satellite-derived position and time. Name the risk properly and it becomes a problem of single-point dependence rather than simple technical shortfall. Explain why that matters, and the implication is plain. A system that draws all of its confidence from one external service, however excellent that service usually is, has already decided how it will fail. The Arctic does not create that vulnerability, but it exposes it sooner and punishes it harder.

This is why resilient PNT begins as a design philosophy rather than a piece of equipment. It asks a blunt operational question: if precise GNSS degrades, what level of function remains, for how long, and for which decisions? That is a more useful question than the usual one about whether a service is technically available. Availability can coexist with untrustworthiness. A receiver can still show a fix while the surrounding system quietly loses confidence in timing, continuity, or integrity. Resilience, by contrast, is measured by retained capability. Can the ship still navigate safely with wider margins? Can the aircraft continue under stricter procedures? Can the surveillance architecture still correlate tracks well enough to avoid false certainty? Can the network keep time long enough to preserve order while fallback references take over?

A layered approach follows naturally from that question. A system relying on several sources of position, timing, or motion knowledge is not magically invulnerable, but it is harder to collapse through a single point of weakness. That layering may include multiple satellite constellations where available, onboard inertial systems, local references, map or terrain matching in some contexts, timing holdover from stable internal clocks, terrestrial radio aids where they still exist, and procedural methods that reduce the demand for exquisite precision when it cannot be justified. The important point is not the shopping list. It is the logic. Each layer provides another way to test, cushion, or replace a part of the GNSS service when the Arctic begins to press against it.

A compass is humble. That is the quiet motif worth keeping nearby. Not because old instruments solve modern navigation by nostalgia, but because resilience often depends on the unglamorous presence of independent reference points. A compass gives direction when coordinates feel slippery. An inertial system gives motion continuity when signals waver. A local chart, a known route, a radar shoreline fix, a timing holdover clock, a second constellation, a terrestrial beacon, a disciplined operating procedure - each is modest compared with the apparent elegance of satellite navigation, and each can become disproportionately valuable when the main reference begins to thin. Resilience grows from such humility.

The aviation world offers a useful public example. Aircraft operating at high latitudes do not rely on a single idea of navigation confidence. They layer certified systems, cross-checks, inertial capability, route procedures, communication practices, and contingency methods because they assume, correctly, that satellite-derived performance may not always deserve simple faith. The lesson is not that aviation has solved Arctic PNT once and for all. It is that professional resilience appears in behaviour long before it appears in hardware. Crews cross-check. Systems compare independent sources. Procedures widen margins when confidence drops. The resulting architecture is resilient not because it is immune to degradation, but because it is designed to remain governable under it.

A second example comes from remote surveying, infrastructure monitoring, and scientific field operations in northern environments. These users often depend on very precise positioning, yet the best practitioners rarely act as though correction-enabled GNSS alone settles the matter. They preserve reference marks, validate against known points, compare sessions, and use inertial or local methods to bridge gaps when the primary service becomes questionable. Again, the point is not that all Arctic operations resemble geodetic work. It is that high-consequence users tend to behave as though single-source confidence is insufficient. Their resilience lies partly in tools, but equally in how they define acceptable certainty.

This distinction between tools and posture matters because there is a common temptation to treat resilient PNT as a technology race alone. The language of alternatives can quickly slide into a catalogue of clever replacements for GNSS, as though resilience meant finding a new master rather than refusing mastery by any one service. That is too narrow. A system can possess several advanced sources of position and time and still remain brittle if its users assume they will all be available, well integrated, and self-validating at once. Conversely, a less spectacular architecture can prove more resilient if it knows how to degrade gracefully, compare references honestly, and adjust operations when precision falls away. In the Arctic, grace under degradation often matters more than technical grandeur.

A credible limitation must be admitted here. Alternatives are not free of their own dependencies. Inertial systems drift. Terrestrial aids have coverage limits and infrastructure demands. Local corrections can fail with backhaul or siting. Internal clocks buy time but not indefinite independence. Map matching and other context-based methods depend on the environment being legible enough, stable enough, or well mapped enough for the task. A layered design can therefore multiply complexity as well as resilience. It can create new maintenance burdens, new integration challenges, and new opportunities for users to misunderstand what has actually been cross-checked against what.

But the limitation strengthens the central argument rather than weakening it. Resilience does not require a perfect substitute for GNSS. It requires that a system not become useless or reckless when precise GNSS degrades. The standard is retained function, not elegant replacement. A ship may continue safely with wider navigational margins and more frequent verification. A surveillance chain may continue correlating events with slightly reduced confidence but without collapsing into disorder. A network may hold timing within tolerable bounds while other references are restored. The question is always the same: what can still be done, and under what discipline, once the best case no longer applies?

This is why operational adaptation belongs alongside technical layering. A resilient system is not one that merely owns more devices. It is one that changes behaviour intelligently when certainty changes. Routes may be altered. Tolerances widened. Human cross-checking increased. Automation may be granted less freedom or more carefully bounded tasks. Product claims may become more modest. A command centre may mark an observation as provisional rather than fused conclusively with other tracks. These adjustments are not admissions of failure. They are the visible signs that a system understands the difference between degraded and lost. In the Arctic, that distinction is crucial because too many failures begin as ordinary confidence carried beyond its rightful limit.

Timing deserves special attention within this broader resilience picture because it often survives in fragments even when positioning degrades more visibly. A system may preserve internal clock discipline for a period, allowing communications and processing to remain orderly while navigation certainty worsens. That can be immensely valuable. Yet timing too needs layers and discipline. Holdover oscillators, network comparisons, local references, and careful monitoring of drift all matter because a preserved clock can keep a system coherent while position is being re-evaluated. The strategic lesson is subtle but important. Resilience may consist not in preserving every function equally, but in preserving enough temporal order that the rest of the architecture can step down without confusion.

The Arctic amplifies the value of such step-down design. In milder theatres, a user who loses precision may find alternative infrastructure, nearby support, or abundant corroboration. In the north, the same loss can carry farther because distance, weather, sparse ground systems, and limited traffic reduce the number of easy checks available. A small degradation therefore becomes a systems question more quickly. What can the platform still trust? What claims can the analyst still make? What route can the crew still follow safely? What data can the network still align? Resilient PNT is useful precisely because it gives practical answers before those questions become urgent in the worst possible moment.

Trust, again, must be translated into visible conduct. A resilient architecture is one in which operators know when to stop pretending they have the same level of certainty as before. A vessel master trusts the design when reduced GNSS confidence leads to changed navigation behaviour rather than quiet continuation. An analyst trusts it when sensor products with weaker geolocation are labelled and handled accordingly. A network engineer trusts it when timing holdover triggers compensating procedures rather than wishful silence. Institutions that lack this behavioural honesty may possess many backup tools and still remain fragile, because no one has decided in advance what degraded confidence is supposed to look like in action.

A useful counter-example lies in tightly bounded systems that operate in narrow environments with plentiful external checks. Some local industrial or urban applications can tolerate high GNSS dependence because the surrounding infrastructure, geography, and redundancy provide rapid correction when something goes wrong. That should not be ignored. Not every system requires elaborate Arctic-style resilience planning. But this only sharpens the Arctic lesson. The farther north one goes, and the more safety, remoteness, or strategic consequence enters the mission, the less one can assume that ordinary surroundings will rescue a brittle design. Resilience becomes not an embellishment but a condition of seriousness.

The compass returns here because it captures the central discipline: keep at least one trusted reference that does not fail in the same way, and know how to use it before the main system begins to wobble. In modern terms that principle scales upwards into constellations, clocks, inertial units, local infrastructure, procedural doctrine, and institutional training. None of these grants invulnerability. Together they make it less likely that one class of degradation will erase the user's ability to navigate, synchronise, interpret, and decide.

The strategic importance of this is larger than navigation alone. A state that can continue to orient itself, maintain temporal order, and make disciplined claims under degraded PNT conditions is harder to confuse, slower to panic, and less likely to overreact to noise. A state that has built its northern operations around the assumption of uninterrupted precision may discover that it loses not only accuracy but composure when that precision thins. Resilient PNT is therefore not merely a technical preference. It is part of what determines whether Arctic surveillance and operations remain governable under stress.

The harder question, then, is not which single alternative can replace GNSS in some decisive future moment. That question is too neat for the Arctic. The more serious one is whether the system in front of us knows how to become less precise without becoming less sane. When the primary signal degrades, what remains of navigation, timing, fusion, and confidence - and has anyone designed the chain so that reduced certainty leads to changed behaviour before it leads to a costly mistake?

Chapter 7

Ground Station Networks and Sovereignty

What does a state truly own when it owns a satellite but not the station that receives its data? The question sounds legal at first and then turns technical, and then political again. A spacecraft may pass over the Arctic exactly as planned. The sensor may collect exactly what the mission requires. Yet the value of that collection still depends on where the data lands, who controls the landing point, how quickly it moves onward, and what happens when the ground beneath the system becomes the least glamorous and most decisive part of the chain.

The romance of space encourages a familiar mistake. It directs attention upward. Launches, orbital tracks, sensor specifications, revisit claims, and the rhetoric of persistence all invite the eye away from the surface. But the Arctic keeps dragging analysis back to Earth. Overhead passes do not become useful awareness by themselves. They become useful only when a station catches them, processes them, routes them, and does so with enough continuity that the system can be trusted under pressure. A satellite without dependable ground access is not absent. It is merely delayed.

The antenna decides more than the orbit admits. That is the central tension here. Ground stations look like support infrastructure, almost administrative in character, until one follows the path of data from collection to decision. Then their strategic weight becomes obvious. Station geography shapes latency. Station ownership shapes access. Station reliability shapes confidence. The state or company that controls the receiving point may not control the sky, but it often controls when the sky becomes actionable. In the Arctic, where distance, weather, and sparse infrastructure already narrow the margin for error, that kind of control is rarely secondary.

This matters because coverage claims often borrow their authority from maps rather than from delivery. A pass over the High North may suggest presence. A direct downlink to a capable northern station can turn that presence into timely use. Routing the same collection through a more distant hub may leave the image just as sharp and the decision far less relevant. The difference is not cosmetic. It changes which missions a system can honestly support. Search and rescue, maritime monitoring, environmental response, military cueing, infrastructure watchfulness, and public evidentiary release each live on different clocks. A station's location relative to those clocks is part of the capability, not an afterthought attached to it.

The stakes deepen when ownership and access no longer align neatly. Many operators do not rely solely on stations they own outright. They rent time, share networks, use commercial services, or build partnerships that spread cost and widen reach. These arrangements can be sensible, even necessary. They can also turn technical dependence into a subtler political fact. Priority rules matter. Visibility into outages matters. Maintenance standards matter. The user may possess the sensor and still find that the decisive variable lies in a contract, a hosting agreement, or a queue managed elsewhere. Information control increasingly follows service access rather than formal possession alone.

That is why sovereignty in Arctic surveillance cannot be reduced to flags, territory, or launch capability. It also inheres in infrastructure that can receive, sustain, and route data under northern strain. A state with modest satellites and dependable ground access may, in some circumstances, possess more usable awareness than a state with finer payloads and thinner control over where their products come down. This is not a paradox once the chain is taken seriously. The Arctic rewards not the loudest architecture, but the one whose weakest terrestrial point is still strong enough to matter when the weather worsens, the queues lengthen, or the politics of access become less friendly.

The path ahead begins with the plain fact that ground stations do not merely support overhead passes but define whether those passes become usable on the relevant timeline. From there the argument moves into hosted ground arrangements and shared access, where the practical gains are inseparable from questions of priority, dependence, and institutional visibility. It then settles into the harsh material life of Arctic infrastructure itself, where power, staffing, maintenance, and continuity stop sounding like background concerns and begin to look like the hidden grammar of system resilience.

A quiet motif runs through all of this: the key. Who holds the key to the station gate, the server room, the maintenance schedule, the antenna time, the backhaul path? The image overhead may belong to one actor, the territory below to another, and the operational truth to whichever institution can actually open the door when the pass arrives. In the Arctic, keys matter because delays are long, alternatives are sparse, and trust is often built on habits users do not notice until one of them fails.

The harder question, then, is not whether a satellite can see the High North. Many can. It is whether the network of stations beneath that vision is placed, governed, and sustained in a way that turns observation into dependable access rather than intermittent promise. When a pass reaches the Arctic sky, who receives it first, who can keep receiving it through winter and failure, and who decides whether that stream of data remains a sovereign capability or a borrowed one?

Why ground stations define usability

In April 2024, a satellite pass over the Arctic could still become two different realities depending on where the data came down. Direct downlink to a capable northern station could place a product in front of operators while the scene still mattered. The same collection, routed onwards through a more distant hub, could arrive as a technically identical image and a strategically weaker fact. Nothing about the sensor had changed. Nothing about the orbit had changed. What changed was the ground.

That is the habit this part of Arctic surveillance must break: the habit of treating the ground station as a supporting character. Space systems are often described from the payload outward. The image, the orbit, the revisit rate, the sensor mode - these are the celebrated pieces. Yet a satellite does not deliver awareness merely by flying overhead. It has to hand its data to somewhere. That somewhere has a location, an owner, a queue, a maintenance schedule, a power supply, a backhaul path, a security regime, and a political setting. In the Arctic, those qualities decide whether a pass becomes usable knowledge or delayed accumulation.

A pass must land. That short sentence is the key to the whole argument. A pass over the High North looks impressive on a coverage map because it suggests presence. Ground stations convert that presence into delivery. Show a polar-orbiting spacecraft sweeping north with excellent sensor performance, and the mission looks healthy. Name the next step properly and the picture sharpens: unless the spacecraft can downlink promptly to a suitable ground site, collection remains trapped in potential rather than turned into service. Explain why this matters, and the implications become strategic. Coverage is not only a matter of what can be seen. It is also a matter of where the resulting data can be caught.

This is why station geography shapes latency so powerfully. A ground station near the path of a polar or near-polar orbit can receive data shortly after collection, often in a window that preserves the decision value of the product. A station much farther away may still receive the same data eventually, but the interval between collection and delivery may lengthen enough to alter the class of mission the system can honestly support. That interval is not merely a technical inconvenience. In the Arctic, where vessel movements, weather, ice conditions, infrastructure activity, and strategic incidents often live on tight or shifting clocks, it can separate warning from hindsight.

Svalbard offers the clearest public example because it has become a canonical site for polar downlink. KSAT's facilities near Longyearbyen matter not because they are mystically northern, but because they sit where many polar-orbiting satellites can hand off data with unusual convenience. That placement shortens the path between orbit and use. A satellite collecting over the Arctic can often be received there quickly enough that imagery, radar scenes, or other products enter operational systems on a more useful timeline than they would if the same data had to wait for a later contact with a station farther south. The lesson is precise. Geography on the ground decides what the orbit can mean in practice.

A second example can be framed through contrast. Imagine a radar image collected over high northern waters where a vessel has appeared unexpectedly near an ice edge. In one architecture, the satellite downlinks directly to a local or near-local polar station and the product is available quickly enough to cue further collection, notify relevant agencies, or compare with maritime tracks while the contact still matters. In another, the satellite stores the same collection and routes it onwards to a distant hub with later downlink and later processing. The image quality may be identical. The operational reality is not. Direct downlink produces a live problem. Distant routing may produce a good record of a problem already moving out of reach.

This is the point at which ground stations stop looking like neutral infrastructure and start looking like strategic assets. Their value lies not only in receiving data, but in changing the speed, sovereignty, and hierarchy of access to data. A state controlling a high-latitude station does not merely own metal, antennas, radomes, and fibre. It controls a gateway through which overhead visibility becomes usable in time. That gateway can support national services, allied co-operation, commercial contracts, scientific access, intelligence workflows, or all of them at once. The station thus becomes more than a node. It becomes an instrument of timing and, by extension, influence.

Information control begins here in a very literal sense. A station operator can determine who receives what, in what order, under which contractual or institutional priorities. Even when the rules are fair and routine, the fact remains. Data is not born equally available to everyone once it leaves the spacecraft. It enters an infrastructure of reception, routing, processing, and distribution. In a crowded or dual-use environment, that infrastructure may privilege one user over another. A civil agency may wait while a defence customer receives priority handling. A commercial client may enjoy contractually guaranteed service. An allied state may possess access rights that remain contingent on another party's infrastructure. Station control therefore frequently becomes information control without needing to announce itself in dramatic terms.

This is why "owning satellites" can matter less than many assume if dependable ground access is missing or politically conditional. A state may possess an impressive space segment and still discover that the decisive question is whether its data can be received, routed, and trusted on a clock it actually controls. Conversely, a state or organisation with modest orbital assets but strong access to well-placed ground infrastructure may exercise more usable surveillance power than a more glamorous rival. The Arctic exposes this inversion because the ratio between orbital opportunity and terrestrial dependence is unusually unforgiving there. One can own the eye and still borrow the hand that catches what the eye has seen.

A credible limitation belongs here. Modern relay systems, crosslinks, and networked constellations can reduce dependence on any single local station. A satellite may move its data to another spacecraft, route it through a mesh, and downlink far from the scene of collection. That is a genuine change, and it weakens the old assumption that local direct downlink is always the decisive path. It would be careless to pretend that the strategic importance of polar stations remains untouched by these newer architectures.

And yet the limitation sharpens the deeper point rather than dissolving it. Relay and crosslinks do not abolish the ground. They relocate dependence within it. Somewhere, the data still has to land. Somewhere, routing still has to terminate in hardware, operators, backhaul, and institutional control. If anything, networked systems make the geography of landing more politically interesting rather than less. The question becomes not whether a local station matters, but which ground nodes now matter most, who governs them, and which users are granted the fastest or fullest paths through them. Ground infrastructure remains the place where orbital possibility becomes service or delay.

This brings sovereignty back into the frame. A station on sovereign territory under sovereign operation offers one kind of confidence. A hosted station on allied soil offers another. A commercial network with flexible access offers a third. Each may be entirely rational. Each also implies a different relationship to control, visibility, and dependence. A state relying on another's polar station for urgent surveillance products is not merely sharing infrastructure. It is accepting that some part of its awareness chain rests beyond direct command. In peacetime that may be efficient. Under strain it may feel thinner than the coverage map ever suggested.

Trust, here as elsewhere in Arctic systems, is visible in behaviour. Operators trust a ground network when they plan workflows around direct receipt rather than hedging with delayed alternatives. Governments trust it when they make claims about awareness without quietly assuming that foreign or commercial partners will keep the gate open exactly as expected. Analysts trust it when they interpret latency as meaningful to the event rather than as a symptom of the infrastructure behind the event. Distrust shows itself just as clearly: duplicate subscriptions, redundant tasking, sovereign backup stations, guarded language about "access" rather than "control". These are not decorative choices. They reveal what users think the station truly guarantees.

The station's strategic significance is therefore not simply that it exists in the right place, but that it compresses distance into a usable decision interval. A direct downlink to a northern station can make the Arctic feel closer to the analyst, the command post, the maritime centre, or the political authority waiting for a product. Routing through a distant hub can make the same Arctic feel remote again, even when the satellites above are identical. This is why station geography belongs inside any honest discussion of coverage. A region is not fully within reach just because the orbit passes over it. It is within reach when the data can descend through an infrastructure aligned with the time the decision still has.

The quiet motif of landing helps clarify the point. A spacecraft pass is only a possibility until the data lands somewhere that can use it. Landings differ. Some are close, fast, and institutionally clear. Others are distant, delayed, and administratively layered. The Arctic turns those differences into strategic facts because time, weather, sparse alternatives, and political sensitivity all amplify the consequences of where the landing occurs. The same overhead pass can therefore belong to two different surveillance systems depending on the station beneath it.

What follows is not a neat conclusion but a harder question. If a ground station can compress latency, prioritise users, shape access, and anchor sovereignty more decisively than many public discussions admit, then what exactly should count as possession in Arctic surveillance? The satellite may be national, commercial, allied, or shared. The image may look objective once it appears. But before it appears, it has to land. Who owns that landing, who governs the queue at the point of reception, and who gets to say that an overhead pass has become usable knowledge rather than merely another moment of expensive visibility?

Hosted ground, partnerships, and access

In 2016, when the Swedish Space Corporation announced an agreement to support OneWeb through its Esrange Space Center in northern Sweden, the news could be read as a straightforward business arrangement: one operator had infrastructure in the right place, another needed access, and both stood to benefit. Yet the deeper significance lay elsewhere. A satellite system that looks sovereign from orbit can depend, on the ground, on borrowed doors. The signal may belong to one actor. The reception path may not.

That is increasingly the normal condition rather than the exception. Ground infrastructure in the Arctic is expensive to build, difficult to maintain, and too strategically placed to be replicated casually by every operator who wants northern reach. Shared stations, hosted access, and commercial ground networks therefore answer a practical problem with undeniable elegance. They reduce the need for each operator to own every antenna, every radome, every backhaul path, every power system, every maintenance team. They turn scarce polar geography into a service. And yet the very efficiency that makes these arrangements sensible also makes them politically revealing, because once access is rented, negotiated, or shared, control becomes layered rather than singular.

The key is borrowed. That is the motif worth keeping close. A hosted ground arrangement gives an operator a way into a station, but not always the same kind of way in as ownership would. Show a constellation needing timely polar downlink and the value of shared or commercial access becomes immediately obvious. The operator can reach northern station capacity without the cost and delay of constructing its own network from scratch. Name the concept properly and it becomes more than outsourcing. It is institutional interdependence in hardware form. Explain why this matters, and the implication is strategic. Technical performance begins to reflect contractual terms, hosting priorities, transparency rules, and the politics of who gets to turn the key first when the queue hardens.

This is one reason Arctic surveillance forces a more mature understanding of capability. Public discussion still tends to treat satellites as the decisive expression of ownership, as though the actor with the spacecraft automatically owns the resulting awareness. But once data must land through a hosted network, a partner station, or a commercial provider, the chain of control fragments. The satellite may be one state's. The first station contact may belong to another state, another company, or a shared consortium. The onward routing may depend on service-level agreements, internal scheduling rules, and priorities invisible to the end user. In such circumstances, owning satellites can matter less than securing dependable access to the right ground.

The benefits of hosted ground are real and should be stated without coyness. It lowers entry barriers. It accelerates service. It lets operators reach high latitudes without carrying the full burden of Arctic construction and sustainment. It can spread costs sensibly across many users. It also provides redundancy where a single sovereign station network would be too thin or too expensive. A small national programme, a commercial Earth-observation firm, or a research mission can become operationally serious far sooner by renting access to an established polar station network than by waiting to build one of its own. That is not weakness. Often it is the most rational possible design choice.

KSAT offers a particularly clear public example because its polar ground network has become central to how many operators access high-latitude downlink and command capability. The company did not invent the logic of hosted ground, but it embodies its contemporary form: multiple sites, shared infrastructure, commercial discipline, and the conversion of scarce geography into a service available to many missions. For operators needing rapid contact with polar-orbiting satellites, such arrangements can transform feasibility. The operator that lacks its own northern station can still achieve near-real operational tempo by buying into a network that already exists. What matters is not merely location. It is dependable admission to location.

A second example lies in the broader use of shared stations for civil and security-adjacent missions in Europe and North America, where hosted access frequently bridges the gap between national ambition and national infrastructure. A state may own a remote-sensing satellite yet route its Arctic passes through stations outside its territory or through stations run by quasi-commercial or allied entities. The practical gain can be immense. The political reading is more delicate. Such arrangements widen access while also exposing just how much supposedly sovereign awareness relies on trust, contracts, and relationships that live below the level of the spacecraft itself. The Arctic makes that dependence harder to ignore because the value of polar station access is so concentrated.

This is where prioritisation becomes unavoidable. A shared station is still a queue, however elegantly managed. Several users may want the same antenna time, the same processing path, the same onward backhaul, or the same fast routing when a crisis sharpens. A hosted arrangement can promise service and still leave unanswered the most important question: whose data moves first when not everyone can be served at once? In peacetime, these frictions may be softened by schedule, contract, and routine. Under stress, they become governance in its barest form. The user discovers whether access meant equality, precedence, or mere eligibility to wait.

Visibility into operations matters for the same reason. A state or company using another party's station network may know it is receiving a service without knowing much about how the service is being organised at the moment it matters most. Are other customers ahead in the queue? Has maintenance reduced capacity? Has a backhaul issue slowed delivery? Have security considerations changed who can inspect, verify, or audit what happened inside the chain? These are not petty administrative concerns. They affect whether an operator can distinguish ordinary latency from selective latency, ordinary outage from political friction, ordinary congestion from a more serious degradation. A borrowed key does not always come with a full view of the building.

The governance implications sharpen further in dual-use environments. A commercial or shared ground network may support scientific, civil, commercial, and security users simultaneously. That mixed ecology often brings efficiency and resilience. It can also blur accountability. If a surveillance product arrives late, was the reason technical, contractual, political, or simply a side effect of how the network balances different classes of user? The answer may be hard to establish from outside. Latency then becomes not only a timing issue but a knowledge issue. The user may suffer delay without being able to determine whether the delay reflects neutral congestion or a hierarchy that places someone else ahead.

A credible limitation deserves admission. Hosted ground is not inherently a threat to sovereignty or a sign of weakness. Shared access can make systems more resilient by avoiding overconcentration in a single national network. Allied station use can strengthen co-operation and spread risk. Commercial providers can often deliver higher professional standards, denser coverage, and better maintainability than smaller sovereign systems struggling alone at the edge of the Arctic. It would be careless to romanticise ownership and dismiss partnership. In many cases, partnership is exactly what makes serious capability possible.

But the limitation clarifies rather than softens the chapter's deeper point. Institutional choices shape technical outcomes. An operator that selects hosted ground for reasons of cost, speed, or flexibility is also selecting a governance model for its latency, transparency, and prioritisation. That model may be entirely suitable. It may even be superior to what sovereign ownership could have achieved. The point is not that shared access is bad. It is that it is never only technical. Once the signal lands on someone else's infrastructure, politics enters in the form of procedure, visibility, queue discipline, and the distribution of trust.

This becomes even sharper when Arctic logistics are considered. Building and sustaining a station in the far north is hard enough that hosted access can appear almost irresistible. Why pour money and effort into duplicating a site, a fibre path, a maintenance chain, and a trained workforce that a trusted partner or commercial network already possesses? That reasoning is often compelling. Yet the same harsh environment that makes sharing attractive also makes dependence harder to escape later. A state that has built its operational habits around a hosted node may discover, in crisis or in prolonged strategic tension, that substituting another node is neither quick nor simple. Efficiency can harden into structural reliance.

Trust is visible in behaviour here too. A state that truly trusts its hosted access may organise critical workflows around it without sovereign duplication. A state that half-trusts it may purchase the service and still build reserve capacity elsewhere, subscribe to competing networks, or maintain procedural hedges against opaque delay. A commercial user may trust a provider enough to accept standard routing. A defence user may insist on dedicated windows, reserved channels, or special handling because ordinary commercial fairness is not the same thing as strategic sufficiency. These behaviours are not administrative quirks. They reveal what "access" is believed to mean under pressure.

The borrowed key returns because it captures both the strength and the fragility of the arrangement. Borrowing a key can be the smartest way into a valuable building. It saves time, cost, and needless duplication. It also means someone else made the lock, owns the door, and may know more than you do about how access is managed when several hands reach for it at once. In the Arctic, where the door often sits in a place too valuable and too difficult to ignore, that arrangement can be both efficient and unsettling.

This is why readers should resist the reflex to equate sovereignty with ownership of the spacecraft alone. Sovereignty in Arctic surveillance often lives lower down the chain. It lives in whether the pass can be received on terms the user controls, whether the station network remains dependable when others are competing for it, whether outages and delays can be audited rather than guessed at, and whether the user can distinguish a technical bottleneck from a political one. A satellite can be sovereign in registry and dependent in operation. Hosted ground makes that contradiction visible.

The harder question, then, is not whether partnerships and commercial access are wise. Very often they are. The more serious question is what kind of dependence has been purchased alongside the convenience. When a pass over the High North matters urgently, and when several users, agencies, or allies all need the same infrastructure at once, who actually holds the decisive form of access: the actor who owns the satellite, or the actor who controls the borrowed key?

Operating in harsh environments

In January 2022, damage to a subsea cable serving Svalbard again drew attention to a stubborn Arctic fact: a ground station can be perfectly placed for polar orbit access and still become operationally fragile through failures that have nothing glamorous about them. No satellite had changed orbit. No sensor had lost its ability to collect. The weakness appeared lower down, in the earthly systems that allow overhead opportunity to become delivered service. For Arctic surveillance, that is not an administrative footnote. It is often the decisive story.

The Arctic does not ask whether infrastructure exists. It asks whether infrastructure can continue. A ground station in a brochure appears static and self-possessed: dish, radome, control room, fibre path, perhaps a neat map proving its excellent latitude. A working station in the High North is something else entirely. It must be heated, powered, staffed, maintained, resupplied, repaired, and defended against weather and wear that do not care whether the mission is scientific, commercial, or strategic. A station can be technically advanced and still live season to season by the grace of generators, access windows, spare parts, and competent people willing to stay with a fault until it yields.

This is why harsh environment operations should be treated as part of capability rather than as a cost appended to it. Show an Arctic ground site receiving data from polar-orbiting satellites and the visible achievement looks clean: passes occur, antennas track, products flow. Name the real condition properly and a different picture emerges. The station is a sustained performance of maintenance, staffing, power management, environmental control, and recovery planning. Explain why that matters, and the implication becomes larger than engineering. Resilience in the Arctic is not what survives one fine day. It is what continues through the week when weather turns, access closes, equipment ages, and a minor fault threatens to become a strategic one.

Cold is only the beginning. That is worth stating plainly because "harsh environment" is too often reduced to temperature. Arctic stations contend with wind loading, ice accretion, snow burial, freeze-thaw stresses, power irregularities, corrosion, limited daylight during key seasons, difficult transport, and the simple but severe fact that repair is often slower there than elsewhere. A failed component in a temperate, well-connected region may be inconvenient. The same component in the far north may alter throughput, force triage, or reduce confidence in a whole chain of operations while everyone waits for the part, the weather window, or the technician who can reach it. The environment magnifies the consequences of ordinary failure.

A station lives by upkeep. That quiet motif keeps the analysis honest. Arctic infrastructures do not merely need maintenance in the sense that all machines do. They need a style of maintenance shaped by distance, climate, and logistical uncertainty. Preventive work matters more because deferred work can grow expensive in continuity rather than only in money. Spare parts matter more because resupply may be slow or vulnerable to interruption. Remote diagnostics matter more because not every problem can justify or survive a long human journey. Staffing models matter more because expertise concentrated in one or two people becomes a form of fragility when weather, illness, rotation schedules, or burnout remove them from the chain.

This is one reason major Arctic stations command strategic respect. Svalbard again offers the clearest public example. Its importance lies not only in latitude, but in the hard-earned capacity to keep a complex site functioning in an environment that strains every assumption of ordinary infrastructure. A polar station of that kind depends on power resilience, environmental protection, trained personnel, maintenance routines, communications backhaul, physical access, and governance arrangements strong enough to absorb repeated stress. The lesson is not that Svalbard is uniquely fragile. It is that any site serving similar missions in similar conditions inherits the same operational truth: without sustained upkeep, good geography decays into disappointing service.

A second example can be drawn from the long history of remote northern radar and communications sites in North America and Greenland, including systems associated with the DEW Line and its successors. Their specific technologies and missions have changed, but the enduring lesson remains. The north has always required more than installation. It requires sustainment. Fuel deliveries, seasonal access, staff rotation, weatherproofing, fault tolerance, and the capacity to restore service after failure have consistently determined whether northern infrastructure counted as presence in any meaningful sense. This remains true even where modern automation has reduced the number of people on site. Fewer people do not eliminate the burden of harsh environment operations; they change its form.

Power deserves special attention because it is often the hidden currency of reliability. A station that cannot depend on stable, redundant energy cannot promise continuous service regardless of how well placed its antennas may be. In the Arctic, power is rarely just a utility assumption. It is part of the mission design. Heating systems, environmental control, de-icing, tracking motors, processing equipment, shelters, and backhaul all rely on it. A power irregularity may not produce immediate darkness. It may instead introduce reduced performance, intermittent resets, degraded heating, shortened equipment life, or the sort of subtle instability that operators initially read as communications trouble or environmental noise. The consequence is that power failure in the Arctic can masquerade as several other failures before it announces itself clearly.

That ambiguity matters because outages and degradations in the north can mimic interference. If a station's throughput drops, tracking falters, timing grows erratic, or a backhaul path becomes unstable, the first operational symptom may resemble jamming, atmospheric disturbance, or unexplained systems degradation elsewhere in the chain. This is where harsh-environment sustainment intersects directly with situational awareness. A user trying to interpret a service interruption needs to know whether the problem originates in weather, ageing hardware, power stress, backhaul trouble, or hostile action. If maintenance histories are weak, monitoring poor, or recovery plans underdeveloped, the station itself becomes a producer of uncertainty. A cold-induced failure can look strategically meaningful until someone proves it was merely poorly recovered.

This is why fault recovery belongs inside any serious account of Arctic capability. Systems are often praised for uptime, but resilience is better measured by what happens after something breaks. How quickly can the site diagnose the problem? Can local staff act, or must outside specialists travel? Are spares already on hand? Can the station degrade gracefully, preserving partial service, or does one failure collapse several functions at once? Can users distinguish reduced capacity from total loss and adjust accordingly? These are non-financial costs in the most important sense. They determine continuity, confidence, and whether an outage becomes a contained incident or a cascade through the surveillance chain.

A credible limitation should be granted. Arctic ground infrastructure is not trapped in an age of brittle machinery and heroic improvisation. Modern remote monitoring, better enclosures, stronger automation, improved materials, modular replacement strategies, and more disciplined reliability engineering have made northern sites more capable and more manageable than many older accounts suggest. Some stations now operate with fewer staff on site, better predictive maintenance, and tighter environmental control than was imaginable a generation ago. It would be careless to write as though the Arctic still defeated engineering by default. It does not.

But the concession sharpens the core point rather than weakening it. Better technology does not repeal harsh environment operations; it professionalises them. Remote monitoring still needs communications.

Modular replacement still needs transport. Automation still needs power and software support. A site with fewer staff may be more efficient and more exposed to the sudden absence of specialised knowledge. Improved resilience often raises the standard by which continuity is judged. Once a system becomes highly reliable, even brief interruptions can cause greater institutional confusion because users have built habits around its apparent certainty. Harshness does not vanish. It changes where the burden sits.

This is why staffing should not be discussed as though it were a human resources matter adjacent to technical capability. In Arctic ground systems, staffing is part of resilience architecture. A station needs people who can work in remote conditions, recognise subtle faults, interpret environmental stress correctly, and co-ordinate recovery under pressure. That may mean permanent presence, rotational models, remote support, or some blend of all three. Each choice carries trade-offs. Permanent staffing builds local familiarity but strains recruitment and retention. Rotations widen the labour pool but can weaken continuity of knowledge. Heavy remote management reduces physical hardship and increases dependence on networks and diagnostics. None of these models is neutral. Each shapes how the station behaves when things stop going smoothly.

The same is true of maintenance philosophy. A site run on minimalist assumptions may look economical until the first serious failure arrives at the wrong season. A site designed with generous redundancy, stocked spares, and conservative upkeep may seem expensive until it quietly avoids the outage that would otherwise distort a regional picture of activity. This is why capability assessments that ignore sustainment are often misleading. They count antennas, throughput, latitude, and processing capacity while leaving uncounted the habits that keep those attributes real through Arctic time. The north turns that omission into a strategic error more quickly than milder environments do.

The distinction between financial cost and continuity cost is especially important here. A repair flight, an extra generator, a larger stock of spare components, or a better enclosure can all be discussed as budget lines. But their deeper meaning lies in what they buy operationally: fewer unexplained gaps, faster restoration, less false suspicion, more stable planning. A state or company deciding whether to fund harsh-environment sustainment is therefore not simply deciding how much to spend. It is deciding how much uncertainty it is willing to manufacture for itself later. Under Arctic conditions, the cheapest station is often the one most likely to produce expensive ambiguity.

Trust again appears in behaviour. Operators trust a station when they treat interruptions as rare enough to be diagnostically meaningful rather than routine enough to be background noise. Analysts trust it when they do not automatically wonder whether a missing product reflects hidden technical trouble. Partner institutions trust it when they base shared workflows on its expected continuity rather than holding large procedural buffers against likely failure. Distrust is visible too: duplicate routing, parallel subscriptions, hesitant claims about coverage, guarded language about confidence, routine fallback to alternative nodes. Those behaviours often tell more truth about Arctic capability than any formal specification sheet.

The motif of upkeep returns because it captures the whole chapter's discipline. Upkeep is not a minor virtue added after acquisition. It is the condition under which the station remains part of the system rather than a static object on a map. A radar image, a timing stream, a command uplink, a direct downlink from a polar pass - all depend on upkeep. When upkeep falters, the station does not simply become less efficient. It becomes a source of doubt about what the wider system is actually seeing and why it is no longer seeing it clearly.

The harder question, then, is not whether an Arctic ground site can be built or even whether it can work impressively in good conditions. Many can. The more serious question is what sort of institution, maintenance culture, staffing model, and recovery discipline stands behind that site when the conditions cease to be good. If a station outage can mimic interference, delay products, and distort situational awareness across a region, then sustainment is not merely one cost among others. It is part of what the capability is. The Arctic keeps asking the same thing in different forms: when the infrastructure goes quiet, who can tell whether the silence belongs to weather, wear, or something more deliberate - and how long can they afford not to know?

Chapter 8

Data Latency and Decision Cycles

How long is "near real time" when the image has already been collected? That is the question that quietly haunts every modern claim about Arctic surveillance. The answer is almost never a single number, because the delay that matters most rarely lives in one place. A sensor may see promptly. A product may still arrive late. A network may move data quickly. Understanding may still lag behind delivery. The Arctic turns this familiar systems problem into a strategic one because distance, sparse infrastructure, harsh conditions, and institutional friction make every hidden minute more consequential.

The public imagination still likes the drama of the instant view: a satellite overhead, a target detected, a picture on a screen, a decision made. Reality is less cinematic. Between collection and action lies a chain of handling, formatting, routing, prioritisation, processing, comparison, and dissemination whose slowest part often defines the system. Not all delay comes from orbit. Much of it accumulates on the ground in queues, in mismatched formats, in competing priorities, in products waiting for the right analyst, in data that has arrived but has not yet become meaning. The Arctic is not unique in this respect. It is simply less forgiving of it.

That is the chapter's central tension. Speed in surveillance is not one thing. It is a sequence of different clocks, each serving a different kind of judgement. A system can be fast at collection and slow at delivery. Fast at delivery and slow at interpretation. Fast at generating alerts and slow at proving that those alerts deserve trust. The friction grows sharper in the High North because decisions there often depend on fleeting conditions - vessel movement, changing ice, short weather windows, sparse corroboration, fragile communications, long logistical tails. A product that arrives after the window has shifted may still be useful, but for a different purpose than the one the system was presumed to support.

This is why latency must be treated as part of capability rather than as an unfortunate gap between capabilities. A surveillance architecture does not merely gather data; it moves data through a decision cycle. The cycle may include tasking, collection, downlink, processing, exploitation, dissemination, fusion with other sources, and human judgement. Any one of these may become the bottleneck. Near-real-time claims therefore often describe a workflow aspiration more than a law of physics. They say, in effect, that the institution hopes to keep the chain moving quickly enough that the product still belongs to the present. The Arctic keeps asking whether that hope survives the ordinary drag of queues and the harsher drag of remoteness.

The stakes extend beyond tempo in the narrow sense. Different missions live on different clocks. A delayed image can be perfectly adequate for pattern analysis, environmental monitoring, treaty verification, or the reconstruction of an incident after the fact. The same delay can be disastrous for warning, interception, route adjustment, or rapid cueing of another sensor. The key question is therefore not whether a system is fast, but what decision it is fast enough to support. Trust appears here in behaviour. Operators trust a system when they act on the product before seeking slower confirmation elsewhere. Analysts trust it when they treat the data as still live rather than already historical. Institutions distrust it when they build workarounds, pad timelines, or quietly reclassify "real time" into "good enough for later".

The Arctic also sharpens the contest between speed and interpretability. Data can be processed closer to the sensor, reduced before transmission, or converted into alerts designed to outrun bandwidth and queue constraints. That often improves timeliness. It can also make the product harder to audit, harder to explain, or less suitable for contested judgement. A fast alert may be exactly what a safety or cueing mission needs and exactly what a politically sensitive attribution decision should treat with caution. What matters is not to choose one virtue and ignore the other. It is to recognise that every effort to accelerate the chain changes what kind of confidence the output can honestly bear.

A further complication follows from integration. Arctic awareness is rarely produced by one source alone. Satellite data increasingly meets airborne tracks, maritime feeds, terrestrial reports, and in some contexts undersea sensing. The act of fusion sounds like an increase in certainty and often is. It is also another source of delay, because alignment across formats, timestamps, geolocation confidence, and institutional ownership can slow the product even after collection and delivery are complete. The more a system relies on integration, the more it must decide which matters more in a given moment: speed of first notice or confidence of combined understanding.

The path ahead begins with the pipeline itself, not as a technical diagram but as the lived route by which data becomes decision. It then turns to the different rhythms of burst delivery and continuous flow, where the usefulness of each depends on the clock of the mission rather than on technological prestige. From there the argument moves into processing nearer the sensor, where bandwidth is saved at the price of new burdens of trust, before widening into the more difficult work of combining space-based data with airborne, surface, and undersea sources. It ends by asking for a language of timeliness and uncertainty strict enough to compare systems honestly rather than flatter them.

A quiet motif runs through all of this: the queue. Some queues are visible - files waiting for downlink, products waiting for processing, requests waiting for antenna time. Others are hidden inside software, routing rules, analytic workflows, or the time it takes for a human being to decide whether the machine has found something meaningful. The Arctic turns queues into strategic facts because the next pass, the next weather break, the next vessel movement, or the next opportunity for corroboration may not wait politely behind them.

The harder question, then, is not whether Arctic surveillance can be made faster. Much of it can. The more serious question is which part of the decision cycle is being accelerated, for whose benefit, and at what cost in interpretability, integration, or honesty about uncertainty. When a system claims to be timely, does that mean it collects quickly, delivers quickly, understands quickly, or merely pushes the queue somewhere less visible while the clock that really matters keeps running?

The collection-to-decision pipeline

In March 2021, when the *Ever Given* blocked the Suez Canal, satellite imagery circulated quickly enough to make the event feel almost simultaneous with its own observation. The public saw a ship, a bottleneck, and the visual proof of disruption. What the public did not see was the chain that made that proof timely enough to matter. An image is not born as a decision. It is tasked, collected, downlinked, formatted, processed, routed, interpreted, and only then placed in front of someone who can act on it. The Arctic makes every link in that chain more visible because it punishes the fantasy that sensing alone produces awareness.

A fast satellite does not guarantee a fast answer. That is the discipline this section must impose. The collection itself may occur at exactly the right moment. The system may still arrive late to its own significance. A ship may alter course. A weather window may close. A second sensor may lose the chance to corroborate. A command post may receive a product that is technically impressive and operationally stale. In the High North, where distance, sparse infrastructure, and difficult conditions already stretch the path from event to interpretation, latency is rarely a singular delay. It accumulates. Often quietly.

The most useful way to understand the collection-to-decision pipeline is to treat it as a sequence of transformations rather than a single act of delivery. Show the process honestly and it begins before the satellite has seen anything at all. Someone defines the question. Someone tasks the system. The spacecraft collects. The data is moved to ground or relay. It is converted from raw form into something analysts can use. It is checked, sorted, compared, and distributed. Only then can it become a product that enters a decision cycle. Name the concept properly and one sees why "near real time" so often misleads. It sounds like a property of physics. More often it is a property of workflow discipline.

That distinction matters because different parts of the pipeline obey different clocks. Tasking may be immediate or queued. Collection may be prompt or delayed by orbital opportunity. Downlink may be direct, deferred, or constrained by communications. Processing may be routine for one product and burdensome for another. Exploitation may require only quick classification or a much slower analytic comparison. Dissemination may be smooth inside one institution and awkward across several. The strategic implication is plain: the speed of the whole system is defined by the slowest stage that still matters to the decision. In Arctic surveillance, that stage is frequently not the satellite.

The pipeline begins with tasking, and tasking is already a source of latency. A system cannot collect what it has not been asked to collect, and the asking is never as simple as public rhetoric suggests. In a crowded architecture, requests compete. Broad-area search, fine-detail follow-up, routine monitoring, environmental watch, and security-driven interest may all seek the same asset. A well-run system does not grant equal urgency to all of them. It decides which question deserves the next look. That choice can save time later or waste it. A hasty tasking decision may produce a beautiful image of the wrong thing. A cautious one may miss the moment when the right thing was visible. The pipeline therefore begins not with data but with institutional judgement.

Collection itself then enters the clock, but collection is often the part of the system people overestimate least accurately. A satellite pass feels like a decisive event because it is visible in diagrams and easy to describe. Yet even perfect collection is only a transfer from ignorance into storage unless the rest of the chain keeps pace. This is especially true in the Arctic, where store-and-forward architectures, limited ground access, or relay dependence may separate sensing from delivery by intervals that change the decision value of the product. A radar scene over northern waters may be collected exactly when needed and still become useful only after the vessel has moved beyond easy follow-up. The sensor has done its job. The system has not necessarily done its own.

The queue is the right motif here because it follows the data from one transformation to the next. The first queue may be tasking. The second may be downlink. The third may be processing. The fourth may be analytic attention. Each queue can be mundane enough to escape public notice and consequential enough to dominate operational outcomes. Arctic systems are especially exposed because alternatives are often few. A delayed pass may not be replaceable by an aircraft, a nearby ship, or a dense sensor network. The data waits, and the event does not.

Processing is often where this becomes most counterintuitive. People like to imagine that latency lives in orbit, in distance, in radio links, in weather. Those matter. But many systems lose more time after the data has already arrived on the ground than before. Raw radar data may need calibration, geolocation, formatting, and conversion into products usable by non-specialist analysts. Optical scenes may require cloud screening, orthorectification, clipping, and metadata handling. Multi-sensor products may wait for alignment with other feeds. Even when these steps are heavily automated, they still impose sequence, compute demand, and quality control burdens. The result is that the data may be present while the product remains absent.

A simple example illustrates the point. A high-latitude SAR collection detects a suspicious contact near ice edge. The satellite downlinks successfully to a polar station. The raw scene enters a processing queue already burdened by other tasks. A quicklook is generated late because a more urgent contract product was ahead in line. By the time the contact reaches the relevant maritime operations centre, the vessel has altered course and the opportunity for an immediate second look has narrowed. What dominated the timeline was not orbit or sensing. It was backlog. This is why claims about speed should always be read against the workflow behind them, not only against the platform that made the original observation possible.

Dissemination adds another layer of ordinary but decisive delay. A product completed on one system is not yet a decision input until it reaches the right person, in the right format, with enough contextual framing to be acted upon. That sounds administrative because it is. It is also strategically serious. A finished product may sit in an inbox, a dashboard queue, a shared repository, or an interagency handoff process that nobody outside the institution ever sees. One recipient may get a fully annotated report. Another may receive only a contact alert. An ally may receive a slower version because dissemination rules differ from internal routing rules. The clock keeps running. Near-real-time claims often break here, in places too prosaic to make for good publicity.

This is why the collection-to-decision pipeline should be understood as a chain of translation rather than a conveyor belt. Raw collection is translated into transportable data. Transportable data is translated into processed products. Processed products are translated into analytic meaning. Analytic meaning is translated into decision relevance. At every stage something is gained and something is lost. Fidelity may be reduced for speed. Context may be thinned to preserve urgency. Confidence may increase while timeliness deteriorates. The pipeline is not merely a sequence of technical steps. It is a sequence of compromises about what kind of knowledge should arrive first.

A credible limitation has to be acknowledged. Not every mission needs the whole chain to move at the same speed. Environmental monitoring, long-horizon pattern analysis, treaty-related review, and retrospective investigation may remain highly valuable even when processing and dissemination take time. For such uses, slower pipelines can still be excellent systems. Indeed, a rush towards speed can damage quality if a mission really requires careful interpretation rather than immediate cueing. The problem is not delay in itself. It is mismatch between the delay and the decision the system is presumed to support.

That concession strengthens the central argument. A pipeline should be judged against the clock of the mission, not against a generic ideal of speed. A system optimised for later certainty may be badly suited to early warning. A system optimised for quick alerting may be entirely unsuited to public attribution or legal defensibility. Confusion arises when institutions slide between these roles without admitting that they are asking one chain to support two very different forms of action. The Arctic is unforgiving of such confusion because there is less room to hide workflow weakness behind abundant alternatives.

This also explains why workflow claims often outpace physical claims. "Near real time" usually means that the institution has tried to compress the steps between collection and use, not that the image materialised in a decision-maker's hands the instant the sensor saw the scene. It may mean quicklook products, pre-prioritised queues, reserved processing capacity, dedicated dissemination pathways, or analysts already placed in the loop before the data arrives. All of that can be highly effective. None of it is magic. The moment any one of those arrangements weakens, the promise of near real time often weakens with it. The phrase is therefore best treated as a description of an organised workflow, not an attribute bestowed permanently by hardware.

Trust appears here in very specific behaviour. Operators trust a pipeline when they act on first products without waiting reflexively for secondary confirmation. Analysts trust it when they assume the timestamps, geolocation, and processing status are current enough to support fusion with other feeds. Institutions distrust it when they build large time buffers, duplicate subscriptions, or parallel tasking pathways because the official chain is too slow or too opaque to carry the weight of urgent decisions. These behaviours reveal more than brochures do. They show what the system is actually believed to support once the queues begin to form.

The queue returns at the end because it is where the chapter's argument becomes hardest to avoid. Everyone imagines the decisive minute as the moment of collection. In practice, decisive minutes are often lost afterwards, waiting for the next handoff, the next processor, the next analyst, the next formatting script, the next approval, the next dissemination rule to yield. The Arctic does not invent this truth. It simply strips away the illusion that the rest of the world can absorb such delay indefinitely without consequence.

The harder question, then, is not whether a satellite can collect data quickly over the High North. Many can. The more serious question is what kind of institution sits beneath that collection, and whether its pipeline is disciplined enough that a product still belongs to the decision it was meant to inform by the time it arrives. When a system claims to be near real-time, which queue has been shortened, which one remains hidden, and who is prepared to admit that the slowest part of Arctic awareness may be the least dramatic one?

Store-and-forward versus continuous delivery

In March 2014, as the search for Malaysia Airlines Flight 370 widened across the Indian Ocean, the world saw a painful demonstration of what delayed data does to urgent decisions. Information still moved. Satellite communications records still mattered. Remote sensing still contributed. Yet much of what became important did not arrive on the same clock as the event itself. The search effort was forced to live inside intervals: intervals between collection and transmission, between receipt and interpretation, between the existence of data and the ability to use it as if it still belonged to the present.

The Arctic makes this difference routine rather than exceptional. A sensor may see something meaningful over ice or sea, but the architecture carrying that observation onward determines whether it behaves like a live warning or a historical clue. Store-and-forward systems collect first and deliver later, usually when the platform reaches a suitable ground station or relay opportunity. Continuous delivery systems aim to keep data moving with much less interruption, often through relay links, inter-satellite routing, or persistent communications paths. Both approaches can be entirely rational. Both can also mislead when their timing is confused with the timing of the decision they are meant to support.

The central question is therefore not which architecture sounds more advanced. It is what kind of decision the architecture is designed to serve, and on what clock. Show a satellite gathering imagery over the High North and the temptation is to treat the moment of collection as the decisive moment of awareness. Name the two delivery logics properly and the picture changes. In store-and-forward, the observation enters a pause before it becomes available to users. In continuous delivery, the system tries to preserve flow from collection towards use with as little waiting as possible. Explain why that matters, and the implication becomes strategic. A system that pauses may be excellent for some missions and dangerously mismatched for others.

Store-and-forward is often misunderstood because the phrase sounds old-fashioned, even second-rate. It is neither by necessity. In many space systems it remains practical, efficient, and entirely appropriate. A satellite collects, stores the data onboard, and transmits it when a ground contact becomes available. This can work very well for environmental monitoring, seasonal change analysis, broad mapping, scientific research, and many forms of retrospective or pattern-based intelligence. If the value of the observation does not collapse quickly with time, then waiting for the next downlink can be a sensible bargain. The architecture avoids some of the complexity, cost, and dependency that continuous delivery demands. Its virtue lies in proportion.

A delayed image can still matter. That short sentence protects the analysis from a common mistake. Not every mission needs immediacy. A sea-ice chart prepared from data that arrived in a burst may remain highly valuable if the decision it supports concerns broad route planning rather than a vessel's next minute of movement. A time series of coastal change does not lose meaning because it was not delivered instantly. A pollution trace, infrastructure change, or seasonal activity pattern may still support strong conclusions after the fact. Store-and-forward systems are not failures of timeliness in the abstract. They are architectures designed around the assumption that some waiting is tolerable.

The trouble begins when that assumption goes unstated. In Arctic security and safety contexts, some decisions decay quickly. A contact near ice edge, a suspicious vessel movement, a temporary deployment, an opening route, a distress event, a change around sensitive infrastructure: these may require action or at least rapid corroboration before the scene alters. In those cases, store-and-forward can become dangerous not because it malfunctions, but because it delivers on the wrong clock. The system may work exactly as designed while the mission fails through mistiming. A product that arrives after the vessel has changed course or after another sensor window has passed is not worthless. It simply belongs to a different category of use than the operator may have imagined.

The contrast with continuous delivery therefore turns on continuity of flow rather than prestige of technology. A continuous architecture seeks to narrow the gap between sensing and use by moving data as it is collected or with minimal interruption thereafter. Relay satellites, crosslinked constellations, persistent communications networks, and highly connected ground infrastructures all push in this direction. The gain is obvious. An observation can enter a decision cycle while the event remains live enough to influence. A maritime centre can cue a second look. A command node can compare the new product with other feeds. A route can be adjusted before ice or weather changes the picture again. Continuous delivery changes what counts as "current".

Iridium's long-standing use of inter-satellite links in high-latitude communications offers one public example of how continuity can alter service meaning. The system's value in northern operations has never lain in raw orbital spectacle alone. It has rested in the ability to keep communications moving across a networked architecture rather than waiting passively for local ground contact. The principle extends well beyond communications traffic in the narrow sense. Once surveillance data can enter a continuous or near-continuous transport path, high-latitude remoteness loses some of its power to slow relevance. A detection becomes easier to treat as operational rather than archival.

A second example sits in modern Earth observation workflows that combine SAR collection with relay or rapid ground-network access. A radar image collected over northern waters under cloud and darkness may be intrinsically valuable, but if it must sit onboard until the next convenient station contact, its role in a time-sensitive mission can shrink sharply. When the same product is routed through a faster delivery path, its operational class changes. It may then support immediate maritime cross-checking, further tasking, or a warning decision while the contact is still part of the present scene. The sensor did not change. The architecture around the sensor did.

This is why store-and-forward versus continuous delivery should be treated as a question of mission fit rather than technological virtue. A broad-area environmental monitoring mission may sensibly privilege store-and-forward because it values coverage, efficiency, and manageable infrastructure over constant flow. A rapid warning architecture may require continuous delivery because its decisions cannot wait for the next burst. A mixed system may deliberately combine both, using continuous paths for alerts and store-and-forward for fuller products or lower-priority collections. The key is to admit that these are different answers to different clocks. Confusion begins when one architecture is sold in the language of the other.

The queue remains the quiet motif here because even continuous delivery does not abolish waiting. It shifts where waiting occurs. In a burst-based system, the waiting is obvious: data sits onboard until transmission becomes possible. In a continuous system, data may still queue inside relay networks, downlink paths, processing chains, or dissemination rules. The advantage is that the queue can become shorter, more distributed, or better aligned with urgent users. But no architecture escapes the logic of scarcity entirely. This is why continuous delivery should not be romanticised into instantaneous omnipresence. It improves the flow. It does not remove the need to govern that flow.

A credible limitation must be admitted. Continuous delivery is not automatically better merely because it sounds faster. It often requires more infrastructure, more dependency on relay or network services, more complex routing, stronger cybersecurity, and clearer governance about who gets priority. It can also encourage users to expect a level of temporal intimacy with the scene that the rest of the chain - analysis, verification, fusion, command authority - cannot always support. A faster stream of data can still produce bad decisions if the institution consuming it has not matched its own workflow to the speed of arrival. Flow without discipline becomes noise.

That limitation strengthens the deeper argument. The right comparison is not between slow systems and fast systems in the abstract. It is between decision cycles and delivery architectures. What is the user trying to decide? How quickly does that decision lose value if the data pauses? Does the mission need first notice, full detail, or something in between? Can the organisation act on a rapid alert, or does it require more interpretation than the continuous path really saves? These questions expose whether the architecture is aligned with use or merely impressive in specification.

This is also where the Arctic imposes intellectual discipline. The region punishes casual language about "real time" because the physical and institutional chain remains long even when delivery improves. A continuously routed product may still need processing, fusion, interpretation, and dissemination. A burst-delivered product may still be fully adequate if the decision sits on a longer clock. The north therefore teaches a useful habit: do not ask whether the system is fast; ask whether it is fast enough for the decision and honest enough about the interval it cannot shrink. That habit matters because too many surveillance claims still confuse the time of collection with the time of use.

Trust appears here in visible behaviour. Operators trust store-and-forward when they design missions around the expectation of delayed but reliable bursts and do not pretend the product is live when it is not. They trust continuous delivery when they are willing to cue follow-on actions before the event has passed out of reach. Institutions distrust both when they build parallel workarounds, treat every delivery as provisional, or quietly keep the urgent decision elsewhere because the official chain cannot bear the timing burden placed upon it. These behaviours reveal what the architecture actually supports.

The contrast also helps clarify a broader strategic point. Surveillance systems do not merely gather facts; they participate in rhythms of action. A burst architecture creates a rhythm of intermittent certainty. A continuous one creates a rhythm of sustained partial presence. Neither is universally superior. The first may favour careful pattern recognition, lower infrastructure burden, and greater efficiency for some missions. The second may favour warning, cueing, and adaptation where events move too quickly for bursts to suffice. The wrong choice is not store-and-forward or continuous delivery. The wrong choice is mismatching either to a decision cycle while continuing to speak as though the fit were obvious.

The harder question, then, is not whether Arctic architectures should aspire to more continuous delivery. Many will, and often with good reason. The more serious question is what happens when a burst-based system is asked to support an urgent decision, or when a continuous system produces a stream faster than confidence can travel with it. Which clock is the mission actually living on, and has anyone been honest about whether the architecture serves that clock - or merely looks modern while the decisive interval slips away?

Onboard and edge processing trade-offs

In February 2022, as commercial satellite imagery and derived alerts flowed around the war in Ukraine, one fact became harder to ignore: some of the most operationally useful products were no longer raw images at all. They were detections, classifications, change flags, and compressed judgements produced before a human analyst had examined the full scene in detail. The gain was obvious. Information moved faster. The harder question followed immediately. What, exactly, had travelled so quickly: evidence, interpretation, or an automated guess dressed in operational urgency?

The Arctic turns that question into a structural one. Distance, sparse ground infrastructure, difficult communications, and short decision windows all reward any architecture that can reduce what must be transmitted and shorten the path from sensing to use. Processing nearer to the sensor - onboard the spacecraft or at the edge of the network close to collection - promises exactly that. Instead of sending every raw pixel or full radar dataset to the ground, the system can detect anomalies, crop scenes, rank targets, compress outputs, or generate alerts before the data begins its longer journey. Bandwidth is saved. Latency falls. The product arrives sooner. Yet the very act of making the product lighter and faster also makes it more interpretive.

That is the central trade-off. Show a satellite over the High North collecting a large radar scene of maritime traffic and ice. If the spacecraft or a nearby edge processor sends the entire raw or lightly processed dataset to ground, users preserve a richer evidentiary record but accept more transmission burden and more delay. If the same system extracts only likely vessel contacts, suspicious changes, or pre-ranked areas of interest, it can move knowledge far more quickly through constrained links. Name the concept properly and one sees that onboard or edge processing is not merely efficiency. It is the relocation of analytic judgement closer to the moment of collection. Explain why that matters, and the implication becomes political as well as technical. The faster product may arrive before confidence has caught up with it.

A filter changes the story. That is the quiet motif worth keeping in view. Raw data, however imperfect, still allows later users to ask their own questions of the scene. A filtered product has already answered some questions in advance and perhaps discarded information judged less important. In the Arctic, that can be a profound advantage. A ship contact extracted quickly from a broad SAR scene may be operationally worth far more than a complete dataset that arrives too late to cue action. A thermal anomaly near remote infrastructure may matter because it is identified and transmitted as an alert rather than buried in a larger file waiting its turn for downlink. But every filter embodies assumptions. It decides what counts as signal, what counts as noise, and what does not need to travel.

This is why processing near the sensor should be understood not only as a communications solution but as an epistemic one. It changes the relationship between evidence and conclusion. In a conventional pipeline, raw data or minimally processed products reach the ground, where human analysts, broader archives, and institutional checks shape the judgement. In an onboard or edge-heavy model, some part of that judgement has already been made before the full evidentiary field is available to those humans or institutions. The Arctic rewards this move because it punishes delay. It also makes the move more consequential because corroboration is often sparse, local follow-up costly, and conditions too difficult for casual second chances.

A useful example can be drawn from maritime surveillance workflows using synthetic aperture radar. A full SAR scene over northern waters may be large, complex, and rich in ambiguous surface information: vessels, rough seas, ice edge features, leads, wind patterns, clutter, and infrastructural traces may all live together in the same dataset. Sending the whole scene preserves analytic depth. Running detection models near the sensor or immediately after downlink and sending only likely contacts, ranked anomalies, or clipped cut-outs can dramatically shorten the time to operational attention. That is immensely valuable when a coastguard or maritime centre needs first notice. But it also narrows what downstream users can inspect. If the algorithm has misunderstood surface conditions or misclassified an ice feature as a contact, the faster product will have accelerated not only attention but also error.

A second example comes from wildfire and thermal anomaly detection in remote northern regions. Systems that process thermal data close to collection can flag likely hotspots, heat signatures, or unusual activity patterns and transmit these compact alerts far more quickly than full imagery products. For fire monitoring, infrastructure watch, or emergency response, this can be indispensable. A prompt alert may preserve time that a larger file would waste. Yet even here the burden of verification remains. A heat anomaly may indicate combustion, industrial activity, sun-heated surfaces, sensor artefact, or something else entirely depending on context and environmental conditions. The system has moved from seeing to suggesting, and the suggestion can outrun the institution's ability to confirm it.

That is why speed and interpretability often compete rather than simply reinforce one another. Speed favours reduction: fewer bits, fewer products, fewer human steps, more direct pathways to action. Interpretability favours retention: richer context, fuller scene access, preserved metadata, visible processing history, and more room for alternative readings. In the Arctic, where the costs of delay are real, the temptation to side with speed is strong. But a fast product that cannot later be explained, challenged, or reconstructed can create a different kind of vulnerability. It may support warning while weakening accountability. It may cue action while complicating attribution. It may save bandwidth while eroding institutional confidence in what exactly the system has done.

This becomes especially important once automation is involved. Onboard and edge processing increasingly draw on classification, segmentation, anomaly detection, and prioritisation routines that can be highly effective in narrowing attention. None of this is inherently suspect. It is, in many settings, essential. But automated products should not be confused with raw truth simply because they arrive early. An automatically generated vessel list, a change-detection flag over snow-covered infrastructure, or a ranked anomaly map of a northern coastline is already an interpretation. The algorithm has imposed categories, thresholds, and exclusions. A system that forgets this may mistake computational confidence for evidentiary confidence.

A credible limitation should be admitted. Not every mission needs to preserve full interpretability at every stage. Search and rescue, maritime cueing, broad anomaly watch, and some forms of early warning may benefit enormously from rapid, reduced products even if those products require later confirmation. In such missions, a fast imperfect alert can be more valuable than a perfect late one. The Arctic often makes this brutally true. A vessel in difficulty, a fleeting contact, a transient opening in ice, or an emerging thermal anomaly may require attention before the best possible explanation is available. Delay can be its own form of error.

But the concession reinforces the deeper point. The right question is not whether onboard or edge processing is good. It is what kind of decision it is being used to support, and whether the institution using it is honest about the confidence the resulting product can bear. A fast contact cue may be fit for retasking another asset and unfit for public accusation. A change flag may justify closer scrutiny and not justify operational escalation. A compact onboard classification may be perfect for bandwidth-constrained triage and entirely inadequate as the sole basis for a contested judgement. Once this is admitted, speed can be treated as one design objective among others rather than as a universal virtue.

The problem sharpens further when accountability enters. A human analyst receiving a raw or minimally processed product can inspect context, question anomalies, compare with archives, and reconstruct why a judgement was reached. A user receiving an onboard-derived alert or pre-classified output may know the result without fully seeing the path that produced it. That opacity is not always fatal. It is often manageable. But it changes the burden of proof. If a fast product triggers a significant decision - a route diversion, a cueing request, a public statement, a military posture change - then someone may later need to explain how the product was made, what confidence attached to it, and what information was discarded in the name of speed. An architecture that cannot answer those questions has bought timeliness at the price of retrospective fragility.

This is why verification burdens rise as processing moves closer to the sensor. The earlier a system interprets, the more carefully downstream institutions must understand what has been interpreted away. Verification may require audit trails, retained raw subsets, confidence scores that mean something operational, model performance knowledge under Arctic conditions, or deliberate preservation of enough contextual data that humans can challenge automated conclusions. None of this eliminates the advantage of near-sensor processing. It simply recognises that automated outputs can move faster than organisational trust in them. The travel time of the product and the travel time of confidence are not the same.

The queue returns here in a transformed form. Traditional pipelines queue large files for downlink and processing. Onboard and edge architectures try to shorten those queues by sending smaller, more refined products. Yet they may create a new queue elsewhere: a queue of products awaiting validation, a queue of alerts needing contextual interpretation, a queue of users asking whether the machine's threshold should really have been trusted in this particular environmental setting. The bottleneck does not disappear. It changes shape. The Arctic, with its severe backgrounds and sparse corroboration, makes that change unusually visible.

Trust reveals itself in behaviour again. Operators trust onboard-processed products when they act on them quickly as cues without demanding the full scene first. Analysts trust edge-generated outputs when they know enough about the pipeline to judge what the automation has preserved and what it has omitted. Institutions distrust them when they treat every fast output as provisional until a richer product arrives, or when they maintain parallel workflows because the automated chain is quicker than it is intelligible. These patterns tell the truth about how much interpretive compression a system can bear before its users begin to worry more about what was discarded than about what was saved.

A useful counter-example lies in very narrow and stable mission domains where the target class is well understood and the cost of occasional error is relatively low. In such contexts, onboard filtering and alert generation can perform brilliantly with modest interpretive risk. But Arctic surveillance rarely enjoys such simplicity for long. Its scenes are seasonally unstable, its backgrounds complex, its corroboration expensive, and its consequences unevenly distributed across safety, science, commerce, and security. That is why the same algorithmic confidence that feels well earned in one domain can feel precarious in another. Near the pole, the environment itself becomes part of the verification problem.

The filter returns at the end because it captures the full dilemma. A filter helps because without it too much may travel too slowly. A filter threatens because once applied, some possibilities no longer travel at all. The harder question is therefore not whether systems should process more near the sensor. Many will, and some must. The more serious question is what kind of Arctic knowledge can safely be filtered for speed without losing the context required to trust it later. When an automated product arrives early, what has actually reached the user first: the event, the interpretation, or the institution's willingness to live temporarily without knowing which is which?

Fusion with airborne, surface, and undersea sensing

In March 2014, as the search for Malaysia Airlines Flight 370 widened across sea and sky, one lesson became impossible to ignore: no single sensor was enough. Satellite handshakes narrowed possibilities. Aircraft searched broad sectors. Ships followed leads that emerged from a mixture of remote sensing, communications analysis, and maritime movement. The search did not fail because there was too little data in the abstract. It struggled because different data arrived on different clocks, in different forms, and with different degrees of confidence. A coherent picture had to be made. It did not arrive ready-made.

The Arctic lives inside that same truth, only more persistently. A satellite may detect a vessel-like contact in difficult weather. A patrol aircraft may later see nothing because the contact has moved or conditions have changed. A maritime transmitter may appear absent, misleadingly present, or simply late. An underwater acoustic hint may suggest activity without identifying it. None of these sources is meaningless. None is complete. The region insists that awareness be assembled from fragments whose value depends less on their individual brilliance than on how well they can be aligned.

This is why fusion matters. Not as a fashionable word for putting everything into the same software environment, but as the disciplined work of deciding which observations belong to the same event, which do not, and what confidence should attach to the combination. Show the Arctic honestly and one sees very quickly that satellites alone do not produce awareness. They produce views, detections, hints, intervals, and anomalies. Name the next step properly and it becomes integration across airborne, surface, and undersea sensing. Explain why this matters, and the implication is strategic rather than merely technical. A state that cannot align its sources may own many sensors and still remain slow, hesitant, or wrong.

The temptation is to describe fusion as if it were additive. More sources, more certainty. Sometimes that is true. Often it is not so simple. Different systems observe different things on different clocks and with different assumptions built into their outputs. A satellite image may carry strong spatial information and weak immediacy by the time it arrives. A patrol aircraft may provide direct visual confirmation and only for the narrow sector it actually reached. A ship's own transmissions may offer identity and route claims while saying little about what is happening nearby. An undersea sensor may register movement or sound without offering the kind of attribution a policymaker craves. Fusion is not a pile. It is a test of compatibility.

A contact becomes a case. That is the quiet motif worth following through this part of the argument. A bright radar return in a SAR scene is not yet a case. It becomes one when it is compared with maritime tracks, past movement, air patrol observations, weather, ice state, and whatever other evidence can bear weight. The case may strengthen or collapse. It may sharpen into likely identification or dissolve into clutter, timing mismatch, or environmental ambiguity. In the Arctic, where follow-up is costly and the scene rarely waits politely for confirmation, this transformation from contact to case is often the real work of surveillance.

Synthetic aperture radar offers the clearest example because it is so central to Arctic observation and yet so often incomplete by itself. SAR can detect ships, changes in sea ice, surface disturbances, and suspicious patterns under darkness and cloud. It is indispensable. It is also rarely the final word. A SAR detection over northern waters may indicate a probable vessel or anomaly, but the decision-maker still wants to know whether it corresponds to known maritime traffic, whether an aircraft or coastal radar has seen the same object, whether AIS data supports or complicates the interpretation, and whether the timing of all these sources actually overlaps closely enough to make comparison honest. The image is persuasive. The case requires more.

A practical example can be imagined without strain because it resembles what maritime centres confront repeatedly. A SAR pass detects an object near the edge of broken ice in waters where traffic is sparse. The return is strong enough to justify attention. A maritime traffic system shows no declared vessel at that exact point, but a nearby track appears several minutes older than the radar scene. An aircraft report later notes disturbed water and possible wake, though visibility is poor. A coastguard cutter receives the product after the contact has shifted again. None of these observations is false. The difficulty lies in deciding whether they describe one vessel, two, or a sensor artefact joined too eagerly to an unrelated track. Fusion is the act of refusing premature certainty while still making the best possible operational judgement.

Airborne sensing adds a particularly interesting tension because it often feels more direct than satellite data while remaining subject to its own severe limits. Aircraft can provide rapid visual or radar confirmation, lower-angle perspective, and flexible tasking once cued. In the Arctic, that makes them valuable partners to space-based observation. Yet aircraft do not hover without cost. They depend on weather, range, crew limits, basing, and their own timing windows. A satellite detection may cue an aircraft beautifully if the product arrives in time. If the aircraft reaches the area after the scene has shifted, the absence of confirmation may say more about latency than about the original detection. Integration therefore requires humility. Later silence does not always invalidate earlier sensing.

Surface sources complicate the picture further. Ships, buoys, coastal installations, and maritime reporting systems bring information rooted in proximity rather than altitude. They can offer contextual knowledge satellite systems often lack: local weather, direct sightings, acoustic cues, traffic behaviour, ice conditions experienced rather than inferred. But they also produce data in formats and temporal rhythms very different from overhead systems. A maritime reporting feed may update on one schedule, a radar image on another, and a shipboard observation in prose rather than machine-readable coordinates. The result is that fusion often fails not because sources disagree conceptually, but because they do not line up cleanly enough in format or timing for the system to compare them without friction.

Undersea sensing pushes this challenge to its most austere form. Acoustic detections, undersea monitoring systems, and submarine-adjacent intelligence rarely provide the sort of crisp visual evidence that public imagination associates with surveillance. They can suggest movement, presence, or environmental disturbance without resolving identity or even precise location in ways other systems would find comfortable. In the Arctic, where undersea conditions matter strategically and where the water column is not a transparent medium for ordinary observation, such sensing can be highly consequential. It can also be deeply difficult to integrate with surface and space-based sources. A sound, a track, a heat anomaly, a radar detection, a declared vessel route, and a satellite image do not naturally belong to one another simply because analysts wish them to.

This is why alignment challenges deserve more emphasis than they usually receive. Timing is the first and most obvious. Sources separated by minutes may describe the same event or miss it entirely, depending on how fast the object or condition changes. Geolocation is the next pressure point. A position derived from one system may not align precisely with another because each carries its own uncertainty, projection, or reference frame. Format follows close behind. One system may output machine-readable tracks; another may generate imagery products; another may offer operator notes; another may provide alerts stripped of context for the sake of speed. The more heterogeneous the inputs, the more fusion becomes a practice of translation as much as of analysis.

The strategic importance of this is easy to miss because the word "fusion" sounds reassuring. It suggests synthesis, convergence, maturity. Yet bad fusion can be worse than isolated uncertainty because it hides mismatch under the appearance of coherence. A contact that seems corroborated by three systems may in fact be three loosely related observations whose timing and geolocation were never close enough to justify the confidence placed in the merge. A maritime anomaly may harden into an intelligence narrative because software linked records that a careful human would have kept apart. A weak undersea indication may receive unwarranted weight when paired with a satellite image whose scene was already stale. The Arctic punishes this especially hard because correction is slow and the cost of chasing the wrong integrated picture can be high.

A credible limitation should be admitted. Fusion is not always necessary, and not every task benefits from it. A single high-confidence optical image under good summer conditions may answer a straightforward question more cleanly than an elaborate multi-source product. A direct radar detection may be enough to prompt a routine maritime check without requiring the whole architecture to awaken. Over-integration can waste time, create false expectations of perfect coherence, and burden users with complexity beyond what the decision requires. The best systems know when not to fuse.

But that concession strengthens the main argument. The reason fusion should be used selectively is precisely because it is work, not magic. It should be applied where the decision needs a stronger case than any one source can provide. In the Arctic, those moments are common because the environment strips every sensor of some degree of completeness. Space systems bring reach. Aircraft bring adaptability. Surface systems bring local context. Undersea sensing brings access to a domain the others only infer. Awareness worthy of the name often emerges not from any one of them, but from the careful alignment of several under explicit acknowledgement of what still remains uncertain.

This is also where trust becomes visible in operational conduct. Analysts trust fusion when they know the system's alignment rules, uncertainty handling, and timing tolerances well enough to accept a combined product without treating it as decorative. Operators trust it when they act on a fused picture rather than on the raw source that first caught attention. Institutions distrust it when they insist on manual cross-checks for every serious case, or when they quietly revert to source-by-source judgement because the integrated picture arrives looking smoother than it deserves. These behaviours reveal whether integration has become a true capability or merely a software promise.

A useful counter-example lies in tightly controlled environments with common standards, shared timing, and a limited set of mission sources. Under such conditions, fusion can become highly reliable and relatively fast because the inputs are designed to belong to one another. The Arctic is moving in that direction in some sectors, but not nearly enough to erase the broader problem. Much of northern awareness still depends on sources owned by different institutions, built for different purposes, and delivered under different governance rules. Shared timelines, common geospatial standards, and explicit uncertainty handling remain uneven. That unevenness is part of the reality the analyst inherits.

The contact returns here because it reminds us what the system is really trying to do. A contact in a SAR image, a report from a patrol aircraft, a vessel transmission, an acoustic hint from below, a thermal anomaly, a weather note from a ship, a coastline radar track - these are all fragments until somebody decides whether they belong together. The decision is both analytic and political. Merge too little and the system remains blind in pieces. Merge too much and it begins to hallucinate coherence. Arctic awareness lives in the uneasy skill of navigating between those errors.

That is why the deepest claim of this section is not technological but epistemic. The Arctic is not watched by single sensors but by chains of comparison. The quality of awareness depends on how honestly those comparisons handle timing, geolocation, formats, and uncertainty rather than on how many sources can be named in a briefing. A fused picture should be understood as a negotiated product, not a natural one. The more complex the mix of space, air, surface, and undersea sensing, the more necessary that honesty becomes.

The harder question, then, is not whether fusion can make Arctic surveillance stronger. It often can. The more serious question is when the integration is good enough that several partial truths become one better case, and when it merely compresses their uncertainties into a single confident-looking output. When a SAR detection seems to line up with a maritime track and an airborne observation, what exactly has been matched: one event across several domains, or several approximations arranged into a story because the system needed coherence faster than the Arctic was willing to provide it?

Metrics for timeliness and uncertainty

In March 2021, when satellite images of the *Ever Given* blocking the Suez Canal circulated with remarkable speed, public discussion settled quickly on a familiar impression: modern observation had become nearly instantaneous. The image seemed to prove that the world could now be seen and understood almost as events unfolded. What that impression concealed was more instructive than the picture itself. The image had been collected, transmitted, processed, selected, and interpreted on a chain of different clocks, each with its own delays and thresholds. The speed that mattered was not one speed.

The Arctic punishes any language that forgets this. A system may collect quickly and still fail to deliver quickly. It may deliver quickly and still fail to become understandable quickly. It may even produce a rapid alert that satisfies an operations centre while remaining too uncertain for a public claim or a sovereign response. Once one looks north, the need for a more honest vocabulary becomes obvious. Words such as *fast*, *timely*, *persistent*, and *near real time* are not wrong, but they are too loose to compare systems whose strengths lie in different parts of the chain. A region this difficult to watch forces a stricter account of what kind of speed is actually being claimed.

That stricter account begins by splitting latency into parts. Show a satellite architecture to a policymaker and the first question is often, "How quickly can it see?" Name that measure properly and one has time-to-collect: the interval between a requirement arising and the moment the sensor actually gathers the relevant data. Explain why this does not settle the matter, and the reason becomes painfully clear. Collection is only the beginning of usefulness. A contact can be observed promptly and still remain unavailable to anyone who might act on it. The implication is straightforward. A system with impressive collection timing may still be slow in the only sense the user ultimately cares about.

Time-to-deliver is therefore a different and indispensable measure. It asks how long it takes for the collected product to reach the person, platform, or institution that needs it. That interval includes downlink, relay, processing queues, formatting, routing, and dissemination. It is often where lofty claims begin to wilt. A radar image of a ship near ice edge may be collected at exactly the right moment and delivered too late to cue an aircraft or redirect a vessel. That is not a minor imperfection. It means the system has changed categories from operational surveillance to retrospective evidence. Time-to-deliver reveals this shift more honestly than any generic boast about responsiveness.

A third measure matters just as much, though it is the one institutions discuss least comfortably: time-to-understand. A product may have been collected and delivered with admirable speed, yet still require interpretation before it can support a meaningful decision. A raw SAR scene, a thermal anomaly, a fused product from multiple sources, or a machine-generated alert may all arrive "on time" in the narrow delivery sense and remain analytically immature. Time-to-understand is the interval between receipt and the point at which a user can say, with appropriate confidence, what the observation means for the decision in front of them. This measure is often slower, messier, and more human than organisations like to admit. It is also one of the most important.

A clock can lie. That is the motif worth keeping in view. One clock may measure when the satellite passed overhead. Another may mark when the file arrived. A third may begin only when the analyst has enough context to trust what the file is actually showing. Institutions often quote the first two because they are cleaner and easier to defend. The third is where operational truth tends to live. The Arctic exposes the difference because environmental ambiguity, sparse corroboration, and the cost of false confidence all lengthen the time between possession of data and possession of meaning. A system can therefore look fast on paper and still feel slow in practice.

This distinction matters because organisations regularly optimise one metric while neglecting the others. A satellite operator may reduce time-to-collect by proliferating sensors and improving tasking. A communications architecture may cut time-to-deliver with relay, crosslinks, or faster downlink. A processing pipeline may produce quick alerts that appear to compress time-to-understand. Each gain can be real. Each can also create a new blind spot if the system's users then assume that the other measures improved by the same amount. They often do not. The result is institutional self-deception. A service described as "rapid" may only be rapid at one stage and merely adequate, or even poor, at the stage the mission actually depends on.

A practical comparison makes the point clearer. Consider a broad-area maritime surveillance system built around fast SAR collection and prompt downlink to a polar station. Its time-to-collect may be strong, and its time-to-deliver may be respectable. But if the resulting detections still require laborious comparison with maritime tracks, weather, ice state, and previous passes before anyone can decide whether the contact matters, then time-to-understand remains the dominant measure. By contrast, a simpler optical scene of a ship in open summer water may take longer to obtain because cloud and light are less forgiving, yet once delivered it may be understood almost immediately by human observers. One system is faster in one sense, the other in another. Honest comparison begins only when the senses are separated.

A second example lies in environmental monitoring. A store-and-forward system may collect and deliver sea-ice or coastal change imagery too slowly for rapid operational manoeuvre and still be excellent for weekly route planning, seasonal assessment, or legal documentation after an incident. In that context, time-to-collect and time-to-deliver may matter less than the stability, comparability, and interpretability of the final product. A decision-maker who confuses those mission clocks may dismiss a useful system as "too slow" or, equally badly, overestimate a fast alerting system whose outputs are poor at durable understanding. Metrics are not neutral. They teach institutions what to value and what to ignore.

Uncertainty should be described with the same discipline. Here too the temptation is to collapse many different conditions into one flattering or alarming phrase. A system may be uncertain because the image is coarse, because timing alignment is weak, because the geolocation margin is broader than the user would like, because the environment is ambiguous, or because the analytic output has been filtered heavily by automated processing. These are not interchangeable kinds of doubt. The more useful question is: uncertain about what? Detection, identification, tracking, attribution, timeliness, or the fit between the product and the decision? The Arctic demands this precision because false certainty and false pessimism are both costly.

One helpful way to talk about uncertainty without pretending to impossible exactness is to distinguish between observation confidence and decision confidence. Observation confidence concerns the product itself: how strongly the system supports the claim that something was seen, located, or measured. Decision confidence concerns what action or judgement the institution feels entitled to make on the basis of that product in context. The distinction matters. A SAR system may provide high observation confidence that a contact exists and low decision confidence about what that contact is without corroboration. A thermal alert may provide moderate observation confidence and still trigger a high-confidence choice to task another asset because the threshold for cueing is deliberately lower than the threshold for public accusation. Once this language is adopted, organisations become less tempted to hide different doubts inside one vague expression.

A credible limitation has to be acknowledged. No metric system, however careful, can fully capture the lived messiness of Arctic operations. Decisions are shaped by judgement, politics, training, institutional culture, available alternatives, and the simple fact that users do not always need the same kind of clarity at the same moment. There will always be cases where a formally slower system proves more useful because its outputs are trusted, or where a fast product matters precisely because it arrives before its uncertainties are fully resolved. Metrics should not pretend to automate common sense.

But that concession reinforces the deeper value of disciplined language. The point of distinguishing time-to-collect, time-to-deliver, and time-to-understand is not to turn surveillance into a spreadsheet. It is to stop institutions from flattering themselves with single-clock stories. The point of distinguishing observation confidence from decision confidence is not to weaken action with academic caution. It is to make clear which stage of uncertainty the organisation is actually choosing to live with. In a region where delays hide in mundane queues and confidence erodes in subtle environmental conditions, this honesty is not bureaucratic decoration. It is part of strategic competence.

The usefulness of these distinctions appears in behaviour. An operator who says a system is "timely" should be able to say for which of the three clocks.

An analyst who says a product is "good enough" should be able to say for which class of decision. A command structure that prizes reduced time-to-deliver without measuring time-to-understand may discover that it has merely accelerated confusion. Another that insists on very high decision confidence for every product may quietly sacrifice opportunities where lower-confidence cues were enough to justify follow-on collection. Metrics do not solve these trade-offs. They make them visible.

This is why vocabulary matters more than it first appears. Systems are often compared through the most flattering number or the most convenient anecdote. One architecture claims revisit. Another claims rapid delivery. A third claims automated alerts. Without a language that separates clocks and kinds of confidence, these claims become almost impossible to compare honestly. The Arctic, with its severe penalties for misplaced optimism and its equally real penalties for excessive caution, is exactly the place where this language is needed most.

The clock returns at the end because it reminds us what institutions most want to avoid admitting: they often optimise the wrong minute. They reduce the time to collect while neglecting the time to deliver. They accelerate delivery while leaving understanding trapped in backlogs, opaque models, or cross-domain misalignment. They seek cleaner confidence scores while losing sight of the fact that decisions live in thresholds, not in perfect knowledge. The harder question, then, is not whether a system is fast or trustworthy in general. It is which clock it has mastered, which kind of uncertainty it has actually reduced, and whether the people depending on it know the difference before the Arctic teaches it to them the hard way.

Chapter 9

Dual-use Constellations and Procurement

What does a state really buy when it buys access to a constellation it does not fully control? The question sounds like procurement language until a crisis begins, imagery appears, and attention turns to who can task the sensor, who receives the product first, and who decides whether the picture stays private, enters a marketplace, or becomes part of a diplomatic narrative. A satellite may orbit above everyone. The rights around it do not.

This is the Arctic version of a broader strategic shift. Space capability no longer sits neatly inside one ministry, one chain of command, or one sovereign industrial base. Commercial imagery providers, analytics firms, hosted payload arrangements, shared buses, common ground segments, and mixed civil-security service models have altered the old picture of national ownership. The change is not merely economic. It has reorganised how visibility itself is produced. A state may possess excellent access without owning the platform. Another may own the platform and still discover that the decisive form of control lies elsewhere - in tasking priority, contractual exclusivity, or the authority to release an image into public view.

The market changed the map. That is the quiet fact under the chapter's argument. High-latitude observation used to depend more obviously on scarce national assets and slower institutional pathways. Now a wider set of actors can obtain imagery, analytics, and derived products from constellations built for mixed purposes and funded through mixed logics. The practical gain is undeniable. More eyes, more iteration, more frequent collection, more avenues for corroboration, and often faster public visibility when something happens in the Arctic. Yet every gain arrives with a harder question. If access widens, who remains able to narrow it at the moment that matters most?

That is the chapter's central tension. Dual-use architectures accelerate capability while redistributing control. They make surveillance more available and more politically entangled at the same time. A commercial provider can support public transparency, allied reassurance, market demand, scientific use, and security-driven tasking without cleanly separating those functions. A hosted payload can give one mission rapid access to space while embedding it inside infrastructure whose priorities are shared, negotiated, or only partly visible. Technical architecture and institutional choice stop being separate stories. The design is already a politics.

The stakes are larger than procurement in the narrow sense. Arctic surveillance does not only inform operations; it shapes expectations, narratives, and red lines. A rapidly released image can harden an interpretation before slower institutions have caught up. A buyer with priority tasking can concentrate attention on a sensitive area and thereby signal concern, resolve, or suspicion without moving a ship or aircraft. A market that seems open can still distribute awareness unevenly because some actors purchase speed, exclusivity, or analytic depth that others cannot. The result is that visibility itself becomes part of statecraft, even when the infrastructure carrying it is commercial in form.

This matters because persistence is never neutral once it is shared across markets and missions. A constellation serving fisheries, shipping, climate analysis, insurance, media, and defence does not produce one kind of Arctic knowledge that everyone then interprets identically. It produces a field of possible observations whose access rules, tasking rights, and release practices affect how incidents are perceived. One actor may see a deterrent signal in concentrated monitoring. Another may see provocation. One may call public imagery transparency. Another may experience it as narrative foreclosure, the moment a contested event hardens into a near-irreversible story before the slower work of verification has finished.

The path ahead begins with commercial imagery and analytic marketplaces, where scale and rapid iteration have widened Arctic visibility while creating new dependencies and asymmetries of access. It then moves into hosted payloads and shared infrastructure, where speed of capability acquisition is purchased alongside more layered governance, before turning to the sharper questions of tasking rights, exclusivity, and what "open" access actually means when priority can be bought or withheld. From there the argument rises into signalling itself, where persistent watching ceases to be mere collection and becomes part of how states reassure, deter, accuse, or unsettle one another.

A quiet motif runs through all of this: the lease. Not because every arrangement is literally contractual in the same way, but because so much of modern Arctic surveillance now operates through leased attention, leased access, leased infrastructure, leased priority, or leased speed. A lease can be efficient, flexible, and rational. It can also leave the tenant discovering, at exactly the wrong moment, which rights were assumed and which were never really theirs.

The harder question, then, is not whether dual-use constellations have made Arctic awareness more available. They plainly have. The more serious question is what kind of control survives once visibility is purchased, shared, hosted, prioritised, and sometimes publicly released through systems whose logic is neither purely commercial nor purely sovereign. When an Arctic incident sharpens and multiple actors reach for the same orbital attention at once, who is actually exercising power: the one who owns the satellite, the one who pays for the tasking, the one who controls release, or the one who gets there first in the market for interpretation?

Commercial imagery and analytic marketplaces

In March 2021, when Maxar released satellite images of the *Ever Given* jammed across the Suez Canal, the event became more than a maritime accident and more than a logistics story. It became a demonstration of how commercial space firms had changed the public life of remote sensing. A private company could collect, process, and distribute imagery quickly enough to shape how governments, markets, journalists, and ordinary readers understood an unfolding disruption. The Arctic has absorbed that same change, with even sharper consequences, because visibility there is scarce enough, politically charged enough, and technically difficult enough that whoever can supply credible images and derived analysis may end up shaping not only knowledge but the tempo of response.

This is not simply a story of more pictures from more satellites. Commercial providers have altered access to high-latitude observation by changing the rhythm, scale, and social location of imagery itself. What was once more tightly held inside national systems or specialist institutions now circulates through a marketplace of collection, processing, analytics, and subscription-based interpretation. A government ministry, a shipping firm, a research institute, a newsroom, an insurer, and a military customer may all draw, in different ways and under different terms, from overlapping commercial infrastructures. The result is not full democratisation. That word flatters the system too much. But it is a real widening of visibility, and one whose implications for Arctic politics are difficult to overstate.

The market changed the witness. That is the central point. A satellite image used to arrive more obviously as a state product, a classified asset, or a specialist scientific output. Now it may arrive as a purchased service, a commercial feed, an analytic dashboard, a licensed archive, or a public release timed for maximum narrative effect. Show an Arctic incident under this new regime and the actors multiply at once. The state is no longer the only one who can see, nor always the first one who can interpret publicly. Name the shift properly and one sees that commercial imagery and analytics have created not merely a new source of data, but a new layer of witness in Arctic affairs. Explain why that matters, and the implication becomes strategic. Markets do not merely reflect security demand. They increasingly shape how that demand is met, timed, and perceived.

The benefits are substantial and should be granted plainly. Commercial providers have often moved faster than public procurement cycles, expanded constellation scale more flexibly, and improved revisit, product diversity, and analytic tooling through repeated iteration. In Arctic use, this can mean more frequent observation of shipping corridors, infrastructure zones, ice conditions, environmental disturbances, and sensitive coastal activity than many states could have achieved alone at the same pace. It can also mean that smaller states, civilian agencies, and non-state actors gain forms of visibility that were once available only to larger powers with dedicated national assets. For a region where remoteness historically protected ambiguity, commercial imagery can compress the distance between event and shared awareness.

This is why commercial services have become attractive not only because they are cheaper or quicker to procure, but because they alter the structure of dependence. A state with limited sovereign collection can still purchase access to a high-latitude imagery stream. An analyst who does not control a sensor can still obtain a subscription to derivative products that flag vessel patterns, change over time, or potential anomalies. A humanitarian or environmental actor can assemble a picture of Arctic developments without waiting for a government to choose disclosure. In such cases, scale matters less as a statistic than as a behavioural change: more actors can watch more often, and some can do so without first persuading a state apparatus to care.

Planet's daily imaging model is one useful public example because it helped normalise the idea that commercial constellations could turn repeated observation into an ordinary service rather than an occasional luxury. The value of such architectures in the Arctic does not lie in any fantasy of perfect constant watch. It lies in the way repeat access reshapes what becomes difficult to hide for long: infrastructure expansion, route use, coastal change, seasonal activity patterns, some classes of environmental disruption, and the tempo of presence itself. A state or company purchasing such a service is not buying omniscience. It is buying a denser baseline against which deviation becomes more visible.

A second example lies in the commercial SAR sector, where providers have extended all-weather, day-night observation into markets once dominated more strongly by state systems. This matters especially in the Arctic because optical visibility remains so seasonally fragile. When commercial radar imagery and analytic products enter maritime monitoring, ice observation, and infrastructure watchfulness, they do more than fill a niche. They change who can plausibly claim to possess evidence under difficult conditions. A suspicious contact in darkness or cloud may now be observed, processed, and circulated through a commercial chain quickly enough to influence public or intergovernmental discussion before slower institutions have consolidated their own reading. The market thus changes not only access, but sequencing.

Yet the advantages come with dependencies that must not be softened into polite afterthoughts. Commercial availability is not the same thing as equal availability. Access depends on contracts, licensing, tasking rights, delivery tiers, analytic subscriptions, and the often quiet hierarchy between ordinary customers and premium or government ones. One actor may receive raw imagery, another only processed alerts, another neither unless a reseller or public release opens the door. Even ostensibly open markets distribute awareness unevenly because money, regulatory relationships, institutional priority, and geographic familiarity all influence who can use the products well and quickly. Commercial visibility is wider than old sovereign exclusivity. It is not flat.

A subscription is not sovereignty. That short sentence helps keep the argument honest. A state may buy commercial imagery and still remain dependent on a firm's tasking logic, station network, processing priorities, export rules, and willingness or ability to serve under pressure. A smaller government or civil agency may find that it has access to products but little real influence over where sensors are pointed during moments of congestion. An allied state may discover that commercial contracts do not perfectly substitute for sovereign tasking when the scene becomes politically delicate. Dependency here is not simply technical. It is institutional and temporal: who gets the first look, the fuller product, the fastest analytic layer, or the right to keep a collection private for long enough to decide how to use it.

This is where commercial imagery begins to shape diplomatic narratives and crisis visibility directly. Publicly released imagery can settle certain kinds of argument before governments have finished their own slower work of verification, qualification, or strategic silence. An image of a vessel in a sensitive Arctic waterway, a construction change at a northern site, a spill, a fire, an unusual concentration of activity, or a route through contested ice can harden interpretation rapidly once it circulates through media and policy networks. The image need not prove everything to become politically decisive. It only needs to become the most legible evidence available in the first hours of attention. Commercial providers, by choosing what to release, how to annotate it, and when to circulate it, can therefore influence not only what is seen but how quickly a narrative begins to set.

This influence is not always intentional in a strategic sense. Markets reward visibility, responsiveness, and product relevance. Firms publish compelling imagery because compelling imagery demonstrates value. Analysts package findings because usable analysis is easier to buy than raw complexity. But once the Arctic is involved, where state sensitivities are high and public evidence is comparatively scarce, commercial timing acquires geopolitical weight whether or not the provider seeks that role. A private release can reassure, embarrass, accuse, or accelerate demands for explanation. It can help deter by making activities visible. It can also provoke by collapsing ambiguity faster than diplomacy can metabolise it.

A credible limitation belongs here. Commercial imagery and analytics do not replace sovereign systems, nor do they render states passive in the face of market power. Governments still regulate, procure, classify, task, and withhold. They can become anchor customers, shape standards, restrict exports, and absorb commercial outputs into larger intelligence architectures that remain state-directed. It would be careless to write as though the market had simply displaced public authority. Much commercial success in this field depends precisely on government demand, state tolerance, or direct public partnership.

But the concession sharpens the deeper point. The relationship between markets and security demand is interactive, not hierarchical in one direction. Security institutions buy commercial products because markets have become capable and flexible. Markets become more capable and flexible because security and adjacent public demand reward those traits. Civil, scientific, journalistic, and commercial uses then benefit from infrastructures partially sustained by strategic appetites, while strategic actors in turn find that they are operating in a visibility environment shaped partly by non-state consumption and public release practices. One should not reduce one side to the other. The power of the present arrangement lies precisely in their entanglement.

This entanglement becomes especially important in the Arctic because perceptions of monitoring can matter almost as much as monitoring itself. A region believed to be watched by a dense commercial market is not politically the same as one believed to be visible only through a handful of sovereign systems. Expectations change. Denials become riskier. Surprise becomes harder to maintain in some domains and easier to stage-manage in others through selective release. A state may seek reassurance from commercial availability, alarm from the same availability when sensitive activities are exposed, or advantage from being able to purchase fast interpretation while others still wait for raw products. The market is not neutral territory. It is a shaping environment.

Trust, as ever, appears in behaviour. Governments trust commercial imagery when they cite it publicly, buy it for routine Arctic monitoring, or use it to supplement sovereign gaps without constant embarrassment about dependency. Analysts trust commercial analytic marketplaces when they treat derived products as worthy of early attention rather than mere marketing gloss. Institutions distrust them when they demand sovereign confirmation before every serious use, maintain parallel procurement as insurance, or speak about commercial products as "open" while quietly negotiating priority rights unavailable to ordinary customers. These patterns reveal the real settlement between market visibility and state confidence.

The subscription returns as a motif because it captures both the power and the limit of this new order. A subscription opens the stream. It does not guarantee equal command over the stream's direction, timing, or public life. One can buy access without owning precedence. One can receive imagery without controlling release. One can depend on a provider while never quite knowing how the provider's other customers, contracts, or political constraints will shape the next moment of scarcity. That is not a reason to dismiss commercial services. It is a reason to understand them as infrastructures of visibility with their own politics.

The harder question, then, is not whether commercial imagery and analytics have made the Arctic more visible. They plainly have. The more serious question is what kind of Arctic visibility they have created: one distributed more widely, timed more quickly, and narrated more publicly, but also tiered by contracts, influenced by release choices, and inseparable from the market logics that now help decide who sees first and who gets believed fastest. When the next Arctic incident sharpens into a diplomatic event, will the decisive witness be the state that owns the area, the state that owns the sensor, or the firm whose image enters the public imagination before either of them has decided how the story ought to be told?

Hosted payloads and shared infrastructure

In July 2022, NASA launched the Tropospheric Emissions: Monitoring of Pollution mission, or TEMPO, not as a free-standing satellite but as a hosted payload on a commercial communications platform. The arrangement was presented, rightly, as a practical success: faster access to orbit, lower duplication of effort, and a more efficient use of existing space infrastructure. Yet it also illustrated a harder truth that Arctic surveillance cannot evade. A mission may own its instrument and still not own the full environment in which that instrument lives, communicates, and competes for attention.

The old fantasy of neat separation no longer holds. Civil and security functions, public and private money, sovereign ambition and commercial service logic now meet inside shared buses, shared ground segments, shared communications links, and shared operational routines. That is not necessarily a problem. Often it is the reason capability appears at all. But when systems are shared, authority is also shared, or at least layered, and that means technical design begins to carry political meaning long before anyone writes a public doctrine about it.

This is the section's central tension. Hosted payloads and shared infrastructure accelerate capability while entangling control. Show a government, research agency, or security institution trying to acquire Arctic awareness quickly, and the attraction of riding on an existing satellite bus or using an already established ground network is immediate. Launch comes sooner. Costs are spread. Infrastructure that would take years to build from scratch is already there. Name the arrangement properly, however, and one sees more than efficiency. One sees a negotiated system of dependencies. Explain why that matters, and the implication becomes unavoidable: the architecture does not merely carry a mission. It distributes power inside it.

A seat on the bus. That is the quiet motif worth keeping in view. A hosted payload gains access to orbit by taking a seat on something larger, more established, and usually not built solely for its own priorities. The gain is real. A mission that might otherwise wait in procurement limbo or struggle to justify a dedicated spacecraft can begin collecting sooner and more regularly. In the Arctic, where conditions change fast and new demands for visibility can emerge before institutions are ready, such acceleration has obvious strategic appeal. A payload placed quickly can begin building archives, routines, and operational habits while a more sovereign system remains a paper ambition. The bus gives motion. It also sets the route.

This is why hosted arrangements should never be described as mere engineering convenience. They change the time horizon of capability. A state or agency that cannot yet afford, justify, or deploy a full sovereign architecture may still acquire a meaningful Arctic role by sharing orbital real estate or terrestrial support with others. Commercial providers have encouraged this logic because they can offer mature buses, launch integration, network services, and operations expertise more quickly than many public systems can build them internally. The same is true on the ground. Shared antenna networks, common processing environments, and hosted command paths allow missions to become functional through partnership rather than through solitary build-out. That is the practical revolution: capability through borrowing structure rather than owning every layer outright.

A useful public example lies in hosted payload programmes more broadly, where government or institutional missions ride on commercial platforms for reasons of speed and access rather than because the mission is trivial. The point is not only that these missions reach orbit sooner. It is that their practical life in orbit becomes partly governed by the host's power budget, communications architecture, operational constraints, and maintenance logic. A payload may be sovereign in purpose and dependent in operation. In the Arctic, where reliability, timing, and prioritisation often matter as much as raw sensing, that difference can become more significant than the public launch story suggests.

A second example appears whenever multiple missions share a satellite bus or ground segment that serves both civil and security uses. A weather or environmental payload may coexist with a communications or imaging function whose users have very different urgency profiles and political stakes. On paper, the arrangement looks rational: one platform, several functions, better use of launch and infrastructure. In practice, the harder question emerges when the system is under stress or demand spikes. Which mission gets the cleaner downlink window? Which one receives priority if power, bandwidth, pointing opportunities, or processing attention become constrained? The hardware may be shared equally in design. The service rarely is in action.

That is why governance is not something added after the satellite is built. It is already embedded in the architecture. Shared buses and ground networks require rules, and rules create hierarchies whether or not the institutions involved like to admit it. Some hierarchies are contractual. Some are procedural. Some emerge from habit. A national security customer may possess priority rights over an environmental one. A commercial anchor tenant may outrank a smaller public mission in practice if not in rhetoric. A host may reserve the right to preserve its own continuity before supporting the passenger. None of this needs to be scandalous to be strategically important. The instrument of control may not be ownership of the payload at all. It may be the order in which competing needs are served.

Tasking priority is where this becomes painfully concrete. A sensor capable of observing the Arctic is not useful simply because it exists. Someone has to decide what it looks at, when, and for whom. In a dedicated sovereign mission, those questions are already political, but at least the political chain is relatively visible. In a hosted or shared arrangement, the same questions pass through more layers. The host's obligations, the passenger's rights, the ground segment's queue, the analytic pipeline's commitments, and the surrounding commercial or allied agreements all shape what is actually possible. The sensor may be nominally yours. The priority schedule may be the real owner.

This is why "owning the payload" can be a weaker form of control than public language usually implies. If another actor controls the bus, the communications path, the first station contact, the maintenance cycle, or the priority logic for tasking and downlink, then ownership of the sensing instrument is only one piece of sovereignty. The decisive question is often: who decides what happens when not everything can happen at once? In the Arctic, where orbital windows, communications margins, weather, and decision timelines already create scarcity, this question is not marginal. It is the core of the arrangement.

A credible limitation must be admitted. Shared infrastructure is not automatically a trap. Many hosted arrangements work extremely well, and some are more resilient than dedicated systems precisely because their costs, maintenance, and operational burdens are spread across stronger institutional shoulders. A shared bus may be better supported than a bespoke small mission. A common ground network may offer more redundancy and professional discipline than a thin sovereign one. It would be careless to romanticise purity of ownership and dismiss partnership as weakness. For many Arctic missions, shared architecture is the only realistic path to relevance.

But the concession strengthens the deeper point. The virtue of shared infrastructure lies in acceleration and access; its price lies in entanglement. The more a mission depends on a host or shared network, the more its technical fate and political freedom become linked to decisions it does not entirely command. Those decisions may concern routine maintenance, spectrum use, operational windows, customer priority, export controls, data handling, or crisis response. None of them looks like classic strategic coercion when viewed individually. Together, they can shape what the mission can do, how quickly it can do it, and whether its owners can claim true control over the capability they paid to place in orbit.

This is especially important in the Arctic because perceptions of monitoring can matter almost as much as monitoring itself. A state may believe it possesses a meaningful surveillance option because it has funded a payload, secured a contract, and integrated the outputs into its workflows. In a calm period, that belief may be justified. Under pressure, the relevant test is harsher. Can the payload be tasked as urgently as the moment requires? Can the data move on the needed clock? Can the host's other commitments, the shared ground segment's queue, or allied and commercial obligations delay or redirect the service? If the answer is uncertain, then the capability may be more conditional than the procurement story admitted.

Trust reveals itself here in behaviour. An institution that truly trusts a hosted arrangement will build critical workflows around it without quietly duplicating sovereign alternatives. One that half-trusts it will speak the language of partnership while preserving backup paths, reserve subscriptions, or secondary tasking methods in case the hosted route proves less authoritative than it appears. A security actor may insist on reserved tasking rights or dedicated windows not because it distrusts the engineering, but because it understands that shared systems tend to reveal their politics at the moment of scarcity. Those protective measures are often read as bureaucratic caution. They are better understood as a recognition that architecture is already governance.

The seat on the bus returns here because it captures both the gain and the limit. A passenger reaches orbit sooner by not insisting on their own vehicle. That is often wise. But the passenger does not set every term of the journey merely because they paid for a seat. The route, the stops, the maintenance schedule, and the right to yield or press ahead in traffic are still influenced by the operator of the whole system. The same is true on the ground. Shared antenna time, processing capacity, and dissemination paths may all work beautifully until several missions need them at once. Then the seat's status becomes visible.

This is why technical architectures must be read as political documents in hardware form. A hosted payload, a shared bus, a common ground network, or a multi-mission platform does not merely solve engineering and budget problems. It encodes choices about whose urgency counts most, whose failure matters most, and whose mission can be delayed without rewriting the public meaning of the system. The Arctic, with its tight windows, sparse alternatives, and sensitivity to delay, exposes those choices earlier and more sharply than more forgiving theatres do.

The harder question, then, is not whether hosted payloads and shared infrastructure are wise. Often they are the wisest option available. The more serious question is what kind of sovereignty survives the acceleration they offer. When the bus is full, the ground segment crowded, and the Arctic incident suddenly time-sensitive, who truly controls the watch: the actor who paid for the instrument, or the actor who controls the order in which instruments are allowed to matter?

Tasking rights, exclusivity, and transparency

In March 2021, when commercial imagery of the *Ever Given* blocking the Suez Canal spread rapidly across governments, markets, and newsrooms, the public saw a vivid demonstration of modern visibility. What it did not see was the quieter question behind the image: who had the right to look first, to look again, and to decide whether that attention would remain a private service, a paying privilege, or a public fact? The picture appeared to belong to everyone once released. Before release, it belonged to a chain of tasking rights, priorities, and institutional choices that are far less democratic than the image itself suggested.

The Arctic sharpens this question because the region is still difficult enough to watch that concentrated attention carries political meaning of its own. A sensor pointed repeatedly at a sensitive coast, a shipping corridor, an offshore site, or a military facility is not merely collecting data. It is declaring interest. Sometimes that interest deters by implying vigilance. Sometimes it reassures by proving that ambiguity will not be allowed to thicken. Sometimes it unsettles precisely because the watched actor cannot tell whether the monitoring is routine, precautionary, commercial, or preparatory. In the Arctic, perceptions of monitoring often matter almost as much as monitoring itself because the region remains sparse enough that attention is legible.

That is the central problem. Tasking governance decides who can concentrate surveillance, on what timetable, and with what degree of privacy or public visibility. Show a shared or commercial constellation and it is easy to imagine openness: many buyers, many passes, many products. Name the more exact issue and the picture changes. Someone holds the right to point the sensor, to reserve capacity, to exclude others temporarily, or to demand priority when a scene becomes sensitive. Explain why this matters, and the strategic implication follows quickly. Control often resides less in ownership of the spacecraft than in the ordering of access to its gaze.

The queue decides. That is the quiet motif worth keeping in view. Satellite surveillance, especially in dual-use systems, is never simply a matter of whether a sensor exists. It is a matter of who moves to the front of the tasking queue when many customers, agencies, or states want the same look. A constellation can seem broadly available and still operate through a hierarchy of rights that only becomes visible at the moment of scarcity. In such systems, exclusivity is often temporal rather than absolute. One actor does not need permanent monopoly to exercise real control. It is enough to gain the first look, the repeat look, or the right to delay others until the scene has changed.

This makes tasking rights more consequential than many public descriptions admit. A system may advertise open access, broad service availability, or market-based tasking while also offering premium priority, reserved windows, or government preference clauses. None of this is inherently improper. Indeed, it is often how complex constellations remain financially and operationally viable. But the practical result is that "open" access can mask a layered reality. Some users buy access to the archive. Some buy routine tasking. Some buy responsiveness. A smaller number buy precedence. The difference between those tiers is not merely commercial. It shapes which observations become politically usable first.

A useful public example lies in the broader commercial satellite imagery market that matured through firms such as Maxar and Planet. These providers widened access to high-latitude observation and made repeated Arctic collection far more thinkable for actors who did not possess sovereign constellations. Yet the very success of such systems has also clarified that access comes in levels. Governments, major institutions, and premium clients can often secure tasking behaviour unavailable to casual buyers or public observers. This is not a scandalous revelation. It is how markets ration scarce attention. The important point is that market rationing can have geopolitical effects when the area being watched is not merely economically interesting but strategically charged.

A second example can be drawn from an Arctic maritime incident, as it illustrates how escalation risk arises from seemingly administrative control. A sensitive vessel movement is reported near contested or politically delicate waters. Several actors want imagery. One government customer holds priority tasking rights with a commercial provider and rapidly concentrates repeated collection on the area. Another actor, relying on standard access, must wait for archived products or slower coverage. The first actor now possesses not just information, but the power to define the event's first evidentiary narrative. It can brief allies, reassure domestic audiences, or imply a stronger pattern of concern simply by being first and most persistent in its gaze. The difference was not orbital. It was contractual.

This is why exclusivity should be understood in several senses rather than one. Exclusive access to a whole system is rare and often unnecessary. More common, and more important, is exclusive access to speed, to priority, to repeatability, or to temporary secrecy. A buyer who can direct immediate retasking enjoys a different surveillance reality from one who can only purchase what has already been collected. A customer who can keep a product private while deciding how to use it enjoys a different form of control from one who receives only the public release after the interpretive struggle is already half over. The Arctic turns these distinctions into strategic facts because many incidents there remain ambiguous long enough that the first sustained observer may strongly shape what the incident comes to mean.

Transparency complicates the picture in ways that are both hopeful and dangerous. Commercial availability can increase transparency by making it harder for a state to monopolise visual evidence of activity in the High North. Journalists, researchers, smaller governments, and non-state observers may all gain some ability to inspect a claim or verify an event. That is a genuine shift. It reduces certain forms of informational privilege and can restrain denial. Yet transparency is never simply the opposite of control. A provider can release imagery publicly and still preserve private priority arrangements for others. An "open" marketplace can widen after the crucial first phase of attention has already been shaped by closed tasking rights. Public visibility may therefore begin as the residue of earlier, less visible governance.

This is where escalation risk enters more sharply. A state or company that can rapidly concentrate sensor attention on a sensitive Arctic area sends a signal whether or not it intends to. Repeated tasking implies concern, interest, or suspicion. If the pattern becomes known, the watched actor may interpret it as monitoring, pressure, or prelude. Even if the imagery never leaves private channels, the act of concentrated observation can alter expectations. If the imagery is then released publicly, the signal intensifies. What might have remained a bilateral or institutional concern becomes a narrative object visible to allies, markets, media, and domestic audiences. Transparency, in such moments, can harden positions rather than soften them.

A credible limitation deserves acknowledgement. Not every tasking decision carries strategic meaning, and not every concentration of observation should be read as escalation. Commercial providers serve many ordinary needs: shipping, insurance, environmental assessment, scientific monitoring, journalism, infrastructure watchfulness. Arctic scenes may attract repeated collection for reasons that are commercially routine rather than politically charged. It would be careless to interpret every retasked satellite as an act of strategic theatre. Much of modern surveillance is mundane in motive even when its tools are geopolitically significant.

But that concession strengthens the deeper argument. The reason tasking governance matters is precisely that ordinary and extraordinary motives often share the same infrastructure. A commercial provider may task for routine customer demand in one week and for urgent state concern in the next. A system built for many users may appear neutral until one actor purchases the right to make its attention momentarily unequal. Because the same constellation can carry civil, commercial, and security logics simultaneously, outside observers may struggle to tell when ordinary market activity has become geopolitical concentration. That ambiguity is itself part of the risk.

This is why the distinction between open and controlled access requires more scepticism than promotional language usually invites. Open access may mean that many users can eventually obtain data. It does not necessarily mean equal ability to direct collection, equal insight into who else has tasked the system, equal knowledge of what has been withheld, or equal speed in receiving results. Controlled access may mean overt state monopoly, but it may also mean subtler forms of private ordering through contracts, embargo periods, or invisible priority classes. A serious reader should therefore ask not whether a system is open in the abstract, but open to what: archive access, routine purchases, urgent tasking, exclusive retasking, or public release?

Trust appears here in very visible institutional behaviour. States trust a constellation's openness when they rely on market access rather than sovereign reserves for sensitive Arctic awareness. They distrust it when they demand exclusivity clauses, reserve capacity, or private release windows because ordinary access does not satisfy their political need for control. Analysts trust transparency when public imagery can be compared against private claims without too much delay or distortion. They distrust it when they suspect that the most decisive looks were never publicly visible, or only became visible after the critical framing battle had already been won elsewhere. These behaviours reveal what the architecture actually provides beneath its public rhetoric.

The queue returns because it is where technical governance becomes strategic power in its most ordinary form. A provider may never deny service outright. It needs only to decide who moves first. In the Arctic, where a few hours of concentrated attention can change how an incident is interpreted, firstness matters. The actor who can point the sensor earliest, repeat the look most persistently, or delay rivals by even a modest interval may gain the ability to set the evidentiary weather in which everyone else must speak.

The harder question, then, is not whether Arctic surveillance systems should be more open or more controlled in some abstract moral sense. The more serious question is who can concentrate attention, with what visibility to others, and how that concentration is likely to be read by those being watched. When an actor can buy priority, reserve secrecy, and then choose the moment of release, where exactly does monitoring end and signalling begin - and who gets to decide whether the difference still matters?

Strategic signalling and escalation pressures

In February 2022, Maxar's public release of satellite imagery showing Russian military deployments near Ukraine did more than document a crisis. It helped set the emotional and diplomatic weather in which that crisis was interpreted. The images did not create the confrontation, and they did not settle every dispute about intent. They did something subtler and, in some respects, more powerful: they shortened the distance between collection and public narrative. Once the pictures circulated, governments, journalists, analysts, and ordinary citizens were no longer arguing in the dark. They were arguing in the presence of visible evidence, or at least in the presence of something that looked enough like evidence to harden expectation.

The Arctic gives that dynamic a distinct and dangerous edge. It remains sparse enough that concentrated surveillance can itself become a message. A sensor repeatedly tasked over a shipping corridor, an offshore installation, a military site, or an ice-bound transit route is not only gathering information. It is signalling concern, vigilance, suspicion, or resolve - sometimes deliberately, sometimes by the mere fact of where attention has suddenly thickened. In a region where ambiguity has long been part of strategic life, persistent observation changes the terms on which actors reassure one another, read one another, and misread one another.

This is the core tension. Surveillance is often described as if it were a neutral collection followed by a neutral interpretation. It is neither. Show an actor that knows it is being watched more closely than before, and the watch itself begins to alter behaviour. Name the concept properly, and it becomes signalling rather than sensing alone. Explain why that matters, and the implications reach beyond operations into politics. A constellation that improves awareness can also raise the stakes of movement, compress diplomatic room, and create new expectations about what should have been seen, what should have been disclosed, and what silence now seems to imply. Persistence, in other words, is not a passive condition. It changes the atmosphere in which decisions are made.

That change can deter. It can reassure. It can provoke. Which of those meanings dominates depends not only on the act of monitoring but on who is doing it, who knows about it, how publicly the results are used, and what prior distrust already surrounds the relationship. A state may interpret repeated surveillance of Arctic waters as a stabilising sign that irresponsible behaviour will be noticed quickly. Another may read the same pattern as a form of strategic pressure, especially if the observation is paired with public commentary, rapid tasking surges, or selective release of imagery designed to imply narrative control. The signal is never self-interpreting. The receiver supplies half its meaning.

A camera pointed twice. That is the quiet motif worth keeping in mind. Once may be routine. Twice may still be routine. But in a sensitive setting, repetition acquires social meaning. The second look says more than the first because it suggests priority. The third look begins to imply concern or focus. The public release of one of those looks changes the sequence again, because it tells not only the watched actor but everyone else that attention has been concentrated and may continue. The Arctic is especially susceptible to this dynamic because so much of its strategic significance rests on movement across large spaces where watching is itself an expensive and therefore legible act.

This is why persistence should be treated as a political condition rather than a simple technical upgrade. A more persistent surveillance architecture does not merely reduce uncertainty for its owner. It also raises expectations among allies, publics, markets, and rivals. Allies may assume quicker reassurance and faster warning. The public may infer that suspicious activity cannot remain hidden for long. Rivals may conclude that certain forms of manoeuvre will be observed and possibly publicised. Once those expectations exist, the failure to detect, the failure to disclose, or the decision to remain silent acquires a new meaning of its own. Surveillance capacity thus creates red lines indirectly, by teaching everyone to expect a certain degree of visibility, whether or not the system can always deliver it cleanly.

That expectation can be stabilising when it discourages reckless acts or helps prevent misinterpretation of ordinary activity. It can also become destabilising when the mere appearance of attention begins to feel accusatory. This is particularly true in the Arctic, where many activities remain dual-use by nature. A vessel may be commercial, scientific, logistical, or strategic in overlapping ways. Infrastructure may support civil life while also serving security ends. An increase in surveillance over such activities can therefore generate concern without necessarily clarifying intent. The watched actor may respond not to what the observer knows, but to what they fear the observer is preparing to claim. Monitoring thus enters the realm of signalling, not because the sensor says so, but because strategic context fills the image with anticipated judgement.

A useful public example lies in the release of satellite imagery during the build-up to the full-scale invasion of Ukraine. The relevance here is not regional similarity but signalling logic. Public release did not merely inform external audiences. It also communicated to Russia that its deployments were being watched, interpreted, and made legible to the world in near real time. Such imagery could reassure allies and publics by demonstrating attention and preparation. It could also harden narratives by making certain interpretations politically more costly to revise later. Once a scene has been widely seen and framed, diplomacy does not return easily to a more elastic ambiguity. The image becomes part of the event.

A second example, closer in kind to Arctic conditions, can be imagined around a sensitive northern maritime incident. A commercial or state-affiliated provider rapidly releases imagery showing a concentration of vessels near disputed or strategically delicate waters. The release may be intended to reassure domestic audiences that authorities are alert, or to deter further movement by exposing it. Yet the same release can also narrow diplomatic room. It can force public responses before private channels have matured, harden suspicions about intent, and encourage outside observers to treat a still-ambiguous event as already resolved in meaning. The image may be accurate. Its political timing may still raise the temperature.

That is why strategic signalling in surveillance should be distinguished from operational guidance. The question here is not how to monitor more effectively or how to respond tactically. The question is how persistent visibility alters the mental terrain in which states and other actors operate. A surveillance architecture that can rapidly revisit, concentrate tasking, and distribute imagery publicly changes the grammar of reassurance and accusation alike. Silence becomes conspicuous. Delayed release becomes meaningful. Public release becomes a choice about tempo as much as transparency. Even a decision not to publish may signal caution, uncertainty, or a desire to preserve ambiguity for diplomatic reasons. The technology does not merely gather facts. It structures when and how facts become politically usable.

A credible limitation must be admitted. Surveillance does not always intensify tension. Much depends on context. In some circumstances, routine and mutually understood observation can lower the risk of miscalculation by reducing surprise and discouraging adventurous interpretations of normal activity. The existence of credible monitoring may reassure smaller actors and stabilise expectations about what the larger players can plausibly deny. It would be careless to imply that persistence always provokes or that public release always hardens the worst narrative. Sometimes visibility reduces fear precisely because it constrains imagination.

But the concession strengthens the deeper point. The stabilising effect of surveillance depends on shared understandings that are often thinner in the Arctic than they first appear. The region combines alliance activity, commercial expansion, environmental change, indigenous presence, infrastructure growth, military concern, and legal ambiguity in ways that resist simple signalling. An observation that looks routine to one side may look concentrated and strategic to another. A public release intended as reassurance may be read as narrative warfare. A pattern of repeat tasking meant only to clarify a technical anomaly may appear, from outside, as proof that a sensitive site has crossed into the centre of strategic attention. Persistence is not neutral because attention is never neutral once actors begin asking what the attention is supposed to mean.

This is why perceptions of monitoring matter almost as much as monitoring itself. An actor may change behaviour because it believes it is being watched closely, even if the actual quality of the monitoring is uneven. A government may feel compelled to respond to imagery already in circulation, even if it privately retains doubts about the interpretation. Markets may react to released observation before institutions have agreed on what it shows. Journalists and outside analysts may amplify a surveillance narrative that then becomes politically harder for states to soften. The image therefore acts not only as evidence but as a timing device. It synchronises outside attention around a particular scene and can thereby compress escalation choices.

Trust, once again, becomes visible in behaviour. States trust surveillance as reassurance when they cite it to calm allies or publics rather than to accuse. They trust it as deterrent when they allow visibility itself to stand as warning without immediate public drama. They use it provocatively when they pair concentrated observation with public framing designed to corner another actor's options. The same image can play different roles depending on when it is released, how often similar images have been released before, and whether the audiences involved believe the observer is trying to illuminate or to discipline. Those behavioural differences reveal more than slogans about transparency ever will.

The camera pointed twice returns at the end because repetition is the bridge between mere seeing and strategic meaning. A single observation may inform. Repeated observation, especially if known or made public, begins to teach others what kinds of action will be noticed, what kinds of ambiguity will be tolerated, and where invisible lines are starting to form. The Arctic, with its vast spaces and relatively few decisive nodes, is unusually exposed to this pedagogy of attention. That is why persistence changes red lines even when no formal declaration accompanies it. People infer from the pattern of watching what matters, what alarms, and what may draw a response.

The harder question, then, is not whether Arctic surveillance can improve awareness. It can, and often does. The more serious question is what kind of political weather that awareness creates once it is made persistent, concentrated, and sometimes public. When an image is released during a northern incident, is it clarifying events, warning an adversary, reassuring an ally, disciplining a narrative, or nudging everyone involved towards a more rigid interpretation than the facts themselves require? In the Arctic, the answer may matter as much as the image.

Chapter 10

Interference, Jamming, and Spoofing

How does a state know whether a failing signal is an accident, a weakness, or an attack? That question sits at the centre of Arctic interference, and it is more dangerous than it first appears. A link drops, a navigation solution becomes doubtful, a ground node behaves erratically, a timing reference begins to drift, and the first impulse is often to ask who did it. Yet the High North is a place where geography, sparse infrastructure, severe weather, and the electromagnetic environment itself can complicate that judgement before any adversary enters the story. The Arctic does not only strain systems. It strains interpretation.

The problem is not confined to dramatic moments. In October 2018, during NATO's Trident Juncture exercise in northern Norway, reports of GPS disruption in Finnmark drew exactly the sort of attention one would expect. Navigation anomalies near a strategic exercise are never treated casually. But the deeper lesson was harder and more durable: once interference enters the picture, technical symptoms and political meaning become entangled. A degradation may be intentional, incidental, environmental, or some unsettled mixture of all three. The signal goes thin. So does certainty.

That is why interference in the Arctic cannot be understood as a simple contest between a transmitter and a receiver. The region's radio environment is shaped by more than hostile intent. Sparse ground networks, long distances, awkward geometry, high-latitude propagation effects, and dependence on a small number of critical links all help determine what kind of disruption is felt and how quickly it is interpreted. The same symptom can therefore belong to different stories. Static on the line may indicate routine congestion, poor siting, equipment trouble, environmental conditions, deliberate jamming, or a failure somewhere else in the chain masquerading as something more sinister. The Arctic turns that ambiguity into a strategic condition.

This is the chapter's central tension. Modern surveillance systems are often presented as though their main vulnerabilities sit in the satellite itself, high above the scene of operations. In practice, many of the most consequential choke points lie lower down: in communications links, navigation signals, timing references, ground stations, relay paths, and processing architectures that can be disturbed without anyone touching the headline platform. That matters because a state may believe its orbital capability remains intact while the practical value of that capability has already been thinned by pressure elsewhere. The platform survives. The service does not.

The stakes run in two directions at once. Underreaction leaves real vulnerabilities untreated and invites complacency about systems whose weaknesses are already visible in peacetime. Overreaction carries its own danger. If routine interference, environmental instability, or maintenance failure is quickly read as intentional disruption, then technical noise can begin to shape diplomatic posture and military expectation. The Arctic is especially exposed to this risk because verification is costly, reaction windows can be short, and the region's strategic assets are close enough to make suspicion feel plausible even when certainty is weak. Static can be read as intention before the evidence deserves it.

That is why interference has to be treated as both a technical and a political problem. A communications outage is not only a matter of link budgets and equipment health. It also becomes a test of institutional judgement: who investigates, how quickly they classify the event, what confidence they attach to their early explanations, and whether they speak publicly before the evidence has settled. A navigation anomaly does not merely affect route confidence. It can change how operators interpret the wider environment and how governments frame risk to allies, publics, or rivals. The same degradation may be experienced as inconvenience, warning, provocation, or proof depending on how it is named. Naming matters.

A quiet motif runs through all of this: static. Static is rarely silence. It is the presence of disturbance without immediate clarity about its source. In the Arctic, systems often continue operating while confidence in them weakens. The picture arrives late. The fix persists but no longer feels clean. The network stays up but behaves oddly. That is often the real form of disruption in high latitudes. It does not announce itself with a clean break. It introduces doubt into systems that depend on timing, continuity, and trust, and it does so in ways that invite premature stories about blame or resilience.

The path ahead begins with the electromagnetic environment itself, where geography, infrastructure scarcity, and strategic proximity shape how interference should be read before intent is assigned. It then moves into the different ways disruption can travel through the chain, showing why communications, navigation, timing, and ground support may be more vulnerable in practice than the spacecraft overhead. From there the argument turns to the hardest problem of all: detection and attribution under persistent uncertainty, where sophisticated monitoring still leaves room for doubt and where that doubt can become a source of instability in its own right.

The harder question, then, is not whether Arctic systems will face disruption. They will, in forms both ordinary and deliberate. The more serious question is how a state distinguishes noise from coercion before the distinction itself becomes part of the crisis. When the signal turns rough in the High North, who can tell whether the static belongs to the environment, the architecture, or an adversary - and how much escalation begins in the gap between those possibilities?

The contested electromagnetic environment

In October 2018, during NATO's Trident Juncture exercise in northern Norway, reports of GPS disruption in Finnmark quickly entered public discussion as a security issue. That was understandable. The setting was sensitive, the systems involved were important, and the Arctic is not a region where signal anomalies are treated with casual indifference. But the episode also revealed something more enduring than the immediate controversy. In the High North, a disturbed signal is never just a disturbed signal. It sits at the intersection of geography, infrastructure, physics, and politics, and the first explanation offered is not always the best one.

A bad signal means several things. That is the starting discipline. A link may thin because of poor geometry, sparse ground support, awkward antenna placement, weather effects, equipment stress, local congestion, ionospheric variability, or deliberate interference. These explanations do not look equally plausible in every context, but they often look plausible enough to compete in the first hours of an incident. The Arctic sharpens that competition because the region already imposes severe ordinary strain on radio systems. When a disruption appears, the analytical challenge is therefore not only to observe it, but to decide whether it belongs to the environment, to the architecture, or to an actor.

The Arctic radio-frequency environment is distinctive before anyone chooses to contest it. Show a map of the region and three facts stand out at once. Distances are long. Infrastructure is thin. Strategic assets sit close enough together that suspicion is never far from any technical anomaly. Name the issue properly and it becomes more than electromagnetic clutter in the narrow engineering sense. It is a communications environment shaped by latitude, terrain, sparse redundancy, changing propagation, and the concentration of military, civil, scientific, and commercial functions in a space that feels empty until one begins tracing where the critical nodes actually lie. Explain why this matters, and the implication becomes immediately strategic. A system operating in the High North inherits ambiguity before any deliberate disruption begins.

This is why ordinary interference and intentional disruption must be distinguished analytically rather than morally. Ordinary interference includes the accumulated frictions of a difficult environment: weak margins, natural variability, overlapping users, equipment misalignment, infrastructure faults, or routine operational noise. Intentional disruption includes deliberate attempts to deny, corrupt, or manipulate communications, navigation, or timing. The problem is that the symptoms can overlap. A navigation service may degrade under natural conditions in ways that resemble jamming to the hurried observer. A communications path may behave erratically because of architecture and maintenance issues while inviting political suspicion because of where it failed. The Arctic teaches that diagnosis must precede accusation, even when accusation feels intuitively satisfying.

Static is not evidence. That quiet motif is worth holding onto because it resists one of the region's most dangerous habits. Static can mean vulnerability. It can mean weather in the broadest sense, including near-space weather. It can mean weak siting, overextended infrastructure, poor resilience planning, or hostile action. A mature analytical stance begins by asking what kind of static this is, where in the chain it appears, how often similar effects have occurred under less dramatic conditions, and what other systems say at the same moment. Without that discipline, technical symptoms are quickly turned into political claims, and political claims in the Arctic can travel faster than verification.

Geography matters more here than many discussions admit. High latitude look angles, sparse terrestrial backup, and the long reach between key nodes all make radio systems less forgiving. A weak link in a crowded southern environment may inconvenience one user and leave several alternatives intact. The same weakness in the High North can dominate a whole service pathway because there are fewer cheap detours. A ground station fault, an awkwardly placed terminal, a degraded backhaul route, or a navigation anomaly near a critical corridor can therefore feel more menacing than its raw technical scale would suggest. The problem is not merely that Arctic systems are exposed. It is that exposure is concentrated.

A useful public example remains the recurring concern around GNSS disruption in northern Scandinavia. The relevance is not only that such incidents have been reported, but that they reveal how quickly navigation degradation becomes a diplomatic object. Civil aviation, maritime operations, military exercises, and public authorities all depend on shared confidence in what a positioning service is doing. When that confidence weakens, users do not experience a tidy engineering problem. They experience uncertainty about route safety, timing integrity, and the intentions of nearby actors. The same technical symptom thus enters several political worlds at once. That is exactly why analytical caution matters.

A second example can be imagined from communications rather than navigation, and it is often more revealing because the politics are less instantly visible. A northern ground node begins to show degraded throughput and erratic delivery during a period of heightened sensitivity. Users suspect external interference. Later inquiry suggests that local power irregularity, stressed environmental controls, or a failing backhaul component played a major role. No hostile transmitter needed to exist for the event to feel strategically consequential. The outage still altered awareness, still delayed products, still changed decisions, and still risked being misread as deliberate action. The lesson is uncomfortable but necessary: vulnerabilities that are merely technical in origin can still produce political effects very similar to those of intentional pressure.

That is why interference in the Arctic must be treated as both a technical and a political category. Technical, because it arises within measurable systems of propagation, power, timing, link quality, and environmental conditions. Political, because the meaning attached to those disturbances depends on proximity, prior distrust, public framing, and the strategic value of the capabilities affected. A state does not respond only to signals. It responds to what it thinks the signals say about intent. In a region where verification is hard and reaction can be pressured by alliance commitments, media attention, or institutional anxiety, misclassification becomes one of the central risks. One can escalate through explanation as well as through action.

A credible limitation deserves acknowledgement. Not every disruption in the High North is ambiguous, and not every case of interference should be buried under endless caution. Some patterns are clearer than others. Some incidents arrive in contexts that make deliberate action more plausible, not less. Some infrastructures are resilient enough, and some monitoring good enough, that ordinary environmental noise can be separated from hostile manipulation with reasonable confidence. It would be careless to pretend that the Arctic is so complex that intention can never be identified. That is not true.

But the concession strengthens the larger argument rather than weakening it. The point is not that attribution is impossible. It is that the electromagnetic environment already contains enough difficulty that any serious interpretation must account for ordinary strain before leaping to extraordinary conclusions. A system may fail because it was attacked. It may also fail because it was fragile in a place that punishes fragility. The difference matters enormously. One explanation points outward to adversaries. The other points inward to neglected resilience. The Arctic is a region where actors often prefer the first story and urgently need the second one not to be forgotten.

This has direct implications for how capability should be judged. A radio service that functions well only under clean conditions is not truly reliable in the High North, even if it performs beautifully on a specification sheet. A navigation architecture that cannot distinguish its own environmental limits from hostile disruption is not merely technically weak. It is politically hazardous. A ground network that allows routine faults to masquerade as interference is not simply under-maintained. It is manufacturing uncertainty for itself and for others. Resilience, therefore, cannot be measured only by whether a system stays on. It must also be measured by whether a system can remain interpretable when conditions grow rough.

The static returns here because it captures the chapter's deeper warning. Static does not only obscure the message. It can become the message if institutions are too quick to read intention into noise or too embarrassed to admit that ordinary vulnerabilities remain unresolved. The Arctic is particularly unforgiving of both errors. One invites overreaction. The other invites complacency. Between them lies the real task: building analytical habits strong enough to separate the politics of interference from the physics of difficulty without pretending they can ever be wholly divorced.

The harder question, then, is not whether the Arctic electromagnetic environment is contested. It is. The more serious question is what kind of contest is actually taking place when a signal weakens, a link fails, or a timing service grows unreliable. Is the disturbance revealing an adversary, a design weakness, a maintenance failure, or a natural condition that the system should have been built to tolerate? Until that question is answered with more care than haste, the most dangerous interference in the High North may be the interference between technical judgement and political imagination.

Disruption modes across the chain

In October 2018, during NATO's Trident Juncture exercise in northern Norway, reports of GPS disruption in Finnmark did more than raise questions about navigation safety. They exposed a habit of thought that remains surprisingly persistent in discussions of space power. When something goes wrong in an Arctic surveillance system, many observers look first to the satellite. Yet the satellite is often the least interesting place to begin. The more revealing question is simpler and more unsettling: which part of the chain actually failed?

A space system can keep flying perfectly while its practical value collapses below it. A communications link can thin. A timing reference can drift. A downlink can stall. A ground node can degrade. A navigation signal can become untrustworthy without disappearing altogether. The headline platform remains aloft, apparently intact, while the service it was meant to provide becomes hesitant, partial, or unusable. In the Arctic, where long distances, sparse infrastructure, and tight operational margins already make every dependency more visible, this difference matters enormously. It is the difference between a platform-centric story and a systems one.

The central point is therefore not merely that disruption can occur at many points, but that those points differ in meaning. Show an outage in a high-latitude surveillance architecture and the first temptation is to ask whether the satellite has been interfered with. Name the chain properly, however, and one sees a series of weaker joints: command links, payload communications, relay paths, downlink windows, ground terminals, timing sources, navigation signals, and the local networks that carry products onward once they land. Explain why this matters, and the implication becomes strategic. Many of the most consequential choke points sit below the spacecraft because they are cheaper to stress, harder to diagnose quickly, and more likely to produce ambiguous symptoms.

A chain breaks low. That is the quiet motif worth keeping in view. Space systems attract attention upward because satellites are visible in imagination even when invisible to the eye. But the Arctic keeps dragging analysis downward, to the places where information must move through radios, antennas, processors, clocks, and power supplies exposed to severe conditions and sparse redundancy. If a surveillance system fails to deliver timely awareness, the fault may lie not in the orbital asset but in the path beneath it. Resilience planning begins to mature at exactly the moment institutions stop equating "the space system" with the spacecraft alone.

Communications links are the most obvious example. A sensor may collect without trouble and still fail the mission because the resulting data cannot be moved on the required clock. This can happen through ordinary weakness as well as deliberate interference. Link margins may already be thin at high latitude. Weather, ice accretion, poor antenna geometry, congestion, or local infrastructure stress may reduce performance further. Deliberate jamming or other forms of radio interference can then push a marginal service over the edge. The important analytic point is that the user often experiences only the last step: the product is late, incomplete, or absent. The symptom appears as a data problem. Its source may lie in the communications path rather than in collection itself.

Navigation and timing services illustrate a different mode of disruption. Here the chain does not necessarily stop. It becomes less trustworthy. A platform, aircraft, ship, or network may continue operating while confidence in position, timing, or synchronisation erodes. That erosion can spread widely because PNT does more than place icons on a map. It supports route confidence, timestamp integrity, network order, sensor fusion, and the comparison of one source with another. A degradation in PNT integrity can therefore alter many behaviours at once without ever touching the imaging payload directly. The system still appears to function. It no longer means what operators thought it meant.

This is why loss of PNT integrity and loss of imagery downlink should never be treated as interchangeable failures. The first often corrodes confidence across several layers simultaneously. The second more plainly interrupts one stream of information. A lost downlink may delay or prevent delivery of an otherwise good observation. A loss of PNT integrity may leave data flowing while making the broader architecture less sure about where, when, or how confidently that data should be interpreted. In operational terms, one resembles blindness in a particular direction. The other resembles uncertainty about the coordinates and clocks by which the whole system organises itself. Both are serious. They are serious in different ways.

A brief comparison makes the distinction concrete. Imagine a high-latitude SAR satellite collecting a scene of suspicious maritime activity. In one case, the radar image is taken cleanly but the imagery downlink is degraded, perhaps by link interference or ground-segment trouble. Analysts receive nothing, or receive it too late. The missing product is obvious, and the immediate consequence is a gap in observation. In the second case, the image is collected and delivered, but PNT services supporting maritime tracks, aircraft routing, or timing alignment across networks have become unreliable. Analysts now possess the image yet struggle to match it confidently to other feeds or to trust the broader sequence of events around it. The first failure withholds evidence. The second contaminates the context. An institution that does not distinguish these modes may respond with the wrong remedy and learn the wrong lesson.

Ground networks introduce yet another class of disruption because they are where technical weakness and political ambiguity often meet. A northern station or terminal can fail through maintenance problems, power irregularities, backhaul weakness, environmental damage, or deliberate targeting of the network path that carries products onward. To the distant user, these failures may look frustratingly similar at first. A service that suddenly degrades during a tense period may invite assumptions of hostile action when the real cause lies in sustainment or local infrastructure. The reverse danger also exists. An organisation accustomed to technical fragility may normalise symptoms that deserve more concern. In the Arctic, where the ordinary environment already produces friction, distinguishing the exceptional from the routine is one of the hardest parts of resilience.

This is why disruption should be mapped as a chain of effects rather than a catalogue of isolated threats. A communications problem may create analytic delay. A timing problem may create false mismatch between sources. A ground-segment outage may masquerade as signal denial. A local navigation anomaly may ripple outward into route change, sensor fusion difficulty, and institutional suspicion. The Arctic magnifies these interactions because redundancy is thinner and recovery often slower. One weak point is rarely only one weak point once the service enters the real tempo of operations.

A credible limitation needs stating clearly. Not every outage or degradation reflects deliberate hostile action, and not every ambiguous symptom should be read as a strategic probe. High-latitude systems live under severe ordinary stress. Equipment ages. Weather intrudes. Power fluctuates. Backhaul breaks. Natural RF conditions complicate clean reception. It would be careless to describe the entire Arctic chain as a constant battlefield of intentional disruption. Much of what goes wrong is simply the cost of operating difficult systems in difficult places.

But that concession sharpens the real argument rather than weakening it. The presence of ordinary failure modes makes system-level reasoning more, not less, important. A mature resilience posture does not begin by assuming malign intent, nor by dismissing anomalies as normal Arctic roughness. It begins by asking where in the chain the symptom has appeared, what dependencies lie beneath it, which other services are behaving oddly at the same moment, and whether the outage pattern fits the known stresses of the architecture. That analytical discipline is itself part of resilience. Without it, institutions may escalate on noise or ignore meaningful warning signs because they have grown too familiar with technical inconvenience.

The political stakes of misreading the chain are considerable. If a state interprets degraded PNT as an attack on national resolve rather than as a localised systems problem, it may overstate the coherence and hostility of what is happening. If it treats a downlink outage as routine when the wider pattern suggests coordinated interference, it may underreact and leave the system exposed. If it sees every missing product as evidence of hostile contestation, it may quietly conceal the more embarrassing truth that its ground architecture is brittle. If it insists every anomaly is benign, it invites surprise. The Arctic does not forgive either reflex.

Trust becomes visible here in institutional behaviour. Operators who understand the chain build fallback modes appropriate to different failures rather than relying on one grand notion of "space resilience". Analysts who understand the chain distinguish between missing evidence and evidence rendered ambiguous by degraded context. Decision-makers who understand the chain resist the urge to compress every disruption into a single political meaning before technical diagnosis has caught up. These are not merely procedural virtues. They are signs that the organisation has grasped where real choke points sit and how differently they wound the overall system.

The chain breaks low returns at the end because it captures the chapter's most important inversion. The most dramatic platform is often not the most vulnerable part, nor the most politically dangerous place to misunderstand failure. A satellite may continue its orbit beautifully while the surveillance architecture below it becomes confused, delayed, or uncertain through much smaller interventions or much older weaknesses. The Arctic exposes this because it places so much weight on links, clocks, ground sites, and delivery paths that already live close to their margins.

The harder question, then, is not whether a hostile actor can threaten a space system by touching something other than the satellite. Of course it can. The more serious question is whether the institutions depending on Arctic surveillance know how to read different disruptions for what they are. When the product fails to arrive, when the clock grows doubtful, when the route shifts, or when the ground node falls quiet, do they know which part of the chain has truly been hit - and what kind of confidence has been lost along with it?

Detection, attribution, and uncertainty

In October 2018, during NATO's Trident Juncture exercise in northern Norway, reports of GPS disruption in Finnmark quickly moved from technical concern to political implication. That shift was understandable. Navigation anomalies near a major exercise, close to sensitive borders and strategic assets, do not remain mere engineering curiosities for long. Yet the incident also exposed a more enduring Arctic problem. A disrupted signal may be detected quickly and still remain difficult to explain with confidence. The signal weakens first. Certainty follows later, if it arrives at all.

That sequence matters because interference is often discussed as though detection naturally leads to attribution. In practice, the path is far rougher. A receiver shows degraded performance. A link behaves erratically. A timing reference drifts. A downlink fails to hold. Those are real symptoms, but symptoms are not explanations. In the Arctic, where natural variability, sparse infrastructure, awkward geometry, long distances, and stressed ground systems already make radio performance difficult, the move from noticing disturbance to naming its cause is rarely clean. Sophisticated monitoring can narrow the field. It does not always close the case.

This is the central discipline: detection and attribution are not the same act. Show a disruption in a northern system and the first task is to establish that something abnormal has happened at all. Name that properly and one is still only at detection. Explain the next step, and the difficulty appears immediately. Attribution requires deciding whether the anomaly reflects routine environmental strain, local technical weakness, accidental interference, deliberate jamming, spoofing, or some layered combination of these. The implication is uncomfortable but necessary. A system can be good at seeing that it is in trouble and still poor at saying why.

A signal goes strange. That quiet motif is worth keeping because it captures how uncertainty actually enters operations. Rarely with theatrical clarity. More often a signal becomes rough, intermittent, mistimed, or subtly implausible. The GPS fix persists but feels wrong. The communications service does not disappear; it becomes unreliable. The imagery arrives late, or arrives with timing and positional context no one fully trusts. In those moments, institutions are tempted to supply intention before evidence has supplied it. The Arctic is especially vulnerable to that temptation because the region is strategic enough that malice is always imaginable and sparse enough that verification is often slow.

Detection is the easiest part to oversell. A modern monitoring architecture may include receiver logs, spectrum awareness tools, network telemetry, timing comparisons, station health data, and multiple user reports across a region. This can create the impression that anomalies ought to be easy to classify. But more sensors do not abolish ambiguity. They often multiply it in a more disciplined form. One receiver may show degraded PNT integrity while another nearby performs adequately. One station may report poor downlink quality while another sees only modest degradation. A maritime user may experience a practical outage before a network manager sees enough evidence to call it one. Detection is therefore distributed and uneven. The first report is rarely the whole report.

That unevenness matters because attribution depends not only on what is observed but on how those observations line up in time, place, and system context. A suspected spoofing event cannot be assessed cleanly if timestamps between reporting systems are themselves under strain. A presumed jamming footprint may be hard to distinguish from local equipment or siting weakness if the same ground node has a history of fragility. A degraded navigation service may look deliberately targeted until weather, ionospheric conditions, or infrastructure stress are pulled back into the picture. Attribution is therefore an act of assembly. It requires technical evidence, environmental context, maintenance history, and operational judgement to be read together rather than in isolation.

A useful public example remains the recurring concern over GNSS interference in northern Scandinavia. What matters here is not only that such disturbances have been reported, but also that they illustrate how quickly a technical event can become a strategic suspicion. Civil aviation, military users, regulators, and neighbouring states all interpret the same anomaly through slightly different thresholds of concern. Some focus on operational safety. Others on hostile intent. Others on the adequacy of existing monitoring. This plurality does not mean truth is unreachable. It means that attribution in a contested northern setting is not a purely technical verdict delivered from nowhere. It is the convergence, or failure to converge, of several institutional ways of seeing.

A second example can be imagined from the imagery chain rather than navigation. A polar-orbiting system collects a valuable SAR scene over a sensitive Arctic area, but the product fails to arrive on the expected clock. One explanation is interference with a communications link. Another is ground-station trouble, backhaul disruption, processing backlog, or a timing fault somewhere below the satellite. If a state treats every such missing product as hostile action, it may manufacture escalation from ordinary systems weakness. If it treats every outage as routine friction, it may normalise real coercion. The problem is not that both explanations are equally likely in every case. It is that they can initially look similar enough to compete, particularly under pressure.

This is why uncertainty persists even when monitoring is sophisticated. People often imagine that enough instrumentation should dissolve doubt. In some cases it does. But sophisticated monitoring often produces probabilities, patterns, and narrowing ranges of explanation rather than courtroom certainty. It can show that an anomaly was regionally clustered, temporally aligned, or inconsistent with ordinary equipment behaviour. It may still struggle to identify the exact source, method, or intent with the confidence political actors would prefer. In the Arctic, where distances are large and direct inspection costly, this residual uncertainty can endure longer than institutions find comfortable. The system knows more than before and still not enough to end argument.

That residual uncertainty matters for strategic stability because actors rarely respond only to evidence; they respond to what they believe the evidence implies about future risk. A state that interprets ambiguous interference as deliberate coercion may raise readiness, alter deployments, or harden public rhetoric. Another that assumes the first state's reaction is opportunistic or inflated may respond in kind. A cycle begins not from proven intent but from asymmetric thresholds for acting under doubt. The Arctic is especially sensitive to this because the theatre is sparse, distances are long, and the costs of waiting for perfect certainty may appear too high to decision-makers already primed for suspicion.

This is why a cautious framework is not the same thing as a timid one. Caution here means separating several questions that political argument likes to collapse. Was there a real disruption? Where in the chain did it first appear? What alternative explanations remain technically plausible? What prior system weaknesses were already known? Which users were affected similarly and which were not? What evidence speaks to deliberate manipulation rather than ordinary strain? How much of the current judgement rests on context rather than direct proof? These questions do not delay seriousness. They make seriousness less reckless.

A credible limitation should be granted. Not every case deserves prolonged agnosticism. Some interference patterns are strong enough, repeated enough, or contextually sharp enough that deliberate action becomes the most convincing explanation. It would be careless to imply that uncertainty always paralyses judgement or that sophisticated actors can never reach firm conclusions. They often can. The problem lies elsewhere. Conclusions that may be compelling inside classified or technical channels are not always equally robust when translated into public accusation, alliance signalling, or escalatory posture. Confidence is not a single threshold. It changes with the consequence attached to the claim.

That concession strengthens the deeper argument. What matters is not whether attribution is possible in principle, but what kind of attribution is sufficient for which decision. A navigation warning may require only modest confidence that the service is degraded. A systems engineering fix may require stronger confidence about where the failure sits in the chain. A public accusation or deterrent signal may require yet another standard. Trouble begins when institutions slide between these levels without admitting that they are changing the burden of proof. The Arctic is fertile ground for such slippage because the technical environment already produces ambiguity and the political environment rewards confident stories.

Trust becomes visible here in behaviour. Operators trust their diagnostic framework when they widen margins, switch modes, or re-route services without needing to settle the full political meaning of the disruption at once. Analysts trust it when they present competing explanations with disciplined ranking rather than forced certainty. Governments distrust their own evidence when they delay public attribution or use more conditional language than the media would like. Distrust of another actor may, by contrast, lead them to speak more firmly than the available proof alone would justify. These choices are not rhetorical decorations. They reveal how uncertainty is being managed and where strategic stability is most vulnerable to strain.

The signal goes strange returns here because it captures the true beginning of many Arctic crises of interpretation. Not with proof, but with abnormality. From that point onward, the most dangerous move is often the most human one: to let the abnormality rush ahead of explanation because explanation is slow, the region is tense, and the architecture is already difficult to read. A cautious framework does not ask institutions to ignore danger. It asks them to distinguish danger from story too quickly told.

The harder question, then, is not whether disruption reports from the Arctic should be taken seriously. They should. The more serious question is what kind of seriousness the situation actually demands. Does the available evidence support a technical warning, a resilience response, a quiet diplomatic query, a public accusation, or merely a refusal to pretend that the signal's strangeness has already become a settled fact about intent? In the High North, strategic stability may depend less on denying uncertainty than on resisting the urge to treat uncertainty itself as proof.

Chapter 11

Cybersecurity and Command Links

How does a space system fail without anything visible happening in space? That question unsettles because it reverses the image most people carry in their heads. They imagine danger as a bright event: a satellite struck, a signal jammed, a launch interrupted, a dramatic loss of hardware overhead. Yet some of the most consequential failures begin in quieter places - an account with too much access, a software update that arrives trusted and leaves suspicion behind, a terminal configured carelessly, a cloud workflow altered just enough that the right data reaches the wrong queue. The satellite keeps flying. The system's integrity does not.

That quietness is part of the problem. A compromised surveillance architecture can continue to look healthy from a distance. Images may still arrive. Links may still appear available. Products may still move through dashboards and dissemination channels. Only later does the harder question emerge: were they the right products, on the right clock, under the right authority, and with a provenance anyone can still defend? In the Arctic, where distance, sparse redundancy, and compressed decision windows already burden the chain, hidden compromise can be more strategically damaging than visible interruption. It does not merely stop observation. It can bend trust.

The deepest vulnerability therefore sits lower than public imagination expects. Spacecraft hardware matters, but the broader exposure often lies in the ground segment, the user terminal, the software stack, and the institutional habits through which commands, updates, credentials, and products move. A surveillance system is now as much a set of permissions, logs, interfaces, automated processes, and cloud dependencies as it is a set of sensors and antennas. That is the central tension here. The same architectures that make Arctic awareness faster, more distributed, and more scalable also enlarge the surface through which manipulation, confusion, or quiet degradation can enter.

A password is a gate. That is the modest motif worth keeping in view because it resists the temptation to think of cyber risk as something abstract and grand. Gates can be strong, poorly latched, badly monitored, or left open by habit rather than malice. The same is true of command paths, dissemination routes, software supply chains, and operational recovery plans. A compromised account can alter tasking, redirect outputs, delay products, or expose patterns of interest without any cinematic breach of the spacecraft itself. The Arctic makes such subtleties matter more because time lost to uncertainty is often time lost to action, and because the cost of verifying what happened after the fact can be unusually high.

The stakes run beyond secrecy in the narrow sense. Cyber compromise in this context is not only about stolen data or dramatic system loss. It is about the integrity of the chain: whether commands are genuine, whether data has been altered, whether an update behaves as intended, whether recovery is fast enough that the interruption does not itself become strategically meaningful, whether institutions can prove to themselves and to others what the system did and why. Arctic surveillance depends on credibility as much as collection. A product that arrives on time but under doubtful provenance may be less useful than a delayed product whose path can still be trusted.

That is why software practice belongs inside any serious account of Arctic resilience. Modern systems depend on frequent updates, third-party components, distributed development, and automated maintenance precisely because static systems age too quickly to remain useful. Improvement and exposure arrive together. A system that never updates becomes brittle. A system that updates constantly inherits new governance burdens: who approved the change, who reviewed the code, who can roll it back, who noticed the anomaly, who had the authority to act while the remote site slept. Technical sophistication does not dissolve institutional responsibility. It multiplies it.

The same logic shapes the language of secure links. Authentication, encryption, and access control are essential, but their presence should not be treated as a magic phrase that ends inquiry. A secure link is not simply a link wrapped in reassuring vocabulary. It is a relationship between identity, key management, software behaviour, user discipline, and auditability. If any one of those is handled carelessly, the promise narrows. In a dual-use Arctic system shared across agencies, contractors, and operating environments, that narrowing can remain hidden until a fault, compromise, or disputed incident forces everyone to ask who actually had authority and how anyone knows.

The path ahead begins on the ground, where terminals, cloud workflows, and operator habits often present a broader attack surface than the spacecraft they serve. It then turns to software supply chains and the uneasy bargain between rapid improvement and accumulated trust, before moving into the basic ideas behind authentication, encryption, and access control as shields that matter but never settle everything by themselves. From there the argument shifts into continuity and recovery, where resilience is measured not by the absence of faults but by the ability to sustain useful service through them, and it closes in the human systems of auditing, separation of duties, and reporting that make technical control more than a design aspiration.

The harder question, then, is not whether Arctic surveillance systems can be made more secure. They can, and they must be. The more serious question is what kind of confidence remains when the chain is stressed but not obviously broken: when the image still arrives, the account still works, the update still appears routine, and the command still looks valid. At that point, what exactly is the system trusting - its engineering, its governance, or merely its own habit of assuming that a closed gate is still locked?

Ground segment as the primary attack surface

In February 2022, as Viasat's KA-SAT network was disrupted at the opening edge of Russia's full-scale invasion of Ukraine, the most striking lesson was not about a satellite falling silent in orbit. The more revealing fact was that the damage spread through ground equipment and user terminals, with effects felt far beyond any single military theatre. A space-enabled service had been degraded through the earthly machinery that made it useful. The spacecraft remained part of the story. It was not the easiest part to touch.

That lesson travels directly to the Arctic. Public imagination still places the drama of vulnerability overhead, in the satellite bus, the sensor, the gleaming hardware beyond the atmosphere. Yet modern surveillance systems live on the ground as much as in space. Their commands, credentials, updates, interfaces, terminal configurations, cloud workflows, and dissemination rules all create points of entry broader and more various than the spacecraft itself. In the High North, where systems already depend on sparse infrastructure, long support chains, and remote teams, that broader exposure becomes a defining condition of resilience rather than a technical side note.

The key claim is simple and disturbing. The ground segment is often the easier place to bend a space system because it is where the system becomes social. Show a satellite architecture on a slide and the spacecraft looks singular and crisp. Name the full operational reality and the picture expands at once: ground stations, user terminals, contractor networks, cloud processing, credential stores, update services, ticketing systems, admin consoles, and human operators spread across organisations and time zones. Explain why this matters, and the implication becomes larger than cybersecurity in the narrow sense. A compromise on the ground can alter what gets tasked, where products are routed, which users receive them, and how quickly anomalies are noticed, all without a visible event in space.

A password opens the door. That quiet motif is worth keeping because it prevents the subject from drifting into abstraction. A compromised account may seem mundane beside the grandeur of an orbiting platform, yet its consequences can be strategic. An intruder does not need to seize total command of a satellite to damage the mission. It may be enough to adjust dissemination permissions, suppress alerts, alter tasking requests, delay processing queues, or redirect outputs to quieter channels. In the Arctic, where latency itself is often a security variable, even a modest change to dissemination paths can alter who knows what, and when, while the spacecraft continues to operate as though nothing extraordinary has happened.

This is why user terminals deserve more attention than they usually receive. They are often physically dispersed, administered unevenly, exposed to local conditions, and used by people whose main expertise lies in operations rather than cyber hygiene. In the Arctic, terminals may sit on vessels, in remote stations, at austere field sites, or inside institutions whose maintenance burdens are already stretched by weather, distance, and staffing. Such terminals are not marginal accessories. They are where the wider system meets the human world. A weakly managed terminal can become a route into credentials, a source of false trust in corrupted outputs, or a point from which service is degraded locally while the central architecture continues to believe itself intact.

Cloud processing deepens the same vulnerability in a subtler register. Space systems now rely heavily on cloud-hosted storage, automated workflows, analytic environments, identity systems, and shared data services because the old model of isolated ground rooms and self-contained pipelines no longer scales. That shift brings real advantages in speed, flexibility, and integration. It also means that a surveillance architecture increasingly inherits the cyber exposure of its software and service ecosystem. A cloud environment holding imagery, metadata, tasking tools, and user permissions may present a richer attack surface than the spacecraft because it concentrates authority in a place built for access. The Arctic sharpens the consequence because remote users often depend on that environment more completely than users in denser theatres with easier fallback.

A practical example makes the point better than any slogan. Imagine a northern monitoring network whose satellite products normally flow from collection to cloud processing and then to several civil and security users through role-based dissemination rules. A compromised account with sufficient privilege does not need to rewrite the whole system. It only needs to alter distribution settings so that one class of product goes first to the wrong recipients, or arrives late to the right ones, or loses the automatic alert that normally accompanies it. The resulting degradation may first appear as ordinary workflow trouble: why did this product arrive here first, why was that one missing, why did the maritime centre not receive the cue in time? The space segment still functions. The mission has nonetheless changed.

A second example lies in the history of satellite service disruptions that have propagated through terrestrial infrastructure rather than through direct compromise of orbital assets. The KA-SAT incident is the clearest public case because it demonstrated how interference with ground-side systems and terminals could disable service at scale without any need for spectacular action in orbit. The relevance here is not to collapse all Arctic risk into the same pattern, but to show the principle plainly. Space-enabled capability can be strategically damaged where it is managed, authenticated, and consumed, not only where it flies. Once that principle is admitted, resilience planning has to move its centre of gravity downward.

This is where institutional discipline becomes as important as engineering. A strong spacecraft design cannot compensate for sloppy credential practices, overprivileged accounts, weak separation of duties, inattentive monitoring, or improvised operational workarounds that quietly bypass formal controls. The reason is structural. Cybersecurity in the ground segment is partly a problem of design and partly a problem of habit. Who can approve a tasking change? Who can modify dissemination paths? Who reviews anomalous login behaviour? Who can push updates to a terminal in the field? Who notices when a product goes missing from the queue and knows that this is unusual enough to investigate? These are governance questions, but in a distributed surveillance system they become part of the engineering outcome.

A credible limitation should be admitted. Spacecraft hardware is not invulnerable, and it would be foolish to imply that the orbital segment no longer matters as a target or source of cyber risk. Command links, onboard software, and supporting systems all remain important. Some missions also maintain strong segmentation between ground tools and space control for exactly this reason. The point is not that the spacecraft can be ignored. It is that public fascination with it can obscure where wider exposure often resides in practice.

That concession strengthens the deeper argument. The ground segment is usually broader, more numerous, more heterogeneous, and more organisationally entangled than the spacecraft. It includes vendors, contractors, remote users, shared services, update processes, cloud identities, audit systems, and human discretion. It is also where dual-use realities become hardest to separate. A single architecture may serve researchers, civilian agencies, commercial users, and security institutions through overlapping ground infrastructure and partially shared credentials or workflows. Such complexity does not automatically produce weakness, but it does mean that resilience depends on how well institutions govern access, not only on how cleverly engineers harden equipment.

This matters for Arctic surveillance because compromise in such an environment can be strategically ambiguous. A lost image, a delayed alert, a misrouted product, a changed tasking queue, or a silent terminal may first resemble ordinary harsh-environment friction. Weather, power stress, and communications weakness already create enough noise that cyber compromise can hide among them for longer than organisations would like to admit. The danger cuts both ways. Institutions may overreact to routine failure by reading hostile action into it. They may also underreact because they have grown used to systems misbehaving at the margins. The broader the ground attack surface, the more important disciplined interpretation becomes.

Trust, here, is visible in operational behaviour. An organisation that truly trusts its ground segment will know who can do what, will be able to reconstruct why a dissemination path changed, and will detect quickly when a product's journey through the system departs from the norm. An organisation that half-trusts it will maintain quiet alternative channels, duplicate notifications, side messages, and personal confirmation habits because the formal architecture does not fully command belief. These improvised habits may keep a mission alive. They may also indicate that the official system has already become too porous, too opaque, or too institutionally fragmented to carry the confidence placed in it.

The password returns because it captures the inversion this section insists upon. The glamorous asset is overhead. The decisive vulnerability may be a gate on Earth, opened not by brute force but by ordinary access granted too widely, monitored too loosely, or understood too narrowly. Arctic resilience, therefore, depends not only on hardened terminals and well-designed clouds but on administrative restraint, careful auditing, alert operators, and an institutional culture willing to treat mundane access decisions as strategic infrastructure.

The harder question, then, is not whether a ground segment can be defended perfectly. It cannot. The more serious question is whether the institutions relying on Arctic surveillance understand how much control sits below the spacecraft and how quietly that control can be altered. When a product is late, a queue shifts, a tasking decision changes, or a dissemination path quietly diverges, who can say with confidence whether the system is encountering weather, error, or compromise - and how much of that answer depends on discipline rather than hardware?

Software supply chains and update practices

In December 2020, the SolarWinds compromise startled institutions far beyond the company itself because it exposed a harsh truth about modern technical systems: sometimes the most dangerous way into a network is through something already trusted to keep that network healthy. The episode did not belong to Arctic surveillance, yet its lesson reaches there with unnerving precision. A system can be improved, patched, updated, and professionally maintained while becoming more exposed at the same time. The very pathway used to keep capability current can become the pathway through which confidence begins to erode.

That tension sits squarely inside contemporary space systems. Satellites, ground stations, user terminals, cloud pipelines, analytics platforms, scheduling tools, and command interfaces no longer behave like sealed machines that change rarely and cautiously. They depend on software that is revised, refined, corrected, and extended far more often than older public imaginations about space still allow. A surveillance architecture serving the Arctic may rely on code written by different teams, libraries maintained by outside vendors, automated deployment routines, cloud services, firmware updates, and remote support personnel spread across several organisations and time zones. The gain is real. So is the burden. A system that never updates decays. A system that updates constantly must learn how to trust itself repeatedly.

This is the central trade-off. Show a modern Arctic surveillance network honestly and software sits everywhere: in terminals exposed to weather and weak connectivity, in processing chains that turn raw scenes into usable products, in orchestration tools that manage tasking and routing, in identity systems that decide who can do what, and sometimes in the spacecraft itself. Name the practical benefit and it is easy to recognise - faster improvement, quicker bug fixing, better analytics, more flexible workflows, and the ability to respond to new operational demands without rebuilding hardware. Explain the cost, and the argument sharpens. Every update widens governance burdens because every update asks an institution to decide who may change the system, how that change is verified, when it is deployed, and what happens if trust in the change proves misplaced.

A patch can travel far. That quiet motif helps because it captures the mismatch between the apparent modesty of software maintenance and the scale of its consequences. A patch may look like a routine technical event, a housekeeping act at the edge of administration. In Arctic operations, however, the same patch may alter how a remote terminal authenticates, how a processing queue prioritises products, how imagery is formatted for users, how a dashboard displays alerts, or how a command interface behaves when connectivity weakens. None of those changes is automatically suspect. All of them matter because Arctic systems often run close to their margins. A small software change can therefore shift the timing, reliability, or interpretability of surveillance in ways that exceed its modest bureaucratic label.

This is one reason software supply chains deserve to be treated as operational architecture rather than as background procurement. A space system rarely runs on code written by one organisation alone. It depends on operating systems, security tools, commercial libraries, firmware, cloud services, vendor-supported components, and development practices shaped by several entities that may not share the same risk culture. In the Arctic, where remote operations frequently rely on automation and distributed support because physical access is slow and costly, this dependence grows deeper rather than shallower. The system becomes not just a chain of hardware and links, but a chain of inherited trust. Each outside component extends capability. Each also adds another promise that must be believed, monitored, and, at times, doubted.

A useful example lies in the broader reliance of remote infrastructure on automated update mechanisms. Arctic terminals and ground systems are often too dispersed, too numerous, or too hard to reach for every change to be performed manually on site. Remote updates are therefore not a convenience but a necessity. They allow operators to correct faults, improve performance, and keep security controls from stagnating. Yet the same mechanism that permits rapid recovery also creates an avenue through which a flawed or poorly governed update can spread quickly across a fleet of terminals or services. The Arctic magnifies this because rollback may be slower, site visits harder, and local staff too thinly spread to compensate with immediate manual intervention.

A second example can be imagined from the processing layer rather than the terminal. Consider a cloud-based imagery pipeline serving several Arctic users. A third-party component used for metadata handling or access control is updated to improve efficiency and compatibility. The update functions technically, yet introduces a subtle change in how products are routed or labelled. A maritime operations centre begins receiving some alerts later than before. Another user receives more than it should. The satellites still collect. The links still carry data. The compromise, if compromise it is, or the flaw, if flaw it is, does not announce itself dramatically. It reveals itself in trust: who received what, why it arrived on that path, and whether anyone can reconstruct the reason with confidence.

This is where governance burdens become unavoidable. Software updates are often described as engineering events, but they are institutional decisions in motion. Someone approves the change. Someone defines the testing threshold. Someone decides whether the urgency of a patch outweighs the risk of deployment under Arctic operating conditions. Someone chooses whether updates should be automatic, staged, delayed, or blocked when connectivity is uncertain. Someone decides who may sign code, who may push it, who may reverse it, and who audits what happened afterwards. These questions are not embellishments attached to technical excellence. They are the conditions under which technical excellence can be trusted.

The difficulty is sharpened by the rhythm of remote operations. Arctic surveillance often depends on distributed teams because geography makes centralised, physically proximate support unrealistic. Engineers, analysts, operators, and vendors may work across time zones and institutions, handing off responsibility through software platforms and procedural routines rather than face-to-face oversight. That model can be highly effective. It can also weaken shared situational awareness about what a change really means on the ground. A developer may see a harmless performance improvement. A field operator may inherit a new failure mode in a place where recovery is slow. A security team may approve an automated practice whose consequences are easy to reverse in a city and painful to unwind at a remote node near the ice. Software culture thus becomes part of Arctic operating culture whether institutions admit it or not.

A credible limitation must be acknowledged. There is no serious alternative to frequent software change in systems of this complexity. A space architecture that refuses third-party components, avoids updates, and insists on perfect internal control would quickly become too rigid, too expensive, and too stale to meet evolving technical and operational demands. The point is not to romanticise a simpler past. Nor is it to imply that outside software is inherently suspect. Modern capability depends on shared tools, reusable components, and ongoing revision. Much of the impressive agility in contemporary Earth observation and command-link resilience comes from exactly these practices.

But the concession strengthens the central argument rather than weakening it. Because frequent updates and third-party dependencies are unavoidable, the quality of software governance becomes part of operational trust. Institutions cannot ask whether change should happen. They must ask how trustworthy their process for living with change has become. Can they verify what they install? Can they stage deployments sensibly? Can they separate urgent security patching from opportunistic feature growth? Can they observe the effects of change quickly enough to catch quiet drift in dissemination, permissions, or timing before that drift becomes strategically meaningful? In the Arctic, those questions matter more because the cost of late recognition is higher and the opportunities for immediate local correction are fewer.

This is why software practice should be linked directly to operational trust rather than confined to technical management. A system trusted in the Arctic is not one that merely updates often or securely in the abstract. It is one whose users believe they understand the provenance of its behaviour. When a product arrives on time, a queue changes, a terminal behaves differently, or a processing chain becomes more efficient, they need confidence that the change was intentional, authorised, and reversible. That confidence is not born from code alone. It comes from documentation, testing discipline, clear ownership, audit trails, careful rollout, and an institutional willingness to treat software maintenance as a strategic act.

Trust becomes visible in behaviour. Operators who trust their update practices do not fear every patch, but they do know which changes are expected and why. Analysts who trust the software chain can distinguish between a new feature and an unexplained deviation. Managers who trust governance know who to wake when an automated deployment behaves oddly at a remote site. Institutions that do not trust their own software practice reveal it quickly: shadow systems proliferate, updates are delayed until they become liabilities, vendors are blamed for surprises that internal oversight should have anticipated, and manual workarounds become the quiet constitution of the mission. These behaviours often say more about cyber resilience than any formal statement of compliance.

The patch returns here because it captures the moral economy of the whole problem. A patch promises care. It says the system is being tended, corrected, improved. That promise is often true. Yet the same act asks the receiving institution to believe that the channel of improvement remains worthy of confidence, that the unseen contributors behind the change have not altered something more than intended, and that the organisation can still explain its own system after the change lands. In the Arctic, where remoteness and timing pressures leave little room for easy reversal, that belief must be earned repeatedly.

The harder question, then, is not whether modern space systems should update frequently or rely on outside components. They already do, and for good reasons. The more serious question is what kind of governance makes such dependence compatible with operational trust. When the next update reaches a remote terminal, a cloud pipeline, or a command interface serving the High North, who can say with confidence not merely that it was authenticated, but that its consequences were understood, observed, and kept within bounds before the Arctic had to teach the system what it had really changed?

Authentication, encryption, and access control concepts

In February 2022, when Viasat's KA-SAT network suffered a disruptive cyber event linked to the opening phase of Russia's full-scale invasion of Ukraine, the most sobering lesson was not merely that service could be interrupted. It was that the trust placed in a link can fail long before the spacecraft itself appears in trouble. Commands, user terminals, and service pathways all depend on a prior act of belief: belief that the right person is speaking, that the message has not been altered, and that the route through which it travelled remains worthy of confidence. A link may stay up. Trust may already be down.

That distinction matters acutely in Arctic surveillance. A "secure link" is often invoked as though it were a settled property, like orbit altitude or antenna size. It is nothing of the sort. Security in command and data links is not a single switch turned to *on*. It is a layered set of decisions about identity, secrecy, permission, and evidence. When those layers hold, systems behave as if integrity were natural. When they weaken, the resulting uncertainty can spread far beyond technical teams. An image may arrive, but can the institution prove it came from the source it claims? A command may execute, but was it truly authorised? In the High North, where delayed verification can be costly and redundancy thin, these questions are not academic.

The most useful way to think about authentication, encryption, and access control is to see them as answers to three different questions. Show a command link in operation and the first question is identity: who is trying to speak? Name the answer properly and one has authentication, the practice of testing whether an actor, device, or service is really what it says it is. Explain why this matters, and the implication becomes immediate. If identity is weakly established, every later safeguard inherits uncertainty. A perfectly hidden message sent by the wrong party remains a dangerous message. A beautifully encrypted command is not safe merely because it is unreadable to outsiders if the system cannot distinguish the legitimate sender from an impostor.

Encryption addresses a different question: what may others learn from what is being sent? The ordinary language of secrecy makes this seem straightforward, yet the Arctic complicates it by putting such weight on distribution, latency, and trust across long chains. Encrypting a link can protect the content of commands or data from casual interception or unauthorised reading. That is crucial, especially where communications pass through shared or exposed infrastructure. But encryption does not, by itself, guarantee that the content is correct, that the sender is genuine, or that the receiving institution still understands the provenance of the product once it has been decrypted and moved through other systems. Secrecy is valuable. It is not the whole of integrity.

Access control asks a third question: even if an identity is real, what is it allowed to do? A password opens the door. That quiet motif is worth keeping because it strips the issue of false grandeur. Cybersecurity in space-ground systems often fails not because nobody thought about secrecy, but because too many doors open too far for too many people, services, or automated processes. A legitimate user account may possess more permissions than its role truly requires. A vendor tool may be allowed to act broadly because convenience has outrun discipline. A cloud service may inherit rights that were never properly narrowed after a crisis ended. Access control exists to stop identity from becoming a blank cheque. It is the difference between being admitted to the building and being handed every key.

These three ideas are often discussed together because they depend on one another in practice. A system that authenticates poorly cannot make strong access decisions. A system that encrypts well but assigns permissions carelessly may preserve secrecy while still enabling corruption from within. A system that limits permissions elegantly but leaves transmission unprotected may still bleed information or invite manipulation. The important point is not that every measure must be perfect. Perfection is not available. The important point is that each measure answers a distinct kind of doubt, and none should be mistaken for the others. In Arctic surveillance, where service may continue through periods of strain and ambiguity, this distinction is essential because the most dangerous failures are often those that remain superficially plausible.

A useful public example comes again from the wider implications of the KA-SAT disruption. The event demonstrated, among other things, that service integrity in a space-enabled network can be compromised through terrestrial pathways and control arrangements rather than through any spectacular failure of orbital hardware. The relevance here is conceptual. A network may possess encryption, authenticated channels, and formal permissions on paper while still proving vulnerable if those mechanisms are badly governed, inconsistently deployed, or undermined through adjacent systems. "Protected" is therefore not a meaningful word unless one can say from what, by which means, and with what residual uncertainty.

A second example can be imagined from an Arctic dissemination chain. A remote sensing product is generated from a polar pass and routed through cloud processing to several authorised users. The image itself remains unaltered. The encryption protecting transport works as intended. Yet a compromised identity or mis-scoped access control rule changes where the processed product is sent and which alerts accompany it. One operations centre receives it late. Another receives it first without the usual contextual note. To the outside observer, nothing dramatic has happened. There is no cinematic breach, no satellite going dark, no obvious sign in space. But provenance and trust have been bent. The system has not simply transmitted data. It has redefined who counts as the right recipient at the right time.

This is why secure command links deserve special caution in the way they are discussed. When people hear that a command path is secure, they often imagine a clean promise: nobody unauthorised can issue instructions; nobody can tamper with what is sent; nobody can see inside the exchange. Real systems are more conditional. Authentication can be strong and still rely on imperfect account hygiene. Encryption can protect content while leaving metadata, workflow timing, or downstream handling more exposed than decision-makers realise. Access control can be formally elegant and still be eroded by exceptions, emergency privileges, shared credentials, or under-audited service accounts. A secure link is therefore best understood not as a badge but as a claim that requires inspection.

That inspection should focus less on technical mystique than on practical questions. Who can issue commands, and how is that identity established? How are permissions separated so that no single account, team, or automated process quietly governs too much of the chain? What evidence exists after the fact to show which commands were sent, by whom, through which system state, and with what result? How are keys, credentials, and privileged roles managed across remote sites, distributed teams, and vendor relationships? The reader does not need implementation detail to think well about these matters. They need to know that confidentiality, integrity, and authority are different promises, each of which can fail alone or in concert.

A credible limitation must be admitted. None of these safeguards can promise invulnerability. Authentication can be undermined by compromised identities or weak operational discipline. Encryption can protect data in transit while doing little for data mishandled at either end. Access controls can be carefully designed and then bypassed by human improvisation, poor review, or the quiet accumulation of exceptional cases. It would be careless to speak as though correct concepts automatically produce correct institutions. They do not. The difference between theory and practice is where most of the serious risk lives.

But the concession strengthens the central point. Because no safeguard is absolute, the right way to ask about protection is not "Is this link secure?" but "What confidence does this architecture justify, and against which kinds of failure?" That question is particularly valuable in the Arctic, where long chains of custody, distributed operations, intermittent connectivity, and multi-agency workflows already make provenance harder to hold onto. A product that arrives from a distant system through several hands and automated stages needs more than a general aura of security. It needs an account of why it should still be trusted at the moment a decision depends on it.

This is where operational trust and cryptographic trust begin to diverge. A system may satisfy technical requirements for authenticating commands and encrypting data while still failing to earn operational confidence if users cannot reconstruct its path, interpret its permissions, or understand the provenance of unusual behaviour. Conversely, an institution may trust a system because it has grown familiar with it, even when its formal protections are weaker or less well-governed than it assumes. The Arctic punishes both errors. It punishes undue scepticism by slowing response and overburdening already thin decision cycles. It punishes unwarranted faith by letting compromised or misrouted products carry more authority than they deserve.

Trust becomes visible in behaviour. Operators trust authentication when they rely on system identities rather than personal workarounds to confirm commands. They trust encryption when they permit sensitive products to move through established channels without private parallel messaging to "make sure". They trust access controls when they accept that not everyone who can see a product should be able to redirect or alter its flow. Distrust shows itself just as clearly: shared credentials, verbal overrides, duplicate informal dissemination paths, or the quiet expectation that one must know the right person rather than trust the authorised system. Those behaviours reveal whether the concepts have become living architecture or remain words in a policy document.

The password returns because it captures the moral simplicity beneath all the technical language. Someone is always deciding who may enter, who may speak, who may listen, and who may carry the message onwards. Authentication, encryption, and access control are ways of making that decision more disciplined and more defensible. They are not ways of abolishing human judgement or institutional fallibility. In Arctic surveillance, where confidence must travel across distance, weather, automation, and politics, that defensibility matters as much as raw secrecy.

The harder question, then, is not whether a link can be made secure in some formal sense. It can, to a degree that may be highly meaningful. The more serious question is what the system can later prove about that security when a product is disputed, a command seems strange, or a dissemination path changes under stress. At that point, what exactly is being trusted: the mathematics of the link, the discipline of the institution, or the hope that the two have remained aligned long enough for the Arctic not to expose the gap between them?

Operational continuity and recovery planning

In February 2022, when the disruption to Viasat's KA-SAT network spread through user terminals and ground systems at the opening edge of Russia's full-scale invasion of Ukraine, the most important question was not whether the service had failed. It had. The harder and more revealing question was what remained possible while failure was still being understood and before full restoration could be achieved. Could users still communicate by another path? Could commands still move? Could the system sustain enough continuity that a strategic shock did not become a total operational blackout?

That question matters even more in the Arctic, because the north punishes every assumption that service restoration can wait politely for normal business hours. A link can fail in darkness, over distance, in weather, in places where the nearest technician is far away and the next good opportunity for corroboration may already be closing. Under such conditions, continuity is not the fantasy of a system that never breaks. It is the discipline of a system designed to remain useful while broken, compromised, or reduced. In Arctic surveillance, that distinction is not administrative. It can determine whether an outage becomes a nuisance, a blind spot, or a strategic event.

The central point is straightforward but often neglected. Continuity is a mode of service, not a slogan about resilience. Show a surveillance architecture under fault, cyber compromise, degraded timing, or communications loss, and the familiar question is, "How quickly can normal service be restored?" Name the more important question properly and it becomes, "What can the system still do before normality returns?" Explain why this matters, and the implication becomes clear. In the Arctic, the interval between disruption and recovery is often the decisive interval.

A system that restores perfectly but too late may still have failed on the clock that mattered.

A fallback path matters. That is the quiet motif worth holding onto. Not because fallback is glamorous - it rarely is - but because it reveals whether continuity has been treated as real architecture or as hopeful language. A fallback dissemination path, an alternative terminal, a degraded but trusted mode of product delivery, a simplified alert channel, a manual approval route, a secondary communications service, a cached local dataset, a retained timing holdover capability: these are all ways of saying that a system has more than one posture. When the preferred path fails, the mission does not have to vanish. It may become narrower, slower, or less elegant. But if it remains governed and useful, continuity has done its work.

This is why recovery planning should be understood as part of latency management rather than as an entirely separate security topic. The book's broader argument has already shown that delay is not an incidental inconvenience. It shapes the real meaning of awareness. Recovery inherits that same logic. A disruption that lasts only a short time in engineering terms may still be strategically consequential if it covers the only window in which an Arctic contact could be cued, confirmed, rerouted, or publicly framed. Conversely, a system that remains partially available through a degraded mode may preserve enough situational awareness that the later return to full service feels like restoration rather than rescue. Recovery speed therefore matters not in the abstract, but in relation to the decision cycle that the service is meant to support.

A practical example shows why. Imagine a polar-orbiting system collecting radar imagery of maritime activity near sensitive northern waters. A cyber fault or ground-side compromise interrupts the usual cloud-based dissemination path just after collection. In one architecture, the product waits until the primary route is restored, by which time the vessel has moved and the opportunity for immediate follow-up has faded. In another, a fallback path sends a lower-fidelity alert and essential metadata to the relevant users while full dissemination remains impaired. The second system is not unbroken. It is continuous. The difference lies not in perfection, but in the ability to preserve a meaningful fraction of the mission while the preferred chain is still damaged.

A second example comes from the history of remote Arctic infrastructure more broadly, where continuity has long depended on degraded modes rather than on all-or-nothing expectations. Stations, networks, and field systems in the north have often survived difficult periods not because they avoided failure entirely, but because operators knew which functions had to be preserved first, which could be sacrificed temporarily, and how to route around local damage while waiting for fuller repair. The specific technology changes across decades. The operational lesson does not. In harsh environments, continuity belongs to systems that already know how to become less than themselves without becoming useless.

This is why recovery planning cannot be reduced to technical restoration procedures. It is also a theory of operational triage. Which services come back first? Which users receive them first? Which products can be simplified without becoming misleading? Which permissions remain active in degraded mode? Which automated functions should be disabled rather than trusted when integrity is uncertain? A continuity plan that does not answer such questions is not really a plan. It is a promise to make decisions during the worst moment rather than before it. In the Arctic, where pressure, distance, and sparse redundancy already narrow the room for improvisation, that is an expensive way to learn what the system values.

A credible limitation must be admitted. Not every service can be preserved meaningfully under degradation, and not every fallback is worth the complexity it adds. Some capabilities depend so heavily on full-bandwidth transmission, strong timing integrity, or uncompromised cloud processing that degraded operation risks producing more confusion than help. It would be careless to imply that every system should keep doing something under all conditions merely for the sake of continuity. Sometimes stopping a function is the more disciplined choice, especially when integrity is in doubt.

But the concession strengthens the core argument rather than weakening it. Continuity is not the refusal to fail. It is the intelligent ranking of what must remain trustworthy when failure has already occurred. That may mean preserving alerts while suspending full analytics. It may mean keeping low-bandwidth dissemination alive while halting automated routing until permissions are revalidated. It may mean favouring human review over speed for a time. The point is not to continue everything. It is to know, in advance, what kind of partial service is still better than silence on the clock the Arctic imposes.

This is where continuity planning and institutional trust become inseparable. A technically elegant fallback route is useless if operators do not know it exists, do not recognise when to invoke it, or distrust the data it carries. A secondary dissemination path may reduce outage impact only if the receiving users are prepared to treat it as authoritative enough for the decisions it supports. A degraded manual workflow may preserve mission continuity only if responsibilities and thresholds are already understood across agencies and shifts. The human system therefore matters as much as the engineering one. Continuity lives in rehearsal, authority, and judgement, not only in backup hardware.

The Arctic makes this painfully visible because delayed restoration often has strategic meaning even when the underlying compromise or fault is eventually contained. A state may infer hostile pressure from a disruption that lasts through a sensitive window. An ally may lose confidence in shared surveillance if fallback pathways prove weaker than advertised. A local operator may overreact because the absence of timely products feels like total blindness, even when some lower-grade awareness could have been preserved. Continuity planning is thus not only about keeping systems alive. It is about preventing delay itself from acquiring more political significance than the original fault deserves.

Trust appears here in operational behaviour. Institutions that trust their continuity plans do not improvise their first degraded mode in the middle of a disruption. They know which path to fall back on, what quality to expect from it, and what decisions it can still honestly support. Institutions that do not trust those plans reveal it quickly: side channels proliferate, manual workarounds multiply, users cling to stale dashboards because the official backup is unfamiliar, and leaders discover too late that "resilient" meant something closer to "restorable eventually" than "useful under stress". These are not minor cultural details. They are the visible signs of whether continuity has been built into the architecture or merely spoken around it.

The fallback path returns because it clarifies the real moral of the subject. Recovery is important, but recovery after total silence may still be a strategic defeat if the silence covered the only period that mattered. A fallback path does not abolish compromise, fault, or degraded service. It narrows the interval in which those conditions can dictate the whole meaning of the event. In a region as unforgiving as the Arctic, that narrowing can be the difference between a manageable incident and a cascading loss of confidence.

The harder question, then, is not whether systems will fail, be compromised, or enter degraded states. They will. The more serious question is what they continue to provide during that interval, and how quickly operators can move from disruption to a mode that still deserves trust. When the primary path breaks in the High North, does the system fall silent while it waits to become itself again, or does it know how to remain useful enough that the clock of Arctic decision-making does not outrun the recovery effort?

Governance, auditing, and institutional accountability

In February 2022, when the disruption to Viasat's KA-SAT network spread through user terminals and terrestrial service pathways at the opening edge of Russia's full-scale invasion of Ukraine, the obvious questions were technical. What failed? How far had it spread? What could be restored, and how quickly? The less glamorous questions arrived just behind them and proved just as important. Who had authority over key decisions? Who could see what had happened inside the system? Which logs could be trusted? Which organisation had to report what to whom, and on what clock? The event was not only a lesson in cyber vulnerability. It was a lesson in governance under stress.

That lesson belongs squarely in the Arctic. A surveillance architecture in the High North is rarely owned, staffed, governed, and used by one institution alone. Civil agencies, commercial providers, research actors, defence organisations, contractors, cloud vendors, terminal operators, and partner governments may all touch the same broad chain. The result is not necessarily confusion. It can produce powerful capability. But it also means that resilience depends on more than engineering. It depends on whether the human system around the technology can say, with confidence and speed, who changed what, who approved it, who noticed the anomaly, and who had the right to act before the delay itself became consequential.

This is the central claim. Accountability mechanisms are not administrative decoration around a surveillance system. They are part of the surveillance system. Show a technically sophisticated Arctic architecture and it is tempting to focus on sensors, links, encryption, cloud workflows, and fallback pathways. Name the deeper requirement properly and one sees that none of these measures means much without records, separation of powers, reporting discipline, and institutional clarity strong enough to make their effects legible. Explain why this matters, and the implication becomes hard to avoid. A system that cannot explain its own actions under stress is not merely badly governed. It is less secure, less resilient, and less strategically credible than its hardware suggests.

A logbook matters. That quiet motif deserves to stay in view because it is humbler than the subject and closer to its truth. In older forms of navigation and command, the logbook recorded what had happened, who had acted, and in what sequence. Modern digital systems have not outgrown that need. They have multiplied it. A surveillance architecture now depends on audit trails, access histories, system logs, workflow records, and incident reports that perform the same moral function: they make action traceable. In the Arctic, where latency is consequential and remote operations often depend on distributed teams and automation, the ability to reconstruct events is not retrospective luxury. It is part of real-time trust.

Auditing sits at the centre of this because it answers a question no encryption scheme or terminal hardening measure can answer on its own: what actually happened inside the system? Technical controls may prevent some errors and intrusions, but they do not remove the need to examine behaviour. A tasking rule changed. A dissemination path shifted. An account exercised unusual privileges. An update rolled out unevenly. A product arrived late to one user and early to another. Without auditing, these facts remain anecdotes and suspicions. With auditing, they begin to acquire sequence, accountability, and pattern. In an Arctic context, where environmental difficulty already generates noise, that distinction is decisive. Auditing is what stops every anomaly from becoming either a paranoid theory or a dismissed inconvenience.

This is why separation of duties matters so much in dual-use systems. The phrase can sound bureaucratic until one imagines its absence. A single actor able to approve a tasking change, alter dissemination permissions, suppress alerts, and sign off on the incident record would not merely hold too much authority; that actor would collapse the system's ability to verify itself. Separation of duties is therefore less about mistrusting individuals than about preserving the architecture's capacity to produce defensible truth under pressure. In a system that spans agencies with different missions and risk cultures, this becomes even more important. What one organisation treats as an acceptable emergency shortcut, another may see as an unacceptable erosion of evidence and control. Governance must hold those tensions before crisis makes them unforgiving.

A useful example can be drawn from any shared Arctic monitoring environment in which civil, commercial, and security users rely on overlapping infrastructure. Suppose a dissemination rule is altered so that a class of high-latitude imagery products now goes first to a different operations centre, or reaches one user stripped of contextual metadata. Technically, the system may still function. Politically and operationally, the consequences can be severe. If the change was unauthorised, slow to detect, or impossible to reconstruct afterwards, then the institution has suffered more than a routing error. It has lost the ability to say with confidence how its own surveillance chain behaved. That loss is strategic because it undermines both internal decision-making and outward credibility.

A second example lies in incident reporting itself, particularly in systems whose owners and users do not share a single command culture. Commercial providers may report anomalies on one cadence and with one threshold for alarm. Defence users may expect another. Civil agencies may privilege service restoration over evidentiary preservation, while intelligence or security institutions may reverse that priority. None of these preferences is irrational in isolation. Trouble begins when they collide inside the same architecture. If one organisation delays reporting to confirm a fault while another interprets silence as concealment, trust begins to erode precisely when clear reporting matters most. The Arctic magnifies this because long distances and fragile timelines make "we are still checking" a heavier sentence than it might be elsewhere.

This is why governance choices shape resilience outcomes so directly. A resilient system is not simply one with good hardware and strong software controls. It is one in which institutions know who owns the risk at each stage, who is obliged to speak when something goes wrong, and who has the authority to choose between continuity, containment, disclosure, and temporary shutdown. These are not abstract managerial niceties. They determine whether compromise spreads quietly, whether delay accumulates unnoticed, whether an outage is interpreted accurately, and whether a degraded service remains trustworthy enough to use while fuller answers are still emerging. In the Arctic, where recovery windows are narrow and ambiguity politically costly, governance becomes operational tempo by other means.

A credible limitation should be acknowledged. Good governance does not prevent every failure, and it should not be romanticised as a substitute for technical competence. Logs can be incomplete, audits can be ignored, separation of duties can become performative, and incident reporting can deteriorate into ritual language that conceals more than it reveals. Institutions may possess impressive accountability structures on paper and still prove indecisive or evasive in practice. It would be careless to suggest that formal mechanisms guarantee resilience. They do not.

But the concession strengthens the deeper argument rather than weakening it. Because technical controls can fail, accountability becomes more important, not less. The question is not whether governance can make a system invulnerable. It is whether governance can make the system legible enough to recover intelligently, assign responsibility fairly, and preserve confidence while facts are still emerging. In a dual-use Arctic architecture, that legibility is one of the few ways to prevent ordinary faults, cyber compromise, and inter-agency friction from collapsing into the same operational fog. A system that cannot explain itself will often struggle to repair itself, and may find that outside actors define the narrative of failure before it has done so internally.

This is especially important where different agencies bring different notions of acceptable risk. A research organisation may tolerate temporary data loss that a coastguard or defence user cannot. A commercial operator may prioritise service continuity that a security office would briefly suspend to preserve integrity. A civilian ministry may see rapid public reporting as responsible transparency, while another part of the state sees it as premature exposure. These are not pathologies. They are predictable consequences of mixed institutional ecology. Governance earns its keep by making those differences visible before crisis, not by pretending they will disappear once a problem arises. In the Arctic, where multi-use infrastructures are normal rather than exceptional, this pre-negotiation of responsibility is part of capability itself.

Trust reveals itself here in very practical ways. Institutions that trust their governance do not need to guess who altered a permission, who approved an update, or who should issue the first report when something suspicious occurs. They know where the record lives and who is answerable for it. Institutions that do not trust their governance show the opposite signs: side channels flourish, people preserve private records because formal logs feel insufficient, cross-agency suspicion rises quickly, and post-incident reviews become arguments about memory rather than evidence. These are not merely cultural failings. They are signals that the surveillance architecture has been designed without enough regard for how humans actually prove, dispute, and repair action within it.

The logbook returns because it captures the true scale of the issue. However advanced the system becomes, someone must still be able to say: this is what changed, this is who changed it, this is why it was permitted, this is when the anomaly was noticed, and this is how the response unfolded. Without that sequence, technical controls lose much of their meaning. Authentication without auditable use, recovery without accountable decision-making, encryption without incident reporting, continuity without documented authority - these are all partial securities, impressive until tested.

The harder question, then, is not whether Arctic surveillance systems should invest in governance alongside engineering. They must. The more serious question is whether their governance is strong enough to survive the mixed loyalties, uneven risk cultures, and distributed authorities that dual-use systems inevitably create. When the next fault, compromise, or unexplained delay appears, will the institutions involved be able to reconstruct the truth of their own system quickly enough to preserve trust - or will the absence of a reliable logbook become part of the incident itself?

Chapter 12

Space Debris and Polar Orbital Congestion

What does it mean to win better Arctic visibility if the orbit that makes that visibility possible grows steadily less governable? The question sounds like a technical afterthought until one remembers how much of northern surveillance depends on the same narrow families of low Earth orbit. The more states and firms seek persistent watch over ice, sea, and coast, the more they crowd into corridors whose appeal is obvious and whose fragility is easier to ignore. A useful orbit begins to resemble a busy road: still open, still valuable, yet increasingly shaped by the behaviour of everyone else using it.

The Arctic gives this problem a distinctive sharpness. Earth observation missions looking north are often drawn towards similar altitude and inclination bands because those bands offer the sort of repeatable coverage and viewing conditions operator's prize. That convergence is rational. It is also cumulative. Each new platform enters not an empty sky but a traffic environment already carrying the legacy of past choices, past collisions, past fragmentations, past assumptions about what would remain tolerable. The surveillance race therefore acquires a second character alongside the first. It becomes a traffic management problem conducted at orbital speed and under strategic pressure.

That is the chapter's central tension. States and companies pursue persistence because persistence promises awareness, deterrence, reassurance, and competitive advantage. Yet the very effort to sustain that awareness can degrade the environment on which it depends. A satellite that must manoeuvre more often to avoid conjunctions spends fuel it cannot replace. A constellation that promises repeatable timing becomes less predictable when avoidance activity begins to alter pass geometry. A shared orbital corridor can support transparency for years and then become a source of uncertainty because too many actors have treated safe access as an inexhaustible condition rather than a managed one.

A lane narrows. That quiet image is enough. No ornate metaphor is needed. A narrowing lane does not become unusable all at once. It becomes more demanding. Drivers leave less margin. Small mistakes matter more. Everyone becomes more dependent on rules, on anticipation, on the competence and restraint of others whom they do not control. Polar low Earth orbit increasingly carries that logic. The lane remains open, but its use now depends on conjunction screening, manoeuvre discipline, shared expectations, and a tolerance for operational friction that can quietly alter what surveillance systems deliver on the ground.

This matters because debris and congestion are not merely engineering headaches. They influence strategic reliability. A conjunction warning can force a manoeuvre that saves a spacecraft and disturbs the timing of a planned collection. An avoidance decision can preserve platform safety while sacrificing a downlink opportunity or introducing delay into an already narrow Arctic decision cycle. A destructive event long in the past can continue shaping today's operating choices because fragments do not obey political calendars. In that sense, space debris is not dead history. It is active structure. It changes what missions cost, how much risk operators absorb, and how confidently states can promise persistent watch over northern theatres.

The stakes also run deeper than asset protection. Arctic surveillance has repeatedly been linked in this book to credibility: credibility of coverage claims, of warning timelines, of shared transparency, of the chain connecting collection to action. Orbital congestion presses directly on that credibility because it erodes continuity from a distance. A public map may still suggest clean persistence. The operator may know that persistence now depends on more avoidance planning, more fuel discipline, more timing compromise, and more faith that other actors will behave with adequate restraint. The credibility of the surveillance system is therefore tied not only to its own engineering, but to the wider environmental conduct of every user in the same corridor.

That wider conduct is why responsibility enters the story so quickly. Debris is cumulative in a way many security effects are not. A strategic action, a careless disposal practice, a weak mitigation culture, or a decision to treat orbital occupancy as someone else's problem can outlast the moment that produced it and burden later missions with a degraded environment. The Arctic is particularly exposed because so many relevant surveillance architectures rely on orbits that resemble one another enough for congestion and fragmentation to become shared conditions rather than isolated annoyances. Stewardship here is not sentimentalism. It is one of the hidden prerequisites of strategic stability.

The path ahead begins with the logic of why polar low Earth orbit attracts so much traffic in the first place, because only then does congestion appear as a structural consequence rather than a surprise. It then turns towards the long afterlife of destructive events and fragmentation, where past acts continue to shape present risk, before settling into the uneasy everyday work of conjunction assessment, manoeuvre judgement, and the operational burdens those decisions impose. From there the argument opens into norms, mitigation, and responsibility, where the question is no longer merely how to survive a crowded environment, but what kind of conduct keeps surveillance credible enough that it does not undermine its own conditions of possibility.

The harder question, then, is not whether the Arctic surveillance contest can be sustained through more launches, more constellations, and more agile operations. It can, for a time. The more serious question is what happens when the very orbits that made northern awareness attractive become less predictable, less forgiving, and more politically charged because too many actors have treated shared orbital lanes as private opportunity. At what point does the race to see the Arctic more clearly begin to cloud the sky on which that sight depends?

Why polar LEO is crowded

In April 1972, when the first Landsat mission began systematic Earth observation from orbit, it helped establish more than a technical success. It fixed a habit of looking. Regular, repeatable observation from low Earth orbit became not simply possible but desirable, and the most desirable orbits turned out not to be infinitely various. Over time, missions seeking broad coverage, repeated access, and interpretable imagery did not scatter randomly across the sky. They converged. The Arctic lives with the consequences of that convergence because many of the same orbital choices that make northern surveillance attractive also make those lanes busy.

The crowding was not an accident. It arose from a series of rational decisions repeated by many actors who wanted similar benefits. An Earth observation mission often seeks a compromise that is hard to improve upon casually: low enough altitude for useful sensing, orbital paths that pass over high latitudes, and lighting conditions stable enough that images collected on different days can be compared without every scene becoming a new interpretive puzzle. Each requirement narrows the field. Put them together and many operators begin choosing from the same neighbourhoods of orbit. The sky is large. The useful lanes are fewer.

This is why polar low Earth orbit should be understood as an economic and analytical answer before it is seen as a congestion problem. Show a mission planner the Arctic, and several demands present themselves immediately. The system must pass over northern regions frequently. It must also serve the rest of the globe with enough regularity that the mission remains politically and commercially worthwhile. If optical imagery matters, the lighting should be predictable enough that change in the image more often reflects change on the ground rather than a radically different viewing condition. Name that requirement properly and one arrives at the gravitational pull of sun-synchronous and near-polar operating bands. Explain why that matters, and the implication becomes plain. The same orbits become attractive to many users for reasons that are individually sensible and collectively congesting.

A lane fills slowly. That quiet motif helps because it captures how crowding actually emerges. Not through one dramatic decision, but through repeated entry by actors responding to the same logic. A lane does not need to become physically impassable to become strategically burdensome. It only needs enough traffic that collision avoidance, conjunction screening, manoeuvre planning, and schedule discipline begin to consume increasing attention and fuel. In polar LEO, that burden matters especially because many of the missions there are not merely scientific ornaments. They support weather services, imaging markets, mapping, maritime awareness, defence planning, environmental monitoring, and the larger politics of who can watch the Arctic with confidence.

Consistent lighting is one of the strongest reasons for this convergence and one of the easiest to underestimate. Optical Earth observation does not simply want light. It wants comparable light. A scene taken under one sun angle and revisited under a radically different one may remain useful, but comparison becomes harder, shadows change, surface contrast behaves differently, and some forms of analysis lose their neatness. Missions that seek repeatability therefore value orbital arrangements that return them to roughly similar local solar times. This does not produce perfect continuity, especially in the Arctic where seasonal extremes complicate everything, but it creates a powerful organising preference. Once many operators adopt that preference, the result is not just a set of good missions. It is a shared orbital corridor.

Global coverage reinforces the same tendency. A mission aimed only at one nation or one sea lane might accept stranger trade-offs. Many Earth observation systems cannot. They are built to sell or serve globally, to revisit many latitudes, and to make the Arctic one important theatre among several rather than the only one. Near-polar trajectories are attractive because the Earth turns beneath them, allowing broad longitudinal coverage over time while repeatedly sweeping through high-latitude space. For Arctic surveillance this is a gift. For orbital traffic it is an accumulation. Each mission gains by entering the lane. The lane itself grows more crowded because so many missions are making the same rational choice.

This is where the Arctic surveillance race becomes a traffic management problem. A satellite designed to observe northern shipping, sea ice, coastal activity, or strategic infrastructure does not enter an empty sky and simply begin serving its mission. It enters a junction. Other spacecraft are already using similar altitude and inclination bands because they too require repeatability, coverage, and manageable imaging conditions. The surveillance contest therefore does not unfold only in terms of who owns more satellites or better sensors. It also unfolds in terms of who can operate most safely and predictably in a crowded environment without squandering fuel, disrupting pass timing, or exposing their constellations to avoidable risk. Visibility competes with survivability.

A useful public example lies in the long prominence of the Landsat and Sentinel families in Earth observation thinking, not because they are the only missions in relevant orbits, but because they illustrate the enduring attraction of repeatable, globally useful observation from near-polar pathways. The lesson is not about one programme's superiority. It is about a shared architectural instinct. Civil, commercial, and security-linked missions repeatedly gravitate towards similar bands because those bands solve real observation problems. Once that pattern is established across decades, crowding is no longer merely a symptom of recent competition. It becomes the cumulative geography of success.

A second example can be imagined from a more contemporary commercial imaging environment. A constellation operator promising frequent Arctic revisit needs satellites in the right inclinations and altitudes to maintain both northern access and broader market relevance. Another operator, serving a different customer base, may reach a strikingly similar conclusion. Their satellites are not identical, their products are not identical, and their business or mission models may differ sharply. Yet their trajectories converge enough that each must now care about the conduct of the other.

Traffic management ceases to be a background engineering matter. It becomes part of strategic planning, service reliability, and the credibility of every promise made to users about persistence.

A credible limitation should be admitted. Polar LEO is not crowded because engineers are unimaginative or because all missions are lazily copying one another. Many different orbit choices remain available, and some missions deliberately choose alternatives because their sensing goals, communications needs, or risk tolerances differ. It would be careless to suggest that Earth observation has only one viable path. Nor does crowding mean every satellite is perpetually on the brink of disaster. Operators still manage these environments with considerable skill.

But the concession sharpens the deeper point. The concentration matters precisely because so many missions are not forced into identical choices by ignorance, but drawn there by quality. They cluster where observation works well. The better those lanes serve repeatable imaging and high-latitude reach, the more attractive they become, and the more each additional entrant increases the collective burden of safe operation. Collision risk then stops being merely a hazard to platforms. It becomes a constraint on persistence, because manoeuvres consume fuel, alter orbital timing, complicate downlink plans, and gradually narrow the freedom with which operators can promise stable service. A system may still see the Arctic. It may do so under a growing tax of caution.

This is why manoeuvre budgets belong in the same conversation as surveillance claims. A satellite in a busy polar corridor must preserve enough control authority and fuel to avoid conjunctions across a mission lifetime. That reserve is not free. It competes with other desirable features of the mission and can quietly degrade long-term predictability. The more often the environment demands active management, the harder it becomes to speak as though persistence were simply a function of constellation size or sensor quality. It is also a function of how much orbital order remains available to support the mission without constant correction. The Arctic race is therefore partly a race to maintain orderly passage through a lane everyone wants to use.

The lane fills slowly returns because it captures the strategic mood of the problem. Congestion does not arrive as a single dramatic threshold after which the sky is suddenly unusable. It arrives as a mounting operational burden: more monitoring, more avoidance planning, more fuel sacrificed to prudence, more schedule variability, more attention spent on other actors' decisions. For surveillance systems, this means that orbital crowding can begin to shape latency and reliability before any collision occurs. A manoeuvre small enough to preserve safety may still move a pass, shrink a downlink window, or complicate the neat repeatability on which the service model was built. The customer sees a delay. The cause lies in traffic.

The harder question, then, is not why so many Earth observation systems want to be in polar low Earth orbit. The answer is clear enough: the lane is valuable because it solves real problems of coverage and repeatability. The more serious question is what happens when the very qualities that made the lane attractive begin to erode under the weight of success. At what point does a good orbit cease to be merely a good orbit and become a crowded commons in which every new claim to Arctic persistence also becomes a claim on everyone else's room to manoeuvre?

Legacy events and contemporary risk

On 10 February 2009, Iridium 33 and Cosmos 2251 collided in orbit above Siberia, turning two satellites into a lasting argument about what space operations leave behind after the immediate event has passed. The collision was dramatic in its own right, but its deeper significance has only grown clearer with time. A destructive moment in orbit does not end when operators stop watching the debris cloud spread. It persists as a changed environment, one in which later missions must fly through the consequences of a past decision, past failure, or past miscalculation. In polar low Earth orbit, where so many Earth observation systems repeatedly return to similar corridors, that persistence matters especially.

The Arctic inherits that persistence in a direct and uncomfortable way. Many of the satellites used to watch sea ice, shipping, coastlines, infrastructure, and strategic movement depend on orbital pathways that are attractive for good reasons: repeatability, high-latitude access, and broad Earth coverage. Those same pathways also intersect with the debris legacy of earlier destructive events and fragmentation episodes. The result is that contemporary Arctic surveillance does not operate in a clean environment to which risk arrives from outside. It operates inside an environment already shaped by prior acts whose consequences have outlived the moment that produced them.

This is the core argument. Debris should not be understood only as a collection of objects to be counted, tracked, or avoided. It is better understood as cumulative risk embedded in a shared orbital environment. Show an operator planning Arctic persistence and the mission may seem to hinge on sensor quality, revisit, downlink, and processing speed. Name the broader condition properly and another constraint comes into view: the orbital corridor itself now contains inherited hazards created by collisions, fragmentations, and destructive tests whose physical effects continue regardless of whether the political logic that produced them still feels immediate. Explain why that matters, and the implication becomes strategic. A state can inherit operational friction from another actor's past choice without any new hostile act taking place.

A shard stays aloft. That quiet motif captures the whole problem better than more elaborate language. A shard does not need intent. It does not need a flag. It does not need to know which mission it threatens. Once created, it becomes part of the environment that everyone else must interpret, manoeuvre through, and spend fuel to survive. In the Arctic context, that means a surveillance race driven by desire for persistence and repeatable access now unfolds in a sky where older acts continue to tax later missions. This is not merely unfortunate inheritance. It is the way strategic action in orbit acquires environmental afterlife.

The Iridium-Cosmos collision remains useful as a public example because it demonstrated that even without deliberate hostility, a single destructive event can alter the conjunction environment for years afterwards. The lesson was not only that satellites can collide. That had long been understood in principle. The sharper lesson was that the resulting debris does not remain local to the original event in any meaningful operational sense. It disperses across the space through which later missions must pass, adding to the burden of conjunction assessment, manoeuvre planning, and the quiet operational tax of flying in a less forgiving corridor. For Arctic operators, that tax is especially relevant because their preferred orbits are not casual choices but repeated returns to similar regions of space.

A second example lies in the 2007 Chinese anti-satellite test against Fengyun-1C, which is widely remembered not only for its political message at the time but for the debris burden it created afterwards. The enduring importance of that event is precisely that it outlasted its immediate strategic theatre. The fragments entered the wider low Earth orbit environment and thereby altered conditions for many users who had no role in the original act. The relevance for Arctic surveillance is not a matter of replaying one incident's politics. It is the more durable insight that strategic actions in orbit can become environmental facts for everyone else. The debris field stops being merely evidence of a decision and becomes part of the operating climate.

This is why fragmentation should be treated as cumulative rather than episodic. A single event may dominate headlines for a short time, but operators do not experience debris as headlines. They experience it as a background of probabilities, warnings, screening burdens, and altered manoeuvre logic spread across years. One fragment may never come close to a given spacecraft. Another may generate repeated alerts. A field created long ago may not threaten every mission equally, yet still thicken the general conjunction environment enough that planning, fuel management, and pass predictability all grow more constrained. In that sense, debris is closer to environmental pollution than to a single battlefield effect. It accumulates, disperses, and lingers in ways that make individual responsibility harder to isolate while making collective consequence impossible to ignore.

The Arctic sharpens this because many relevant missions share similar orbital preferences. Weather satellites, optical imagers, radar platforms, mapping systems, and surveillance constellations do not all fly in identical trajectories, but enough of them rely on comparable altitude and inclination bands that fragmentation in those neighbourhoods is felt as shared operational burden. The result is that debris becomes a structural issue for Arctic transparency itself. If safer passage through relevant orbits grows harder, then the continuity of observation also becomes harder to maintain. A state may still possess the satellites. It may no longer possess the same freedom to use them predictably and cheaply over time.

This is where contemporary risk becomes more than collision risk in the narrow sense. A debris-rich conjunction environment changes behaviour long before any impact occurs. Operators devote more effort to screening. Warning thresholds matter more. Manoeuvre choices become more frequent and more politically loaded when they affect collection plans, pass timing, or downlink opportunities. Fuel budgets tighten. Predictability softens. The mission's credibility begins to depend not only on whether the spacecraft survives, but on whether the service remains stable enough that users still treat it as a dependable source of awareness. For Arctic surveillance, this means that legacy debris events do not simply threaten hardware. They also threaten the continuity and tempo that make surveillance strategically meaningful.

A credible limitation should be admitted. Not every piece of debris becomes an equal threat, and not every conjunction warning reflects intolerable danger. Space situational awareness has improved markedly, and operators are not passive victims drifting helplessly through an uncontrolled sky. Screening, coordination, and manoeuvre discipline do reduce risk. It would be careless to imply that legacy debris has rendered polar low Earth orbit unmanageable or that every historical fragmentation event produces the same burden for every present mission. The environment remains usable, often highly so.

But that concession strengthens the deeper point rather than weakening it. The fact that operators can manage legacy risk does not make the risk trivial. It means only that management itself becomes a lasting cost of prior actions. A safer environment would demand less screening, fewer manoeuvres, less fuel sacrifice, and less uncertainty about pass stability. Once that is understood, debris stops looking like an unfortunate technical nuisance and begins to look like a strategic inheritance problem. The operators of Arctic surveillance systems are not only managing their own missions. They are also paying, in continuity and manoeuvre budget, for a history they did not fully choose.

This becomes especially important for how strategic competition in space is imagined. Destructive action in orbit is sometimes discussed in terms of immediate coercive effect or signalling value. That framing is too short-lived. The more enduring effect may be environmental. A state or actor can alter the conditions of later observation for many others by creating debris that persists after the original signalling moment has faded. In the Arctic context, where repeated surveillance is central to reassurance, deterrence, environmental management, and crisis interpretation, such environmental degradation is not secondary. It strikes at the conditions that make orderly watching possible. A less predictable orbit can mean a less predictable political picture on the ground.

Trust reveals itself here in operational conduct. Users trust an Arctic surveillance architecture when they assume planned passes, stable revisit patterns, and ordinary downlink schedules will hold often enough to support decisions without constant apology or explanation. They begin to distrust it when manoeuvres, conjunction alerts, or altered timings become frequent enough that persistence feels conditional rather than dependable. These behavioural shifts matter because surveillance credibility rests not only on what the sensor can do under ideal conditions, but on how much environmental friction the system must routinely absorb just to remain itself.

The shard stays aloft returns here because it points to the moral gravity of the issue. A fragment created by one event can outlast the policy language, the governments, and the momentary crisis that brought it into being. It then becomes part of the world others inherit. The Arctic, with its dependence on repeated use of similar orbital corridors, forces that inheritance into view more starkly than many other theatres. It asks operators and policymakers alike to confront a difficult truth: some strategic acts in space do not end when the signal is sent. They remain, quietly altering the lane for everyone who comes after.

The harder question, then, is not whether legacy events still matter to contemporary Arctic surveillance. They plainly do. The more serious question is how long strategic actors can continue treating debris as a technical after-effect rather than as a durable transformation of the security environment itself. When a conjunction warning appears in a polar corridor years after the original event that helped thicken that corridor, whose decision is the operator really managing in that moment - their own, or someone else's long-expired impulse that still has the power to shift a pass, consume fuel, and narrow the room for orderly observation?

Conjunction assessment and operational burden

On 10 February 2009, when Iridium 33 and Cosmos 2251 collided above Siberia, the event entered orbital history as a warning that space traffic was no longer an abstract planning problem. It was operational fact. For operators of Earth observation missions, especially those relying on polar low Earth orbit, the lesson was not only that collisions could happen. It was that avoidance would become a standing burden long before another collision took place. The modern surveillance satellite now flies under a second mission alongside imaging or communications: it must constantly survive the environment created by everyone else.

That burden is felt most sharply not at the moment of impact, but in the long sequence of decisions made to prevent one. A close approach warning rarely arrives as a simple command to move or stay still. It arrives as a problem of judgement under uncertainty. The projected path of one object must be compared with the path of another, the quality of the tracking data must be weighed, the possible miss distance interpreted, and the consequences of action or inaction placed side by side. In the Arctic context, where many observation systems occupy similar orbital corridors and where timing matters for downlink, revisit, and tasking, the decision to manoeuvre is never only about safety. It is also about what the mission will cease to do, even temporarily, in order to remain alive.

This is why conjunction assessment should be understood as a permanent operating condition rather than an occasional emergency drill. Show a polar Earth observation system on a coverage map and it appears elegant: regular passes, repeatable geometry, dependable access to high latitudes. Name the hidden process properly and another picture emerges. The operator is continuously comparing trajectories, reviewing warnings, ranking uncertainties, and deciding whether the risk of staying the course is greater than the cost of moving off it. Explain why that matters, and the implication becomes clear. Persistence is never free. It is purchased partly through fuel, partly through caution, and partly through the willingness to disturb one's own mission plan for the sake of future service.

A warning reshapes the day. That quiet motif captures the lived reality better than the language of orbital mechanics alone. A conjunction warning does not merely introduce a technical note into a log. It can reorder priorities across a control team, alter planned collections, complicate ground-station bookings, and force communication with other operators or traffic-management authorities. In a crowded polar environment, the warning may arrive against a background of other warnings, some of them routine, some of them less so. The challenge is to decide which warning is truly consequential without exhausting the mission through constant defensive motion. An operator who manoeuvres too readily squanders fuel and predictability. One who waits too confidently may accept a risk that later looks reckless.

The conceptual process of conjunction assessment is deceptively simple. Operators receive information about an expected close approach, compare the projected positions and uncertainties of the relevant objects, and decide whether the risk merits a manoeuvre. But each element contains judgement. Tracking data is not perfect. Uncertainty volumes shift as new observations arrive. The object approaching may be an active satellite, an inactive body, or debris with no possibility of coordination. The observing spacecraft may itself be in the middle of a carefully timed sequence of imaging, downlink, or calibration events. The decision therefore sits at the intersection of orbital safety and mission design. In the Arctic, because useful passes and downlink opportunities are often tightly sequenced, even a small orbital adjustment can travel forward into consequences the risk table alone does not show.

This is where fuel enters the story not as a background engineering quantity but as strategic time stored in propellant form. Every avoidance manoeuvre spends some portion of future freedom. A satellite with generous manoeuvre margin can absorb more conjunction events without profound changes to its mission life. A satellite with tighter reserves experiences each manoeuvre as a narrowing of options. That narrowing matters especially in high-latitude surveillance because the value of a platform often lies in its long-term repeatability. An operator planning a multi-year watch over northern routes, coastal installations, or ice behaviour depends on orbital stability as much as on sensor quality. Fuel spent on avoidance is not wasted if it prevents collision, but it is still transformed mission life. The craft survives by becoming slightly less capable of remaining what it was designed to be.

A useful public example lies in the operational culture that followed the 2009 Iridium-Cosmos collision. Operators across low Earth orbit did not simply become more aware of risk in the abstract. They became more dependent on continual conjunction screening and more conscious that close approaches could no longer be treated as rare curiosities. For polar missions, that shift was particularly significant because their orbital lanes already concentrated traffic. The lesson was not merely "avoid collision". It was that avoidance itself would become a recurring demand on planning, staffing, communications, and mission confidence. In that sense, the collision changed later operations even for satellites never physically touched by its debris.

A second example can be illustrated through the downlink problem that matters so much in Arctic systems. Imagine a radar satellite scheduled to collect imagery over northern waters and then downlink the product to a high-latitude ground station in a narrow window chosen to keep latency low. A conjunction warning arrives and the operator decides to manoeuvre conservatively. The satellite survives the encounter, but the altered orbital timing shifts the next pass just enough that the planned ground-station contact is no longer usable. The image is still collected, perhaps even beautifully. Yet delivery is delayed because the spacecraft now reaches the station under worse geometry or outside the booked slot. No collision occurred. No hardware failed. The burden of safe operation has nonetheless turned into latency, and latency in Arctic surveillance is often indistinguishable from diminished strategic value.

This is why conjunction assessment must be read as part of the collection-to-decision chain, not as a separate branch of orbital housekeeping. A manoeuvre can alter more than the spacecraft's physical position. It can change when a target is seen, how well a repeat pass aligns with earlier observations, whether a relay opportunity is available, whether a downlink window holds, and whether the resulting product arrives while the event still matters. In a denser operating environment, these distortions may be absorbed by other assets. In the Arctic, where alternative coverage is often thinner and the environment already punishes delay, the same distortions can be much harder to smooth away.

Coordination complicates the matter further. When the conjunction involves another active satellite rather than untracked debris, operators ideally communicate, compare intentions, and avoid both collision and contradictory manoeuvres. Yet even this apparently straightforward co-operation contains friction. Not all operators share the same thresholds for action. Not all are equally transparent about their planned manoeuvres. Commercial operators, civil agencies, military actors, and newer entrants may carry different risk cultures and different ideas about what counts as prudent behaviour. The result is that conjunction assessment is never merely technical. It is also social. A congested orbit depends on reciprocal legibility, and that legibility is uneven.

A credible limitation should be acknowledged. Not every conjunction warning leads to a manoeuvre, nor should it. A healthy operating regime does not treat every projected close approach as grounds for immediate orbital alteration. Better tracking, improved screening, and more disciplined analysis often allow operators to avoid unnecessary action. It would be careless to imply that polar LEO has become so crowded that satellites spend their lives zigzagging in panic. The system remains workable, and much of its work is managed well.

But the concession sharpens the deeper point rather than weakening it. The burden lies not only in the manoeuvres executed, but in the constant readiness to decide whether a manoeuvre is justified. Every credible warning consumes analytical attention. Every non-trivial warning creates a temporary competition between caution and continuity. Every executed manoeuvre introduces small perturbations that can ripple forward into pass timing, downlink schedules, coverage regularity, and fuel accounting. Conjunction assessment is therefore a tax on predictability even when collisions are successfully avoided. The safer the operator behaves, the more visible this tax can become.

This matters for Arctic surveillance because predictability is itself part of credibility. A system trusted to provide timely northern awareness is not judged solely by whether it remains intact in orbit. It is judged by whether it can continue to deliver useful observations on a clock decision-makers recognise as reliable. Frequent manoeuvres, or even frequent warnings requiring late adjustments, can erode that reliability. Planned revisit patterns become less exact. Downlink bookings become more brittle. Analysts lose some of the neat repeatability that helps them compare changes through time. The spacecraft is safer. The mission is also less steady. That is the trade-off operators live inside.

Trust shows itself here in visible behaviour. Operators trust their conjunction process when they can make avoidance decisions without paralysing the rest of the mission. Ground teams trust it when rescheduled downlinks, shifted pass times, and altered collection windows are understood as manageable consequences rather than unexplained disruptions. Users distrust it when coverage promises begin to feel conditional, when products arrive with irregular timing and insufficient explanation, or when manoeuvre decisions seem to emerge from opaque criteria. A system that cannot explain how safety choices affect service will struggle to sustain confidence even if it is, in a narrow sense, operating responsibly.

The warning reshapes the day returns because it clarifies the chapter's broader concern. Conjunction assessment is not just a technical shield held up against debris. It is a mechanism through which crowded orbits reach down into latency, mission planning, and service reliability on the ground. A warning may save a spacecraft and still cost an image, a timing window, a relay opportunity, or a politically valuable moment of observation. Arctic surveillance makes these trade-offs especially stark because the environment leaves fewer cheap substitutes when one carefully planned pass slips.

The harder question, then, is not whether operators should manoeuvre to preserve safety. Of course they should. The more serious question is what kind of surveillance architecture remains credible when safe behaviour increasingly requires deviations that make its timing less exact and its delivery less smooth. At what point does the burden of conjunction management stop looking like prudent orbital hygiene and start looking like a structural limit on the persistence that Arctic missions were built to promise?

Norms, mitigation, and responsibility

In 2007, when China destroyed the Fengyun-1C satellite in an anti-satellite test, the event did more than send a political signal in the moment. It changed the orbital environment that others would later inherit. That is the enduring fact that matters here. A strategic act in space can continue operating long after its immediate message has faded, not through rhetoric but through debris, altered conjunction risk, and the quiet burden imposed on later users of the same corridors. In polar low Earth orbit, where so many Earth observation missions pass repeatedly through similar bands, that burden is not abstract. It becomes part of the background against which Arctic surveillance must prove it can remain credible.

This is why mitigation and responsibility belong inside the language of security rather than outside it. They are sometimes treated as softer concerns: technical housekeeping, good citizenship, a matter for engineers and regulators after the real strategic competition has been decided elsewhere. That distinction does not survive contact with the Arctic. If a surveillance architecture depends on repeatable passes, stable manoeuvre margins, reliable downlink windows, and long mission life in crowded polar corridors, then the health of that orbital environment is part of the mission. A safer orbit does not merely reduce operational irritation. It preserves the continuity on which transparency, warning, and strategic reassurance depend.

The crucial point is that norms in space matter most when they stop sounding idealistic and start sounding practical. Show an operator trying to maintain persistent watch over northern sea routes, infrastructure, or military activity, and the immediate concerns seem concrete: collision risk, conjunction screening, fuel use, pass timing, downlink reliability. Name the larger framework properly and one sees that all of these depend partly on whether actors share restraint about how they launch, operate, manoeuvre, dispose of, or destroy objects in orbit. Explain why that matters, and the implication becomes difficult to evade. Mitigation is not merely a moral preference. It is a condition of usable persistence.

A lane stays open. That quiet motif is enough. Norms and mitigation practices matter because they help keep the lane open in a meaningful sense: not merely physically navigable for the next few passes, but governable over time for the many users who depend on it. In the Arctic, this matters with unusual sharpness because the value of surveillance lies not only in isolated images but in long sequences of dependable observation. A corridor cluttered by poor disposal practice, unmanaged fragmentation risk, or weak co-ordination can still be used. It simply becomes more expensive, less predictable, and less trustworthy. Continuity then begins to erode before any spectacular failure occurs.

Mitigation, at its most basic, is the effort to reduce avoidable harm to the orbital environment through design choices, operating practice, end-of-life planning, and restraint in behaviour that would needlessly thicken debris risk. None of this requires grand rhetoric to justify it. If one wants an orbit to remain useful for observation, one should not treat it as disposable. Yet the importance of mitigation grows precisely because so much of polar low Earth orbit is used by actors with very different motives. Civil agencies, commercial firms, defence organisations, weather services, research missions, and dual-use constellations may all rely on overlapping orbital bands while carrying very different ideas about urgency, acceptable risk, and institutional responsibility. Norms become important because shared corridors magnify the consequences of dissimilar habits.

This is where responsibility becomes strategically interesting. Responsibility in orbit is not just about who caused a past problem. It is about who behaves as though later users matter. A state or company that designs missions with disposal, co-ordination, and collision avoidance in mind is not merely behaving well in a generic sense. It is making a decision about what kind of environment it expects to rely on in future. In Arctic surveillance, that decision is tied directly to credibility. A system that promises persistent watch but contributes casually to orbital disorder is quietly undermining the conditions of its own promise. Stewardship and self-interest are not opposites here. They are often the same logic viewed from different distances.

A useful public example lies in the long afterlife of destructive anti-satellite activity. The reason such events remain significant is not only that they signal resolve or technological capability when they occur. It is that they alter the conjunction environment for operators who had nothing to do with the original calculation. The message may have been national. The consequences become communal. This matters for the Arctic because many relevant observation systems repeatedly occupy related corridors. A fragmentation event that thickens risk there does not discriminate between scientific, civil, commercial, or strategic missions. It taxes the whole lane. That is exactly why mitigation cannot be dismissed as a merely technical agenda detached from security competition. Competition conducted without restraint reshapes the field on which later competition must occur.

A second example comes from the quieter realm of ordinary operating practice. A mission that maintains good ephemeris quality, communicates its manoeuvres clearly, and manages end-of-life responsibly may never become famous for doing so. Yet such routine discipline can matter more to strategic stability than louder gestures. It reduces uncertainty for others. It lowers the chance that conjunction warnings turn into avoidable crises. It preserves fuel and predictability not only for the mission itself but for those sharing nearby space. In Arctic terms, that means more reliable revisit patterns, more stable downlink planning, and less chance that the surveillance chain is disrupted by environmental disorder of human making. Good conduct is rarely dramatic. Its absence often is.

A credible limitation should be acknowledged. Norms are not self-enforcing, and mitigation practices do not dissolve strategic rivalry. States and companies continue to calculate interests differently, and not every actor will treat shared orbital stewardship with equal seriousness. Some will accept higher environmental risk in pursuit of near-term strategic or economic gain. Others will endorse restraint publicly while behaving more opportunistically in practice. It would be careless to write as though consensus alone could keep polar LEO orderly. The orbital environment remains shaped by power, competition, uneven capability, and unequal willingness to bear constraint.

But that concession sharpens the argument rather than weakening it. Precisely because rivalry persists, norms matter as signals of what kinds of conduct actors are trying to normalise. They do not need to end competition to influence it. They only need to make some behaviours costlier in diplomatic, operational, or reputational terms, and other behaviours easier to defend and coordinate around. In a crowded orbital regime, even partial shared expectations about debris mitigation, avoidance conduct, and environmental restraint can lower the background noise of mistrust. That does not eliminate danger. It makes reliability less hostage to improvisation.

This is why safer orbits support more reliable transparency. The connection may sound indirect until one follows the chain. Transparency in Arctic surveillance depends on the continued ability to place sensors in the right corridors, keep them there long enough to build persistent records, manoeuvre them prudently without constant disruption, and trust that their pass timing and service continuity will remain stable enough to support shared interpretation. If the orbital environment grows more hazardous through neglect or deliberate disorder, transparency becomes more fragile. A state may still claim to watch. Its watching becomes less continuous, less predictable, and therefore less politically reassuring. Environmental stewardship enters security competition at exactly this point: not as a moral add-on, but as the infrastructure of credible observation.

Trust reveals itself here in operational behaviour. Operators trust the orbital environment when they can make collection and downlink plans without assuming repeated disturbance from avoidable debris risk. Governments trust it when they treat persistent surveillance as a dependable source of transparency rather than as a capability always one conjunction crisis away from interruption. Smaller users trust it when they believe the major actors will not degrade the lane so badly that only the richest and most manoeuvrable systems can survive comfortably. Once those forms of trust weaken, surveillance claims begin to look more contingent, and contingency in the Arctic quickly becomes a political problem.

The lane stays open returns here because it captures the practical heart of the matter. Norms and mitigation do not promise purity. They promise room to continue. In an orbital environment already marked by legacy debris, rising traffic, and strategic competition, room to continue is a serious achievement. The Arctic depends on that room because so much of its surveillance value lies in repeated, comparable, and dependable observation over time. A more hazardous orbital corridor is not just a dirtier environment. It is a less reliable basis for watchfulness, reassurance, and restraint.

The harder question, then, is not whether responsibility in orbit is compatible with security competition. It must be, because the competition is already taking place in shared lanes that no serious actor can afford to render unusable. The more serious question is what kind of competition Arctic surveillance systems are preparing for: one in which actors preserve the environmental conditions that make credible transparency possible, or one in which short-term advantage steadily corrodes the very orbits their own future awareness will depend upon. At what point does neglect of mitigation stop looking like ordinary strategic hardness and start looking like a quiet refusal to preserve the lane everyone still claims to need?

Chapter 13

Institutions and Rules in the High North

How can a region be densely governed and still remain strategically under-explained? That is the paradox of the contemporary Arctic. Its institutions are real, active, and often useful. They organise dialogue, sustain co-operation, and preserve a vocabulary of orderly engagement in a geography that would otherwise invite louder misunderstandings. Yet the growth of space-enabled surveillance reveals a harder fact: governance is strongest where actors agree to limit what counts as the subject of governance. Much of the tension now gathering around Arctic visibility lives precisely in what those institutions bracket, soften, or leave only partially named.

The same is true in orbit. Space activity is not lawless, nor is it governed in the tidy way public shorthand sometimes suggests. Responsibility, registration, peaceful use, national supervision, commercial participation, multinational operation - each sits inside an established legal and institutional language. But legal vocabulary does not end political dispute. A system may be lawful in status and still contentious in effect. A satellite may be properly registered and still contribute to a pattern of watching that another actor experiences as pressure rather than reassurance. Once surveillance becomes persistent, legality and acceptability begin to pull apart in ways that matter acutely over the High North.

This is the chapter's central tension. Institutions stabilise some things by refusing to stabilise others. They reduce friction by narrowing agendas, by speaking in certain registers and not others, by preserving co-operation where possible and leaving harder security competition to adjacent channels or to silence. That has been part of the Arctic's relative manageability. It may also be part of its present strain. Surveillance competition grows most easily in spaces where norms are thin, where legal language is broad but operational meaning is contested, and where actors can all claim a form of legitimacy while disagreeing sharply about what kind of watching changes the political weather.

A map has blank edges. That quiet motif matters here because the Arctic institutional landscape often looks fuller than it really is. A map with names, forums, agreements, and working groups can suggest comprehensive order. Yet every map has margins where the labels thin out and the practical questions get harder. In the High North, those margins are exactly where persistent surveillance now acquires strategic force. Institutions can support co-operation, but they do not automatically tell states what repeated imaging means, what level of orbital monitoring counts as reassurance, when commercial transparency becomes signalling, or how to manage rivalry conducted through systems that are both civil and security-relevant at once. The blank edges are where misreading grows.

This matters because misunderstanding rarely emerges from pure absence. More often it emerges from partial coverage. Actors assume an institution is carrying a burden it was never designed to bear, or they assume legal status settles a political argument that it only frames. The result is a dangerous softness in the middle of hard competition. A surveillance architecture may be technically lawful, commercially rational, and strategically inflammatory all at the same time. An information-sharing practice may reassure one audience while alarming another. A government may invoke institutional language to calm a dispute while the actual source of friction sits just beyond the institution's comfortable remit. The Arctic's relative order depends, in part, on these acts of selective framing. So does its fragility.

That fragility becomes sharper because visibility changes incentives. A region long shaped by distance, weather, and sparse on-scene confirmation now supports more frequent watching from space, more commercial imagery, more derived analytics, and more opportunities for public release. This does not simply produce clarity. It changes how actors behave in anticipation of being seen, how they interpret the concentration of attention, and how quickly they feel compelled to respond once an image or analytic claim begins to circulate. Institutions built to foster co-operation in the Arctic can help absorb some of that pressure, but they cannot dissolve it merely by existing. The watching itself alters the context in which their language is received.

That is why the relationship between space law and Arctic politics needs careful handling. Legal ideas provide structure, but they do not spare anyone the work of interpretation. Responsibility tells us something important. Registration tells us something else. Peaceful use, as a phrase, carries weight and ambiguity in equal measure. None of these concepts should be dismissed. None should be treated as self-executing answers to operational disputes over surveillance systems run by states, contractors, consortia, and commercial firms whose products may circulate far beyond the actor that commissioned them. The reader needs a firmer distinction than public argument usually offers: between what a system is allowed to be and how its use is likely to be read.

The path forward begins with the institutional architecture of Arctic governance itself, where co-operation has been real and durable partly because certain security questions were never fully brought into the room. It then turns to the high-level legal language that structures space activity, not to settle disputes in advance but to clarify the terms in which they are argued. From there the argument moves into confidence-building, transparency, and signalling, where the difficult question is not whether openness is good, but when it cools suspicion and when it sharpens it by changing who feels watched, exposed, or cornered.

The harder question, then, is not whether institutions and rules matter in the High North. They matter profoundly. The more serious question is whether they reach far enough, clearly enough, and credibly enough into the emerging politics of persistent surveillance to prevent legal form, commercial access, and strategic anxiety from colliding in the blank edges of the map. When the next dispute turns on who saw what, who released it, and what that visibility was meant to signal, which part of the Arctic's institutional order will actually hold - and which part will prove to have been a margin all along?

Arctic governance and security boundaries

In 1996, when the Ottawa Declaration established the Arctic Council, it gave the High North one of its most important institutional facts: a forum built to support co-operation while deliberately avoiding the hardest military questions. That choice was not a flaw in disguise. It was part of the forum's success. By narrowing its remit, the Council helped preserve a space in which environmental, scientific, and indigenous issues could be discussed without every exchange collapsing into a security argument. Yet the same act of institutional restraint created a lasting boundary. Some of the region's most sensitive strategic pressures were not solved. They were placed just beyond the main table.

That boundary matters more now that surveillance has become more persistent, more commercialised, and more entangled with civil activity. The Arctic is not governed by absence. It is governed by selective presence.

There are institutions, practices, working relationships, and habits of co-operation that remain real and important. But there is also a widening zone in which visibility, infrastructure, orbital services, maritime monitoring, and security competition overlap without being fully stabilised by any single forum or shared rulebook. The Arctic is governed. It is not fully covered.

This is the chapter's essential tension. Institutions shape behaviour not only by what they regulate, but by what they leave outside their comfortable jurisdiction. Show an Arctic council room, a coastguard dialogue, a scientific exchange, or a search-and-rescue framework, and one sees a region with genuine capacity for order. Name the missing piece properly and the picture changes. Hard security competition, especially where it intersects with space-enabled surveillance, often grows in the gaps between institutions rather than inside them. Explain why that matters, and the implication becomes plain. Misunderstanding thrives most easily where expectations are weak, language is thin, and actors can all claim legitimacy without sharing the same idea of what counts as responsible watching.

A map has margins. That quiet motif helps because it prevents the discussion from drifting into easy extremes. The Arctic is neither a lawless frontier nor a neatly governed zone in which every major source of tension has an institutional home. It is a region whose map of governance is dense in some areas and faint in others. Environmental co-operation, indigenous participation, scientific coordination, fisheries management, search and rescue, and practical state interaction have all given the region a degree of structure that outsiders sometimes underestimate. But strategic monitoring, military signalling, space-enabled observation, and the political uses of persistence often sit near the margins of that map. The institutions do not disappear there. Their grip simply weakens.

This is why Arctic governance cannot be assessed by asking only whether institutions exist. The harder and more relevant question is what kind of behaviour they can actually stabilise. Institutions work best where actors accept some shared vocabulary of purpose. Search and rescue is one such area because the need is concrete and the political cost of co-operation is relatively low. Scientific exchange has often worked similarly. Surveillance competition is different. A satellite image can support environmental management, commercial planning, sovereignty performance, military cueing, or diplomatic signalling, sometimes all at once. The same data stream that looks like transparency to one actor may feel like pressure to another. Institutions that were not built to arbitrate such layered meanings will struggle to do so merely by moral authority.

A useful public example lies in the long-standing role of the Arctic Council itself. Its importance should not be minimised. It helped keep co-operation alive in a region often imagined as inherently confrontational, and it gave indigenous organisations an institutional presence rare in many other geopolitical forums. But its deliberate bracketing of military security also illustrates the limits that matter here. That design helped protect co-operation. It also meant that when surveillance intensity, military posture, and strategic signalling began to interact more visibly, the principal regional forum was not designed to metabolise the argument. The result is not institutional failure in the crude sense. It is institutional partiality: success in some domains and thinness where the most contentious monitoring questions now gather.

A second example can be seen in the practical co-operation that has often endured among Arctic coastguards and operational agencies even during periods of broader political strain. Such relationships matter because they show that governance in the north is not merely declaratory. It can be functional, technical, and quietly resilient. Yet even this co-operation has limits. A coastguard channel may help clarify a maritime incident. It may do far less to settle what repeated satellite monitoring of a sensitive area is meant to signal, or whether a rapid public release of imagery was reassuring transparency or strategic accusation by other means. Functional channels reduce some forms of risk. They do not automatically generate norms for all the new forms of visibility that space systems have made routine.

This is where surveillance competition takes on its most Arctic character. It expands in the spaces institutions do not fully cover, precisely because those spaces are politically usable. An actor may increase watchfulness without formally breaching any agreed rule. Another may react strongly without being able to point to a clear institutional violation. Commercial providers may distribute imagery that is lawful, contractually routine, and strategically explosive all at once. The problem is not only that governance is incomplete. It is that incompleteness creates room for competing interpretations to harden without a trusted regional mechanism strong enough to settle them. What one side treats as ordinary monitoring, another may read as an attempt to redraw the emotional boundary between routine observation and coercive attention.

A credible limitation belongs here. Institutions do more than cynics sometimes allow. They shape habits, lower transaction costs, preserve communication, and keep some channels open even when larger politics turn cold. The Arctic has not remained manageable by accident. It has remained manageable in part because actors invested in frameworks that reduced the frequency of total misunderstanding. It would be careless to imply that governance matters only where it fails. Much of the region's relative stability has depended on precisely the kinds of co-operation that are easy to overlook because they become ordinary.

But the concession sharpens the deeper point rather than weakening it. The very success of partial governance can create complacency about what has not been governed. Actors may assume that because some channels are steady, the wider region is institutionally buffered against escalation. Yet surveillance competition, especially where enabled by satellites, dual-use services, and commercial imagery, tests parts of Arctic order that were never fully institutionalised. This is why governance and security boundaries must be examined together. A forum can be effective and still leave strategically sensitive ambiguity intact. A norm can be durable and still say little about whether persistent watchfulness is stabilising or provocative in a given context.

The phrase "security boundary" therefore deserves care. It does not only describe the line between civilian and military affairs. It also describes the point at which co-operative institutional language loses power to interpret what actors are doing. Beyond that boundary, the same behaviour may acquire sharply different meanings. A shared environmental product may remain uncontroversial. A focused sequence of collections over the same area may not. A communication channel may reduce risk after an incident begins. It may do little to shape the incentives that produced the incident in the first place. The Arctic's political problem is not that all boundaries are rigid. It is that some are blurry exactly where better shared understanding is most needed.

Trust reveals itself here in behaviour. States trust governance when they use regional institutions to clarify ambiguity rather than bypassing them at the first sign of strain. They distrust it when they treat those forums as useful for routine co-operation but irrelevant to serious questions of surveillance and signalling. Operators trust norms when they expect others to interpret certain monitoring patterns with restraint. They distrust them when they assume every concentrated act of watching will be read in the harshest available light. These behaviours tell the truth about what governance can stabilise. If actors behave as though the institution ends where strategic watching begins, then that is the real boundary, whatever the public language says.

The map has margins returns because it captures the practical lesson. Governance in the Arctic is not weak because it has edges. All governance has edges. The real question is whether those edges are recognised clearly enough that actors do not mistake institutional calm for strategic settlement. Where margins are thin, misunderstandings do not arrive from nowhere. They grow in the unruled overlap between lawful action, commercial capability, military sensitivity, and the accelerating visibility that space systems now provide.

The harder question, then, is not whether Arctic institutions can preserve co-operation. They can, and often do. The more serious question is what happens when the next episode of persistent surveillance, rapid imagery release, or concentrated monitoring pressure emerges just beyond the part of the map those institutions were built to stabilise. At that point, what holds the region steady: the governance that exists, the norms that are implied, or the hope that actors will show restraint in a space no one has fully agreed how to govern?

Space law basics for surveillance systems

In 1967, the Outer Space Treaty gave the world a vocabulary before it gave it detailed answers. That vocabulary still shapes how states, firms, and institutions talk about satellites today: responsibility, peaceful use, national supervision, registration, jurisdiction, liability. The treaty did not anticipate every commercial platform, dual-use service, cloud-processed imagery feed, or multinational surveillance chain now relevant to the Arctic. But it did establish the grammar in which those newer arrangements are debated. That matters because arguments in the High North are often not arguments about law alone. They are arguments conducted through legal words whose political meaning has widened.

A lawful satellite can still be unwelcome. That short sentence captures the tension that readers need to keep in mind. Arctic surveillance systems often operate through structures that would have seemed less familiar in earlier decades: commercial providers serving governments and private customers at once, payloads hosted on shared platforms, imagery processed in one jurisdiction and consumed in another, and data products that circulate across alliances, agencies, and markets before a political meaning has settled around them. In such a world, the question is rarely just whether something in orbit exists on a legally recognisable basis. The question is what legal status does and does not settle once watching becomes persistent, shared, and politically charged.

The first concept worth holding clearly is responsibility. Show a modern surveillance chain and the temptation is to distribute accountability thinly across manufacturers, launch providers, cloud services, insurers, analytics firms, and end users until no one seems to own the system in any serious sense. Space law resists that temptation. At a high level, responsibility remains tied to states, including for activities carried out by non-governmental entities under their jurisdiction or authorisation. Explain the practical meaning of that principle, and one sees why it still matters in Arctic debates. A commercial or mixed-use system does not float free of public accountability merely because private actors operate important parts of it. The state remains part of the legal story even when the market dominates the operational one.

This is especially important because Arctic surveillance often relies on multinational and commercial actors precisely where public debate most wants clarity. A state may buy imagery from a foreign company, route it through cloud infrastructure in another country, integrate it with national systems, and release selected products into public discussion under its own political authority. Another state may do something similar through a different legal and commercial chain. The activity in orbit may be easy to describe. The institutional identity of the system may not be. Responsibility matters because it stops the whole architecture dissolving into plausible deniability. Someone, in legal terms, remains answerable for the activity even when the operational chain is distributed.

A registry matters. That quiet motif helps because registration can sound dry until one remembers what it is for. Registration links a space object to a state in an identifiable way. It does not answer every political question about what the object is doing, but it gives the system a legal address of sorts. In debates over Arctic surveillance, this matters because registration helps readers distinguish between the nationality of an operator, the nationality of a customer, the place of launch, the place of data processing, and the state with which the object is legally associated. Those are not always the same thing, and public argument often blurs them. Registration does not dissolve ambiguity, but it reduces one kind of it.

The concept of jurisdiction follows naturally from this. A registered object does not become legally ownerless merely because it circles above everyone.

The law preserves a continuing relationship between a state and the objects it places on the register, along with associated questions of control and supervision. For the reader, the practical lesson is modest but important. When a surveillance satellite is discussed in Arctic political argument, one should ask not only who uses the data or who paid for the service, but who bears the formal legal relationship to the object itself. That relationship will not resolve every dispute, but without it the debate quickly drifts into a confusion of flags, firms, and end users.

Peaceful use is the phrase that causes the most misunderstanding because it sounds simpler than it is. In ordinary public discussion, it is often heard as if it meant the absence of all military relevance. That is not a safe assumption. Much of modern space activity is dual-use in the plainest sense: imagery useful for environmental observation may also support military awareness; communications supporting civil users may also matter for security operations; navigation and timing services sit inside both everyday infrastructure and strategic competition. The legal language of peaceful use, therefore, does not function as an easy sorting device between innocent and threatening systems. A surveillance architecture may be lawfully operated and still contribute to political unease, because legal permissibility and strategic reassurance are not synonyms.

That distinction matters acutely in the Arctic. A state may rely on a commercial constellation for maritime awareness, environmental response, and military cueing at once. Another may object not because the satellite lacks legal status, but because persistent monitoring of a sensitive area feels like pressure. Here the reader needs a disciplined separation between legal status and political acceptability. Law asks certain questions about responsibility, registration, and the broad permissibility of activity. Politics asks another set: is this pattern of observation stabilising or escalatory, routine or concentrated, transparent or accusatory? The two sets overlap. They do not collapse into one another. Confusing them is one of the fastest ways to talk past the real problem.

A useful public anchor remains the Outer Space Treaty itself, because it established the high-level principles still invoked whenever states discuss outer space activity in serious terms. Its continuing value is not that it answers every contemporary surveillance dilemma with mechanical clarity. It does not. Its value lies in providing a shared vocabulary through which newer arrangements can at least be argued intelligibly. A second anchor is the Registration Convention, which reinforces the importance of identifying space objects and linking them to states in a formal way.

Together, these instruments help explain why even highly commercial and multinational surveillance systems remain enmeshed in public law, however market-driven their day-to-day use may appear.

A credible limitation should be admitted plainly. High-level legal principles do not settle all the questions that matter most in Arctic surveillance. They do not tell states how comfortable they should feel about repeated commercial imaging of sensitive areas. They do not answer every dispute over whether a system's use is prudent, provocative, or merely unfortunate in timing. They do not erase the ambiguities created by mixed ownership, dual-use payloads, allied data-sharing, or public release of imagery during tense moments. It would be careless to pretend that legal vocabulary supplies full political settlement. Often it does not.

But that concession strengthens the deeper point rather than weakening it. Because law does not settle everything, readers need to understand what it *does* settle, and what remains open to political struggle. Responsibility tells us that private operation does not erase public accountability. Registration tells us that an object in orbit is not a legal mystery even when its services are globally distributed. Peaceful use, understood at a high level, warns against simplistic claims that legality depends on a complete absence of strategic relevance. These concepts do not dissolve disagreement. They help ensure the disagreement starts from something firmer than slogans.

This also clarifies why multinational and commercial actors make the Arctic debate harder, not easier. A service may be bought by one state, run by a firm in another, rely on software teams elsewhere, use a satellite registered under a particular national authority, and distribute products to a mixed civil-security audience. Public controversy will often gravitate towards whichever of these elements is most politically useful to emphasise. Legal analysis cannot stop that selectivity, but it can show that the architecture has several layers of identity and that one should not mistake one layer for the whole. A politically awkward surveillance practice is not automatically unlawful. A formally lawful one is not automatically prudent.

Trust becomes visible here in argumentative behaviour. States that want to calm a dispute often invoke legal status, registration, and routine operation to show that nothing extraordinary is occurring. States that want to sharpen concern often point instead to effect, concentration of attention, or the political context of the watching. Both moves can be intelligible. The reader's task is to notice which question is being answered and which one is being avoided. A speaker who proves registration has not yet proved reassurance. A critic who proves unease has not necessarily proved illegality. That gap is where much Arctic argument now lives.

The registry matters returns because it captures the practical discipline this section is trying to restore. Before deciding whether a surveillance system is acceptable, alarming, routine, or destabilising, one should know what object is being discussed, who is legally tied to it, who operates it, who uses its outputs, and which part of that chain is carrying the political weight of the debate. Only then can the reader separate the legal architecture from the strategic interpretation layered on top of it. Without that separation, discussions of Arctic surveillance drift too quickly into moral theatre.

The harder question, then, is not whether space law supplies a complete answer to surveillance in the High North. It does not. The more serious question is whether actors are using legal language to clarify responsibility and status, or to smuggle political comfort into places where law was never designed to provide it. When a satellite is lawfully registered, responsibly supervised, and formally acceptable in legal terms, what exactly remains to be argued about its watching - and why does that remainder so often matter more than the legal status everyone begins by citing?

Confidence-building, transparency, and signalling

In February 2022, when commercial satellite imagery of Russian deployments around Ukraine circulated rapidly through governments, newsrooms, and public debate, the images did more than document military facts. They changed the atmosphere in which those facts were interpreted. What had been argued through inference and diplomatic warning was now argued through visible evidence, or at least through something that looked sufficiently like evidence to narrow the room for denial. The release reassured some audiences, alarmed others, and hardened expectations almost at once. Transparency did not merely illuminate the scene. It altered it.

The Arctic lives close to that same tension, but under conditions that make it even harder to manage calmly. Distance is vast. Weather obscures. Surface traffic is sparse enough that what is seen can carry exaggerated meaning, and what is missed can encourage imagination to run ahead of proof. Persistent surveillance seems, at first glance, the perfect answer to such uncertainty. More watching should mean less misunderstanding. Sometimes it does. Yet the same persistence can also intensify strategic sensitivity, because repeated observation is never only informational. It can also be expressive. It can say: we are attentive, we are worried, we are suspicious, we want others to know we are looking.

This is the central difficulty. Confidence-building and transparency are often spoken of as if they automatically reduce risk, while signalling is treated as the more muscular and dangerous cousin. In practice the three are entangled. Show an Arctic actor sharing imagery, opening a communication channel, or disclosing a monitoring pattern, and the move may reassure by lowering uncertainty. Name the same act in another political context and it may look like pressure, accusation, or strategic theatre. Explain why that matters, and the implication becomes plain. Transparency is not neutral simply because it is factual. Its meaning depends on timing, audience, framing, and the surrounding level of trust.

A window can calm. That quiet motif is useful because it reminds us what transparency is trying to do at its best. It opens a view where distance, weather, and suspicion would otherwise thicken into rumour. Shared maritime data, notice of unusual activity, rapid clarification through operational channels, mutually intelligible reporting formats, and routine information exchange can all reduce the temptation to assume the worst. In the Arctic, where conditions already limit direct visibility and where misinterpretation can travel faster than physical confirmation, such windows matter. They help actors distinguish an anomaly from an escalation, a routine movement from a strategic test, an environmental event from a hostile signal.

This is why confidence-building mechanisms deserve more respect than they sometimes receive. They are not sentimental instruments for times of harmony. They are practical arrangements for times when trust is incomplete. Communication channels between operational agencies, predictable procedures for sharing certain classes of data, habits of advance notice, and the disciplined use of common reference points all help by reducing the number of dark spaces into which fear can pour. A region as difficult to observe as the Arctic benefits disproportionately from even modest improvements in mutual legibility. When actors can compare notes early, they are less likely to mistake every partial observation for proof of intent.

A useful public example lies in the practical co-operation that has often existed among Arctic coastguards and maritime authorities, even when wider politics have been strained. The value of such contact is not that it dissolves disagreement. It does something more modest and often more important. It creates a path by which an incident, a contact, or a puzzling movement can be queried before it is narrated at full strategic volume. A second example lies in the public release of commercial satellite imagery during crises. Such releases can reduce uncertainty for outside audiences, constrain implausible denials, and reassure smaller actors that events are being watched. But they also demonstrate the opposite risk. Once an image enters public circulation, it can harden a narrative before slower institutions have finished asking whether the scene means what the fastest interpretation says it means.

This is where signalling returns with force. Persistence changes incentives because it teaches actors that watching itself can carry political meaning. A state may share data to reassure allies or calm a public. Another may read the same release as an effort to isolate, embarrass, or pre-emptively frame an opponent. An operator may intensify collection over a sensitive Arctic area for reasons it regards as prudent monitoring. The watched party may experience the same act as concentrated scrutiny and infer that a red line is being drawn. The region's physical remoteness makes these judgments more volatile, not less, because mutual visibility is already thin before the first satellite image appears. The clearer the window becomes, the more carefully everyone studies not only what is visible through it, but who chose to open it and when.

A credible limitation should be acknowledged. Transparency does not always soothe, and secrecy does not always inflame. There are circumstances in which discretion reduces pressure, protects diplomatic room, and prevents every ambiguous event from becoming a public test of resolve. There are also circumstances in which excessive data sharing produces noise rather than clarity, overwhelms decision-makers, or gives adversaries more insight into how a system sees than prudence warrants. It would be careless to treat openness as a universal medicine. Confidence-building is not the same thing as indiscriminate exposure.

But that concession sharpens the real lesson. The question is not whether transparency is good or bad in the abstract. The question is what kind of uncertainty it is reducing, for whom, and at what political cost. A shared operational picture may be excellent for preventing maritime misunderstanding and poor for managing a politically explosive military incident. A public image release may strengthen deterrence by demonstrating attention and weaken stability by cornering actors into immediate public response. A communication channel may prevent tactical confusion and still leave the wider strategic meaning of the watched activity unresolved. In other words, transparency helps most when it is matched to the problem it claims to solve.

This is why the reader needs a framework rather than a reflex. One should ask whether the transparency being offered is reciprocal or one-sided, routine or exceptional, operational or public, clarifying or performative. One should ask who gains reassurance from it and who instead feels newly exposed. One should ask whether the communication channel in question exists early enough to matter, whether the shared data can actually be interpreted in common, and whether the release of information narrows room for dangerous fantasy or narrows room for useful diplomacy. These are not cynical questions. They are the necessary questions in a region where persistence has changed the emotional temperature of observation.

Trust becomes visible in behaviour. Actors who trust a transparency mechanism use it before suspicion hardens into accusation. They pick up the line, compare the track, share the clarification, or release the image with restraint rather than theatrical flourish. Actors who distrust it wait, hedge, or route communication through more political channels, treating the same mechanism as too weak, too partial, or too easily instrumentalised. The same is true of signalling. A state confident that persistent monitoring will be read as reassurance behaves differently from one that expects every act of watching to be read as challenge. Those expectations shape not only what is communicated, but what is chosen to remain visible or hidden.

The window returns because it captures the unresolved nature of the problem. A window can calm because it lets others see. It can also inflame because it frames what they see and tells them that someone chose the moment of visibility. In the Arctic, where weather, distance, and sparse traffic already limit natural clarity, the politics of opening and closing that window have become inseparable from the politics of surveillance itself.

The harder question, then, is not whether confidence-building and transparency should be part of Arctic stability. They must be. The more serious question is when they are serving understanding and when they are serving narrative advantage under the cover of understanding. When the next image is shared, the next operational channel activated, or the next persistent watch pattern becomes visible to those being watched, who will read the gesture as reassurance - and who will see, through the same clear window, the beginning of pressure rather than the easing of it?

Chapter 14

Defining Persistence in Arctic Surveillance

What does it mean to say that the Arctic is being watched persistently? The phrase sounds precise until one asks the first serious follow-up. Persistently in what sense: continuously, frequently, selectively, or only after something suspicious has already happened? The answer changes more than vocabulary. It changes procurement, posture, confidence, and blame. A system praised as persistent under one definition may look intermittent under another, while a critic may denounce a shortfall that the architecture was never designed to overcome in the first place.

That ambiguity has followed the whole argument of this book like a faint but decisive background hum. Satellites over snow do not produce one simple kind of awareness. They produce different temporal arrangements of attention. Some systems stay near the scene. Some return often enough to matter. Some wake only when another source has already suggested that something deserves a closer look. Some are superb at reconstructing what happened after the fact while contributing very little to immediate warning. Yet public language, procurement rhetoric, and even some official doctrine routinely slide between these meanings as though they were interchangeable. They are not.

This is the chapter's central tension. Persistence sounds like a quantity when it is really a relation between observation and decision. Show a coverage map and one can easily mistake repeated access for uninterrupted watch. Show a high-resolution image delivered after delay and one can mistake exquisite detail for useful timeliness. Show a resilient constellation and one can mistake platform number for system strength. The deeper question is always the same: persistent for whom, against what problem, and on what clock? Once that question is asked seriously, many disputes that first looked technical turn out to be disagreements about hidden definitions.

A timetable on the wall helps. That quiet motif is enough. A timetable is not the journey itself, but it tells you what sort of promises are being made and which promises are only being inferred by wishful eyes. Arctic surveillance systems have timetables too, whether or not their advocates speak that plainly. They make promises about return, delivery, confidence, survivability, and recovery. Trouble begins when one timetable is advertised while another is silently assumed. A policymaker may hear "persistent" and imagine constant watch. An operator may hear the same word and mean revisits good enough for a certain class of maritime monitoring. An analyst may mean something else again: the ability to keep a case alive through corroboration and follow-up. The word survives. The agreement does not.

That matters because the Arctic punishes muddled expectation. Crises there often turn not on whether data exists somewhere in the system, but on whether it arrives in time, in trusted form, and with enough continuity that a decision-maker can still use it before the scene changes. A surveillance architecture that collects magnificently but delivers slowly may be persistent in archive and weak in warning. Another that pushes rapid low-detail alerts may be persistent in cueing and thin in forensic reconstruction. Neither description is an insult if it is honest. The strategic danger lies in pretending they are the same capability, then discovering the difference when a contact has moved, a downlink is missed, or a disruption has already spread through the chain.

The same problem extends to resilience. Too much public discussion still treats resilience as a matter of quantity alone, as though adding satellites were enough to make a system durable. But the chapters leading here have shown something tougher and more useful. Resilience lives in diversity of pathways, in governance that can keep systems legible under stress, in software and cyber discipline, in continuity planning, in the ability to manoeuvre through orbital congestion, and in institutions capable of distinguishing ordinary friction from hostile pressure. A system with many platforms may still be brittle if it depends on the same ground chokepoints, the same timing assumptions, the same software habits, or the same commercial gatekeepers. Redundancy without diversity can be a crowded version of fragility.

This is why the future of Arctic surveillance competition will be shaped as much by institutional choice as by any breakthrough sensor. Networking, commercialisation, shared infrastructure, and contested space promise more capability and more ambiguity at once. They can compress latency, widen access, and stabilise awareness. They can also create new dependencies, thinner margins for misinterpretation, and stronger incentives to act on partial persistence as though it were total knowledge.

The next arms race in the High North may not be defined by who sees the most in a simple sense. It may be defined by who defines persistence most persuasively, who builds systems whose timetables fit real decisions, and who preserves continuity under contest without teaching others to read every act of watching as a threat.

The path ahead moves from the meanings hidden inside persistence claims to the harder discipline of judging awareness by decision-relevant timeliness rather than raw collection alone. From there it turns to resilience as something distributed across the whole chain rather than attached to a platform count, before widening into the futures that matter most: not predictions dressed as certainty, but structured uncertainties about commercial power, networked architectures, political signalling, orbital congestion, cyber dependence, and the changing rules by which surveillance becomes either stabilising or provocative.

The harder question, then, is not whether Arctic surveillance is becoming more capable. It is. The more serious question is what kind of persistence those capabilities actually deliver, what sort of resilience they truly embody, and how much of the next competition will be fought not over sensors alone but over definitions, dependencies, and the timetables hidden behind confident claims. When someone says the Arctic is now watched persistently, which timetable are they asking you to trust - and which one are they hoping you do not inspect too closely?

A typology of persistence claims

What does it mean to say that the Arctic is watched persistently? The question sounds technical, yet much of the confusion in strategy, procurement, and public debate begins exactly there. A surveillance system may be described as persistent when it revisits often, when it remains over an area continuously, when it can be called into action quickly after a suspicious event, or when it can keep returning to reconstruct what happened after the fact. These are not minor shades of meaning. They are different promises. When institutions use one sense while inviting audiences to hear another, disputes that appear to be about capability are often really disputes about vocabulary.

The Arctic makes this slippage more consequential than it might be elsewhere. In a theatre of long distances, difficult weather, sparse infrastructure, and narrow decision windows, the difference between constant watch and timely reappearance is not semantic polish. It can determine whether a vessel is intercepted, whether an anomaly is merely logged, whether a false alarm is corrected in time, or whether a later investigation can establish a sequence strongly enough to shape political judgement. A map with many passes may still not amount to the kind of persistence a coastguard, a defence ministry, an insurer, or an environmental authority has quietly assumed. The same architecture can therefore be praised and condemned at once, depending on which unstated definition is doing the work.

This is why persistence needs a typology rather than a slogan. Show a satellite constellation over the High North and one can generate an impressive picture of repeated access, overlapping swaths, queued tasking, and data return. Name the actual claim more carefully, however, and the scene separates into distinct categories of performance. One system may hold something close to continuous coverage over a limited area or through a particular mix of platforms. Another may offer frequent revisit that is good enough for some missions and wholly inadequate for others. A third may be event-driven, springing into concentrated attention only when another source has already suggested where to look. A fourth may be weak at warning but strong at what might be called investigatory persistence: the ability to come back, corroborate, compare, and keep an incident alive analytically over time. The implication is immediate. Not all persistence is persistence of the same kind.

A timetable on the wall helps. That quiet motif is worth keeping because it rescues the discussion from abstraction. A timetable does not merely say that transport exists. It says what kind of reliability is being promised, with what spacing, for whom, and under what assumptions about delay. Arctic surveillance works the same way. Continuous coverage is the strongest and rarest promise. It implies that a scene remains under watch without meaningful temporal gaps for the purpose at hand. Frequent revisit is a different promise altogether. It accepts gaps but argues that they are short enough, regular enough, or numerous enough that the mission still makes sense. Event-driven monitoring is more conditional. It does not promise to see everything all the time; it promises to look hard once something has triggered attention. Investigatory persistence makes a different offer again: not immediate control of the scene, but sustained ability to return, compare, document, and establish pattern or attribution after an event has begun or passed.

These distinctions matter because each category rewards a different architecture. Continuous coverage tends to demand heavier infrastructure, more platforms, different orbital design, or a mixed system able to maintain a near-unbroken watch over a particular objective. Frequent revisit often trades permanence for regular return, which can be enough for monitoring shipping corridors, ice movement, infrastructure change, or repeated military presence so long as the decision does not depend on every minute between passes. Event-driven monitoring privileges responsiveness once a cue exists, which means the wider system may depend less on omnipresence than on fast tasking, reliable communications, and good prioritisation. Investigatory persistence rests on archives, repeatability, comparative imagery, and the institutional patience to keep building a case when the first moment of surprise has already gone. If these are collapsed into one generic word, policy choices become muddled. A buyer may believe they are funding warning and receive something far better suited to reconstruction. A critic may condemn a system for lacking uninterrupted watch when its real strength lies elsewhere and was never honestly described.

A useful public example sits in the ordinary language of commercial Earth observation. Providers often speak of persistent monitoring or persistent insight because the phrase is both attractive and elastic. In some cases the claim is fair if understood as frequent revisit across a broad area combined with analytic filtering that flags change. In other cases the same phrasing may encourage the listener to imagine a form of near-continuous awareness that the underlying architecture does not truly deliver. The issue is not bad faith alone. It is that institutional audiences frequently want to hear the strongest meaning. A ministry under pressure, a parliamentary committee, a newsroom, or a senior commander may translate "persistent" upwards, from repeat access to steady watch, because the stronger sense sounds more politically satisfying. The word becomes a bridge between what is sold and what is hoped.

A second example can be imagined from Arctic maritime surveillance. Suppose a system detects unusual movement near a remote coastal installation. If the architecture offers continuous coverage, the contact may be watched through its approach, loitering, and departure. If the system offers frequent revisit, analysts may see a sequence of appearances separated by uncertain intervals in which important behaviour could have occurred unseen. If it is event-driven, the initial clue may come from another source - a surface report, a radar anomaly, a communications irregularity - and the satellites then concentrate attention. If the system is strongest in investigatory persistence, the value may emerge later, when imagery and supporting data establish whether the movement formed part of a larger pattern. Each of these results can be strategically useful. Each is a different kind of usefulness. The mistake lies in acting as though they belong to one undifferentiated category of persistent watch.

A credible limitation should be admitted. These categories are analytical tools, not natural boxes. Real systems often combine them imperfectly. A constellation may offer something close to continuous watch over one small area, frequent revisit across a wider zone, event-driven surge capacity when retasked, and strong investigatory value because its archive is rich. The world is not neatly segmented, and the best architectures are often hybrids. But this does not weaken the typology. It makes it more necessary. Hybrids are precisely where political and procurement language grows most slippery, because a system can truthfully possess one mode in one context and still imply a stronger one elsewhere. The remedy is not cynicism. It is precision.

That precision should focus less on labels than on questions. What is being observed: a point target, a corridor, a region, a fleet, an incident, a pattern? Over what interval must the scene remain known well enough for the decision to count as timely? Is the system promising to detect the event as it unfolds, to revisit often enough that change cannot remain hidden for long, to concentrate attention after a trigger, or to build an evidentiary sequence afterwards? How much of the claimed persistence depends on other systems doing the first noticing? How much depends on downlink speed, processing queues, and analytic availability rather than on the satellite pass itself? These are not technical curiosities. They are the durable checklist by which persistence claims become intelligible rather than theatrical.

This matters acutely for procurement because budgets are often shaped by words before they are shaped by orbital diagrams. A government that believes it is buying continuous awareness may overpay for disappointment or underpay for a mission it describes too grandly. A commercial customer may seek persistent insight and be perfectly well served by event-driven monitoring tied to fast analytics, yet still be misled if the contract language flatters the service into something it is not. A defence planner may undervalue investigatory persistence because it sounds less dramatic than constant watch, only to discover later that comparative archives and repeated follow-up were the decisive assets in proving a contested sequence of events. Definitions do not merely describe systems. They steer institutions towards certain architectures and away from others.

Trust reveals itself here in behaviour. Users trust a persistent claim when they can align their decisions to its actual timetable without constant surprise.

They distrust it when they build parallel workarounds, supplementary contracts, manual cross-checks, or quieter internal caveats because the public word is stronger than the delivered reality. Analysts trust a system when they know whether a missing interval means failure, ordinary gap, or simply a type of persistence the architecture never claimed to eliminate. Policymakers distrust their own rhetoric when they begin attaching adjectives such as "near", "effective", or "operationally meaningful" to avoid saying plainly what sort of persistence they mean. Those behaviours often tell the truth more clearly than glossy specifications.

The timetable returns because it captures the discipline this subject demands. A timetable does not become deceptive because it fails to offer a train every minute. It becomes deceptive when it invites the traveller to assume that it does. Arctic surveillance claims work the same way. Continuous coverage, frequent revisit, event-driven monitoring, and investigatory persistence are all valuable forms of watchfulness when named honestly and matched to the right decisions. Confusion begins when one timetable is printed and another imagined.

The harder question, then, is not whether persistence exists in Arctic surveillance. It does, in several forms. The more serious question is which form is actually being promised when the word is used, which one the audience is privately hearing, and which one the system can still deliver once latency, weather, orbital geometry, communications, and institutional friction have all taken their share. When someone says the north is watched persistently, what kind of timetable are they asking you to trust - and what kind of decision are they quietly assuming it will be good enough to support?

Designing for latency-aware awareness

In March 2021, when satellite images of the *Ever Given* blocking the Suez Canal circulated with remarkable speed, public attention fixed on the image itself. The ship was visible. The obstruction was obvious. The scene seemed to prove that modern surveillance had become almost instantaneous. Yet the deeper lesson lay elsewhere. The useful question was not simply how clearly the satellite had seen, but how quickly that seeing had been turned into something decision-makers could still use. An image can be sharp and late. A warning can be rough and on time. In the Arctic, that difference is often the whole argument.

The High North is unforgiving of systems that mistake collection for awareness. A satellite may pass over the right place at the right moment and still fail the mission if the data reaches the relevant user after the vessel has moved, the weather has shifted, the aircraft has landed, or the political meaning of the event has already begun to harden elsewhere. This is why latency-aware awareness matters. It asks not what the sensor can theoretically collect, but what the entire chain can deliver on the clock of the decision that matters. In the Arctic, that clock is often measured in hours rather than in the slower rhythms favoured by institutional comfort.

The central claim is simple but easy to resist. Surveillance should be judged by decision-relevant timeliness, not raw collection. Show a sophisticated imaging system and the temptation is to admire altitude, resolution, spectral power, or revisit statistics. Name the actual problem more carefully and another picture emerges. Orbit choice shapes when the sensor can see. Sensor choice shapes what it can detect and how much data it creates. Downlink and processing choices shape when the resulting product can leave the machine world and enter the human one. Explain why that matters, and the implication becomes difficult to avoid: a slower path to exquisite detail may be less useful than a faster path to imperfect warning if the decision will not wait.

A clock is always running. That quiet motif belongs at the centre of this subject. The clock begins before the image appears, because tasking, orbital access, and collection opportunity already take time. It keeps running through downlink, processing, dissemination, and interpretation. By the time the product reaches a command post, maritime centre, analyst, or minister, the event itself has not paused out of courtesy. Arctic systems live under this pressure more intensely because alternatives are sparse and the environment changes fast enough that a delayed picture may become a historical artefact sooner than many buyers or politicians expect. A latency-aware design begins by asking which clock cannot be allowed to run too far ahead.

Orbit is the first author of latency whether institutions admit it or not. A constellation built around frequent revisit from polar low Earth orbit offers one kind of temporal promise. A highly elliptical architecture offers another. A system that depends on store-and-forward delivery lives on a different schedule from one with relay support or dense ground access. None of these choices is neutral. An orbit may be excellent for Arctic geometry and still impose gaps that matter to a rapidly unfolding incident. Another may linger helpfully over high latitudes yet remain tied to communications pathways that delay useful delivery. The point is not to rank one orbit as universally superior. It is to understand that orbital elegance and operational timeliness are related but not identical virtues.

Sensor choice then compounds the same trade-off. A high-detail system can produce images of immense value, especially for identification, attribution, and later scrutiny. But higher fidelity often means larger data loads, more demanding processing, and slower movement through the chain. A coarser but wider or more easily processed sensor may detect less, yet still support earlier action because the product arrives before the scene has drifted out of relevance. In the Arctic, this is not a minor preference question. A broad-area alert that flags unusual presence near ice edge may matter more in the first hours than a later image good enough to count fittings on a vessel's deck. The later image may still prove decisive. It simply belongs to a different moment of the decision cycle.

A practical contrast makes the point more clearly than theory. Imagine two surveillance chains watching northern waters. The first is built for high detail. It collects an excellent radar or optical scene, stores a large file, waits for the right downlink opportunity, passes through a careful processing sequence, and finally delivers a product rich enough for close interpretation. The second is built for rapid alerting. It uses a faster, lower-detail path that identifies a likely contact, transmits a compact alert quickly, and sacrifices some richness of context to preserve time. The first chain may be stronger for later identification, evidentiary use, or diplomatic argument. The second may be stronger for cueing an aircraft, redirecting a patrol, or prompting a second look while the target still inhabits the same piece of sea. Both are useful. Confusion begins when one is purchased or described as though it were secretly the other.

A useful public example lies in the broader contrast between commercial rapid-alert architectures and slower, richer imagery services. The point is not to name winners. It is to see that some systems are designed to compress the path from detection to notification, while others are designed to maximise the evidentiary and interpretive value of the final product. In Arctic use, these design philosophies create different latency profiles even when both systems are technically impressive. One answers quickly to the question, "Is something happening here?" The other answers more powerfully to the later question, "What exactly was it, and how confidently can we say so?" A mature surveillance architecture knows which question it has paid to answer fastest.

A credible limitation should be admitted. Not every mission in the Arctic turns on hours. Some depend on pattern analysis, environmental record-building, infrastructure watchfulness, or post-incident reconstruction, where slower and richer data may be entirely appropriate. A system optimised for rapid alerting can mislead users if it is asked to carry more interpretive weight than its speed allows. A system optimised for depth can be perfectly successful on its own terms while disappointing those who expected operational tempo rather than analytic strength. The problem is not that one architecture is noble and the other flawed. The problem is mismatch between latency profile and decision profile.

That concession strengthens the deeper argument rather than weakening it. Once one stops asking whether a system is merely fast or merely detailed, better questions appear. Fast for which user? Detailed enough for which judgement? Timely at which stage: collection, delivery, or understanding? Dependent on which ground access, cloud workflow, relay path, or human queue? A latency-aware design does not worship speed blindly. It aligns the whole chain to the moment in which the information still has the power to change something real. In the Arctic, that alignment is especially important because distance and weather already strip away so many cheap chances for correction.

This is also why latency-aware awareness belongs to procurement language, not just to operator culture. Buyers who ask only what a sensor can collect are inviting disappointment. Buyers who ask what the chain can deliver in the relevant decision window are already closer to reality. A ministry concerned with maritime ambiguity, search and rescue, or fast-moving strategic signalling may need one latency profile. Another concerned with treaty interpretation, persistent documentation, or infrastructure patterning may need another. Neither should be allowed to hide behind the single flattering word "persistent" if what they really mean is "rapid enough for my purpose". The clock punishes such vagueness later.

Trust shows itself here in behaviour. Operators trust a system when they are willing to act on its products without immediately reaching for slower confirmation by default. Analysts trust it when they know what kind of conclusion its timing and fidelity can honestly support. Institutions distrust it when they quietly build duplicate subscriptions, manual workarounds, or informal warning channels because the official architecture collects beautifully and arrives too late. These habits are not embarrassing side stories. They are the lived evidence of whether a system's latency profile matches its mission.

The clock returns because it is the most democratic part of the whole argument. It does not care how expensive the sensor was, how elegant the orbit looks on a slide, or how confidently a vendor says the system is persistent. It only asks whether the product arrived before the decision closed. The harder question, then, is not whether Arctic surveillance can be made more powerful in abstract technical terms. It can. The more serious question is what kind of awareness that power produces once orbit, sensor, and downlink choices have written their own timetable into the chain. When the next Arctic incident turns on a handful of hours, which matters more: the image that proves everything late, or the alert that proves less but arrives in time to alter what happens next?

Resilience as an ecosystem property

In February 2022, when the disruption to Viasat's KA-SAT network spread through user terminals and terrestrial service pathways at the opening edge of Russia's full-scale invasion of Ukraine, the most revealing lesson was not simply that a space-enabled service could be damaged. It was that the decisive weakness lay below the satellite itself. The spacecraft remained part of the story, but the broader system failed through a chain of ground dependencies, software exposure, and user equipment vulnerabilities. What looked from a distance like a space event was, at closer range, an ecosystem failure.

That distinction matters profoundly for the Arctic. Public language still tends to equate resilience with platform count: more satellites, more coverage, more security. There is some truth in that instinct. A constellation is harder to silence than a single spacecraft. But it is only part of the truth, and often the less interesting part. In the High North, where communications are sparse, maintenance is hard, weather and distance punish weak margins, and data must pass through multiple institutional and technical layers before it becomes usable, resilience is never a property of satellites alone. It belongs to the whole arrangement that allows sensing to become awareness.

This is the central argument. Resilience should be treated as an ecosystem property. Show a surveillance architecture in a briefing and the eye is usually drawn upwards: spacecraft, orbits, revisit, payloads. Name the real structure more honestly and another picture appears: ground stations, downlink paths, timing services, cloud processing, software updates, user terminals, reporting chains, operators, fallback procedures, and the norms that determine who acts when something breaks. Explain why this matters, and the implication becomes immediate. A system with many satellites can still be brittle if too much of its usefulness depends on the same gateway, the same timing source, the same software chain, or the same institutional bottleneck.

A bridge can have many lanes. That quiet motif helps because it makes the problem visible without turning it into ornament. Many lanes do not guarantee resilience if they all lead to the same narrow support pier. In Arctic surveillance, redundancy often works exactly like this. Several spacecraft may pass over the same region. Yet if they rely on the same small number of polar ground stations, the same relay service, the same processing environment, or the same dissemination logic, then the apparent width of the system conceals a thinner reality. The user sees abundance in orbit. The choke point sits elsewhere.

This is why redundancy and diversity must be separated rather than praised under one flattering word. Redundancy means having more than one way to perform a function. Diversity means those ways do not fail for the same reason. A constellation with many identical satellites in similar orbits can offer redundancy against the loss of one platform and still remain vulnerable to common disruptions affecting the whole class. Several ground terminals can offer redundancy and still disappoint if they depend on the same backhaul provider or the same software update pipeline. Multiple data products can appear diverse while all deriving from one fragile timing service or one analytic environment. True resilience therefore grows when systems add alternatives that do not share the same failure mode. The Arctic rewards that distinction mercilessly because common-mode failure there is often hidden until the wrong day.

A useful example can be drawn from the contrast between a constellation supported by several geographically separated ground stations and one supported mainly through a single heavily loaded high-latitude node. Both may appear operationally strong during routine periods. Under strain, the difference becomes sharp. If weather, maintenance trouble, cyber compromise, or backhaul failure affects the primary node in the second case, the surveillance chain may degrade dramatically even though the satellites are healthy and passing overhead as planned. In the first case, service may still suffer, but the architecture has more room to route around the damage. The important point is not that one system has more hardware. It is that it has less concentrated dependence.

A second example lies in sensing itself. An Arctic system that relies heavily on one mode of observation, one collection logic, or one timing assumption may claim persistence and still remain fragile. A more resilient architecture often mixes broad-area detection with finer follow-up, radar with optical or thermal where appropriate, local reporting with space-based observation, and different latency profiles for different decisions. That diversity does not guarantee harmony. It creates something better: options. If one sensor is blinded by weather, another may still detect. If one downlink path is delayed, a lower-bandwidth alerting chain may keep awareness alive. If one product is contested, corroboration may arrive from a different technical and institutional path. The result is not invulnerability. It is a reduced chance that one convenient choke point will silence the whole picture.

This is where governance enters as more than a soft afterthought. Governance determines whether redundancy and diversity actually function as resilience or merely decorate a system diagram. Who can switch to fallback modes? Who decides whether a degraded source remains trustworthy enough to use? Which organisations share data quickly enough to matter, and which keep it trapped behind incompatible procedures? How are incidents reported, and how rapidly can operators distinguish routine harsh-environment failure from hostile disruption? These are governance questions. They are also resilience questions because Arctic systems often fail, or recover, through institutions before they do so through hardware. A technically rich architecture can become brittle if its agencies do not trust one another's products, if its reporting culture punishes early warning, or if its permissions are so centralised that local operators cannot act when the clock is already running.

A credible limitation deserves admission. More diversity is not automatically better, and resilience is not achieved simply by scattering complexity everywhere. Every added pathway introduces new interfaces, more coordination problems, more opportunities for latency, and more burdens of trust. A system can become so elaborate that it is difficult to govern and difficult to understand under pressure. Some shared infrastructure is efficient and entirely sensible. Some degree of common architecture is inevitable. It would be careless to imply that every concentration of capability is a weakness or that every hybrid system is resilient by virtue of variety alone.

But that concession sharpens the central claim rather than weakening it. The aim is not maximal variety. It is the reduction of dangerous shared dependencies. Readers do not need classified details to ask intelligent questions here. Do several key functions rely on the same narrow node? Would one cyber compromise, one power failure, one timing anomaly, one software fault, or one political access denial disable large portions of the chain at once? Are the backup options genuinely independent, or do they merely look separate while sharing the same hidden support? A serious resilience claim should survive those questions. A weak one usually falls apart under them.

This matters especially because disruption usually targets the most convenient choke point, not the most glamorous one. A hostile actor, a harsh environment, or simple operational entropy does not care which part of the architecture looks most impressive in a briefing. It presses where the system is least able to absorb pressure without losing timeliness or trust. In the Arctic, that may mean a communications bottleneck, a polar ground station, a credentialed cloud service, a navigation dependency, or an institutional reporting gap rather than the satellite bus itself. An ecosystem view of resilience therefore changes how strength is recognised. It shifts attention from heroic hardware to mundane survivability.

Trust becomes visible in operational behaviour. Institutions that trust their resilience do not panic when one pathway weakens because they know which alternative is available, what quality of awareness it can still provide, and how its use will be governed. Institutions that do not trust their architecture reveal it quickly: parallel unofficial channels appear, products are cross-checked through personal networks, operators hedge against the formal system, and leaders discover too late that "redundant" meant "repeated" rather than "independent". These are not cultural side notes. They are field evidence of whether resilience is real.

The bridge returns because it clarifies the chapter's practical lesson. A bridge is strong not because it is long or busy, but because its load does not depend fatally on one hidden weakness. Arctic surveillance systems deserve the same standard. More satellites may matter. They matter less than many people think if the same link, node, software chain, or governance habit still carries too much of the weight.

The harder question, then, is not whether Arctic surveillance architectures can be made more resilient by adding platforms. Sometimes they can. The more serious question is whether those additions actually reduce shared dependence or merely decorate the same underlying fragility with extra hardware. When the next disruption arrives, what keeps awareness alive: the number of satellites overhead, or the diversity, redundancy, and governance that determine whether the whole chain can keep working when the easiest point of pressure has already been found?

Futures, constraints, and the next arms race

In February 2022, when commercial satellite imagery of Russian deployments around Ukraine began circulating with extraordinary speed, the world saw more than a crisis documented from orbit. It saw a future arriving in plain view. Private firms, public agencies, analysts, and governments were no longer waiting for one sovereign sensor to settle the picture. They were participating in a wider surveillance environment in which collection, networking, processing, and release had become distributed across institutions with different motives and different thresholds for disclosure. The Arctic will live with the consequences of that shift even more sharply, because distance, weather, and sparse on-scene confirmation give space-enabled observation unusual power over what becomes visible, when, and to whom.

That future is often described too narrowly, as though the decisive question were simply which state acquires the best sensor or the most satellites. The harder truth is less theatrical and more consequential. Arctic surveillance competition is increasingly shaped by commercial access, network architecture, relay pathways, software habits, orbital congestion, governance rules, and the political meaning of persistence. A state may possess exquisite imagery and still lose the practical contest if its downlink is brittle, its products arrive too slowly, its access is contractually fragile, or its institutions cannot decide what to do with a stream of alerts before the scene has already changed. The next arms race will not be fought only in payload specifications. It will be fought in the structure of systems.

This is the central tension. The forces that promise more stability in the Arctic are often the same forces that can make competition sharper. Commercialisation widens access and reduces monopoly over visibility. It also creates uneven tiers of priority, dependence, and public release. Networking reduces latency and weakens some local bottlenecks. It also creates new shared dependencies, richer cyber surfaces, and stronger incentives to act on early partial information. Contested space pushes operators towards resilience, redundancy, and faster adaptation. It also teaches states to watch one another's watching with greater suspicion. The race, in other words, is not simply to see more. It is to shape what seeing means.

A queue forms quickly. That quiet motif is useful because it captures the politics of the near future more accurately than heroic language about domination. Arctic surveillance is increasingly a question of who gets priority in the queue: priority for collection, for downlink, for relay, for processing, for analytic attention, for public framing. Commercial operators, allied states, civilian agencies, and military institutions may all depend on overlapping infrastructures while claiming different forms of urgency. When pressure rises, the queue becomes strategy. A state able to move its requirement to the front may gain a political advantage without adding a single new sensor. Another may own platforms yet still lag because its institutional arrangements place it behind in the part of the chain that matters most.

This is why commercialisation matters so much. It does not merely lower barriers to entry or broaden the market for data. It changes the social location of surveillance itself. Images and analytic products that once would have remained inside narrow public channels now circulate through firms, subscriptions, media, allied exchanges, and specialised intermediaries. That circulation can stabilise by making denial harder and by giving smaller actors access to evidence they could not otherwise gather. It can also accelerate competition by compressing the time between collection and political meaning. A commercial release can harden a narrative before slower diplomatic or military channels have decided how much ambiguity they wish to preserve. The Arctic, where many incidents begin in uncertainty and where natural visibility is often poor, is especially vulnerable to this kind of accelerated interpretation.

Networking deepens the same transformation. Inter-satellite links, relay constellations, edge processing, cloud-based dissemination, and fused operational pictures all promise to reduce the old tyranny of distance. That is a real gain. Yet networking also changes the pattern of vulnerability. A connected architecture can route around some local failures and lower some forms of latency, but it can also become more dependent on common software, common identity systems, common relay agreements, and common operational assumptions. The Arctic has already shown that a system with more pathways is not automatically a system with more resilience. If those pathways share the same hidden support, then the appearance of flexibility conceals a thinner reality. The future is therefore likely to reward actors who reduce common dependencies rather than merely multiplying visible nodes.

A useful public example lies in the role commercial imagery and derived analytics now play in international crises. Their significance does not rest only on technical merit. It rests on the ability to move quickly from sensing to circulation. A second example can be drawn from the Arctic itself in a hypothetical but entirely plausible form: two states observe the same northern incident through partly shared commercial and public infrastructures. One has priority tasking, faster analytics, and a standing practice of controlled public release. The other has good sovereign sensors but slower institutional pathways and weaker confidence in its dissemination chain. The first state may shape the diplomatic weather before the second has settled its own internal picture. The difference does not arise from a miracle sensor. It arises from institutional design.

That is why the book's argument about latency matters so much here. Future competition in the High North is unlikely to be decided simply by who collects the most data. It will be shaped by who can align collection, delivery, interpretation, and decision on the clock that Arctic incidents impose. Some crises will still turn on exquisite detail. Others will turn on whether a lower-detail alert arrived in time to change a route, cue another sensor, or avoid a public misunderstanding. Actors that design for decision-relevant timeliness will gain a subtler but more durable advantage than actors that merely accumulate raw data collection. This is not a prediction about one winner. It is a pathway: systems that treat latency as a political and strategic variable will usually outperform those that treat it as a back-office inconvenience.

A credible limitation should be admitted. Breakthrough sensors may still matter a great deal. Better SAR, stronger thermal discrimination, improved networking in orbit, more flexible processing, and new combinations of commercial and sovereign capabilities will alter the surveillance landscape. It would be foolish to pretend that technology no longer matters. But technology is unlikely to matter in the simple way procurement rhetoric prefers. A breakthrough absorbed into brittle institutions, congested orbits, fragile ground networks, and ambiguous signalling practices may produce less stability than a more ordinary sensor embedded in a disciplined, diverse, and well-governed chain. The most important future changes may therefore come not from invention alone, but from choices about who shares data, who controls priority, who can explain disruption, and who can preserve continuity under stress.

This is where escalation and stability begin to depend less on hardware glamour than on the management of uncertainty. A more densely watched Arctic can deter by reducing room for surprise. It can also inflame by making every concentrated act of observation legible as a possible signal. More commercial access can reassure by widening the evidentiary base. It can also accelerate narrative hardening when partial images enter public life before interpretation has matured. More networking can stabilise by shortening delivery chains. It can also magnify systemic vulnerability if too much confidence gathers around a shared relay, a common cloud, or an under-audited identity structure. The future therefore does not divide neatly into optimistic and pessimistic scenarios. It divides into pathways shaped by whether institutions learn to govern the very visibility they are so eager to expand.

Readers do not need classified detail to think clearly about these pathways. They need a disciplined set of questions. Where are the shared choke points? Who depends on whom for timeliness? Which systems are genuinely diverse rather than merely numerous? Who can buy priority, who can route around disruption, and who can release a decisive image first? What is being called persistent, and on what decision clock? Which transparency measures calm the scene, and which merely move escalation into public view faster? Those questions do not tell us exactly what the next Arctic arms race will look like. They do something better. They prevent us from confusing sensors with systems and capability with stability.

The queue forms quickly returns here because the future is likely to be shaped by these quiet ordering rules more than by dramatic singular events. The next contest in the High North may be fought through contracts, routing rights, relay access, data-sharing arrangements, orbital stewardship, software governance, and the political uses of persistence long before it is fought through spectacular technical leaps. That makes the race both more mundane and more dangerous. Mundane, because its decisive mechanisms may sit in procurement offices, cloud consoles, and reporting chains. Dangerous, because those mechanisms can alter strategic timing without announcing themselves as strategy.

The harder question, then, is not whether Arctic surveillance competition will intensify. It almost certainly will, in one form or another. The more serious question is what kind of competition is being built: one that multiplies visibility while preserving room for restraint, or one that turns every improvement in watchfulness into a faster route towards suspicion, public framing, and brittle dependency. When the next shift comes in the High North, will it arrive as a dazzling new sensor - or as a quieter institutional choice that decides whose queue moves first, whose warning counts, and whose version of persistence becomes the standard everyone else must live inside?

About the Author

Afnan Barakat is a nonfiction writer with a research-driven interest in how technical systems quietly reorganise geopolitics. Rather than treating satellites as distant machines, Barakat approaches space infrastructure as a set of institutions, incentives, and operational chokepoints that shape what governments can know, claim, and contest. That orientation fits the Arctic, where the romance of maps and frontiers often obscures the practical work of downlink schedules, ground access, data workflows, and the politics of who gets timely visibility.

Barakat writes in an editorial voice that aims to be precise without being enclosed by jargon. The guiding concern is integrity: separating what space systems can plausibly deliver from what public language implies they deliver, and showing readers how to ask better questions about coverage, latency, and resilience. The book is informed by the long arc from Cold War early warning and polar communications to today's commercial constellations and hybrid public-private data ecosystems. It is also shaped by a belief that the most consequential security dynamics often emerge at the seams between domains - space and sea, signal and decision, sensor and story - where accountability is hardest and assumptions travel fastest.

www.ingramcontent.com/pod-product-compliance
Lightning Source LLC
Chambersburg PA
CBHW031321230926
51848CB00001B/39
9789377940379